ESSENTIALS for design

ADOBE® PHOTOSHOP® CS

level one

Gary Poyssick

PEARSON

Prentice
Hall

Prentice Hall
Upper Saddle River, New Jersey 07458

Publisher and Vice President: Natalie E. Anderson
Executive Editor: Jodi McPherson
Acquisitions Editor: Melissa Sabella
Editorial Assistant: Alana Meyers
Senior Media Project Manager: Cathleen Profitko
Senior Marketing Manager: Emily Knight
Marketing Assistant: Nicole Beaudry
Senior Managing Editor: Gail Steier de Acevedo
Project Manager, Production: Vanessa Nuttry
Manufacturing Buyer: Vanessa Nuttry
Interior Design: Thistle Hill Publishing Services, LLC
Cover Design: Blair Brown
Cover Printer: Coral Graphics
Printer/Binder: Von Hoffman Press

ABOUT THE SERIES EDITOR

Ellenn Behoriam is president and founder of Against The Clock, Inc. (ATC), one of the nation's leading content providers. Ellenn and her staff have successfully produced many of the graphic arts industry's most popular and well-received books and related series. These works include the *Electronic Cookbook, Workflow Reengineering, Teams and the Graphic Arts, Adobe Photoshop Creative Techniques, Adobe Illustrator Creative Techniques,* and *QuarkXPress 6: Creating Digital Documents,* the foundation for the QuarkXPress Trainer certification programs. The Against The Clock Series, published in concert with Prentice Hall/Pearson Education, includes more than 26 titles that focus on applications for the graphic and computer arts industries.

Against The Clock also worked with Pearson to develop the *Companion for the Digital Artist* series. These titles focus on specific and fundamental creative concepts, including design, Web site development, photography, typography, color theory, and copywriting. The concise and compact works provide core concepts and skills that supplement any application-specific education, regardless of which textbooks are being used to teach program skills.

Under Ellenn's leadership and direction, ATC is currently developing more than 20 titles for the new *Essentials for Design* series. Her staff and long-established network of professional educators, printers, prepress experts, workflow engineers, and business leaders add significantly to ATC's ability to provide current, meaningful, and effective books, online tutorials, and business-to-business performance and workflow-enhancement programs.

ABOUT THE AUTHOR

Gary Poyssick, co-owner of Against The Clock, is a well-known and often controversial speaker, writer, and industry consultant who has been involved in professional graphics and communications for more than fifteen years. He wrote the highly popular *Workflow Reengineering* (Adobe Press), *Teams and the Graphic Arts Service Provider* (Prentice Hall), *Creative Techniques: Adobe Illustrator,* and *Creative Techniques: Adobe Photoshop* (Hayden Books).

ACKNOWLEDGMENTS

We would like to thank the professional writers, artists, editors, and educators who have worked long and hard on the *Essentials for Design* series.

Special thanks to Deborah Zerillo, Editorial Assistant, for her help in keeping us all together.

And thanks to the dedicated teaching professionals: Sharon L. Neville, Technical Communications Consultants; Elouise Oyzon, Professor, Rochester Institute of Technology, Department of Information Technology; Deborah L. Killips, Killips & Associates; and Emily Springfield, Instructional Designer. Your insightful comments and expertise have certainly contributed to the success of the *Essentials for Design* series.

Thank you to Laurel Nelson-Cucchiara, copy editor and final link in the chain of production, for her help in making sure that we all said what we meant to say.

And to Melissa Sabella, Jodi McPherson, and Vanessa Nuttry, we appreciate your patience as we begin this new venture together.

CONTENTS AT A GLANCE

TABLE OF CONTENTS

HOW TO USE THIS BOOK

Essentials courseware from Prentice Hall is anchored in the practical and professional needs of all types of students. The *Essentials* series presents a learning-by-doing approach that encourages you to grasp application-related concepts as you expand your skills through hands-on tutorials. As such, it consists of modular lessons that are built around a series of numbered step-by-step procedures that are clear, concise, and easy to review.

Essentials books are divided into projects. A project covers one area (or a few closely related areas) of application functionality. Each project consists of several lessons that are related to that topic. Each lesson presents a specific task or closely related set of tasks in a manageable chunk that is easy to assimilate and retain.

Each element in the *Essentials* book is designed to maximize your learning experience. A list of the *Essentials* project elements, and a description of how each element can help you, begins on the next page. To find out more about the rationale behind each book element and how to use each to your maximum benefit, take the following walk-through.

WALK-THROUGH

Project Objectives. Starting with an objective gives you short-term, attainable goals. Each project begins with a list of objectives that closely match the titles of the step-by-step tutorials. ▶

OBJECTIVES

In this project, you learn how to

- Open and save an image
- Identify the different parts of the Photoshop working environment
- Learn to use the File Browser to organize your images
- Recognize different tools in the Photoshop Toolbox
- Use a selection tool to isolate part of an image
- Modify an existing image using painting tools
- Move around an image
- Select different viewing options

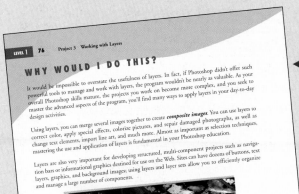

Why Would I Do This? Introductory material at the beginning of each project provides an overview of why these tasks and procedures are important.

Visual Summary. A series of illustrations introduces the new tools, dialog boxes, and windows you will explore in each project. ▼

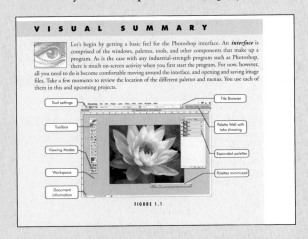

VISUAL SUMMARY

Let's begin by getting a basic feel for the Photoshop interface. An *interface* is comprised of the windows, palettes, tools, and other components that make up a program. As is the case with any industrial-strength program such as Photoshop, there is much on-screen activity when you first start the program. For now, however, all you need to do is become comfortable moving around the interface, and opening and saving image files. Take a few moments to review the location of the different palettes and menus. You use each of them in this and upcoming projects.

FIGURE 1.1

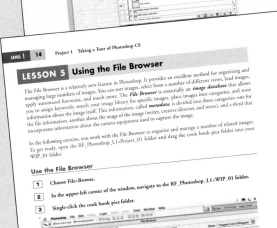

Step-by-Step Tutorials. Hands-on tutorials let you learn by doing and include numbered, bold, step-by-step instructions.

? ◀ If You Have Problems. These short troubleshooting notes help you anticipate or solve common problems quickly and effectively.

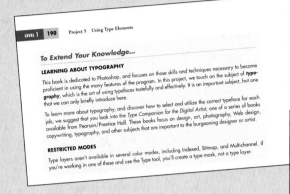

◀ To Extend Your Knowledge. These features provide extra tips, alternative ways to complete a process, and special hints about using the software.

Careers in Design. These features offer advice, tips, and resources that will help you on your path to a successful career. ▶

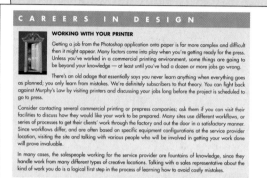

End-of-Project Exercises. Extensive end-of-project exercises emphasize hands-on skill development. You'll find three levels of reinforcement: Skill Drill, Challenge, and Portfolio Builder. ▼

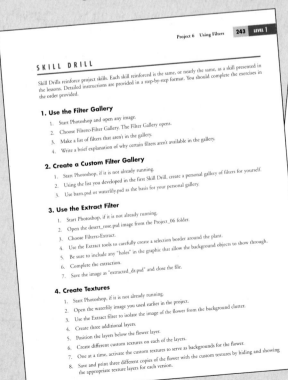

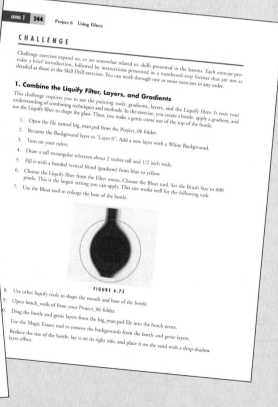

Portfolio Builder. At the end of every project, these exercises require creative solutions to problems that reinforce the topic of the project. ▶

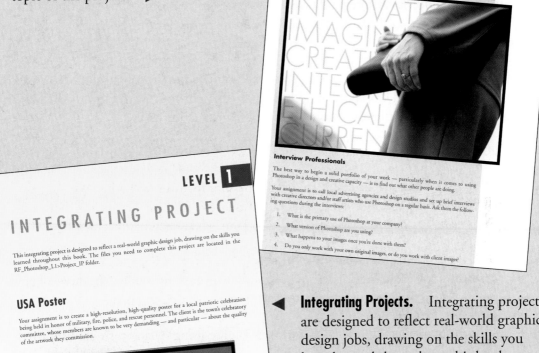

PORTFOLIO BUILDER

Interview Professionals

The best way to begin a solid portfolio of your work — particularly when it comes to using Photoshop in a design and creative capacity — is to find out what other people are doing.

Your assignment is to call local advertising agencies and design studios and set up brief interviews with creative directors and/or staff artists who use Photoshop on a regular basis. Ask them the following questions during the interviews:

1. What is the primary use of Photoshop at your company?
2. What version of Photoshop are you using?
3. What happens to your images once you're done with them?
4. Do you only work with your own original images, or do you work with client images?

LEVEL 1

INTEGRATING PROJECT

This integrating project is designed to reflect a real-world graphic design job, drawing on the skills you learned throughout this book. The files you need to complete this project are located in the RF_Photoshop_L1>Project_IP folder.

USA Poster

Your assignment is to create a high-resolution, high-quality poster for a local patriotic celebration being held in honor of military, fire, police, and rescue personnel. The client is the town's celebratory committee, whose members are known to be very demanding — and particular — about the quality of the artwork they commission.

◀ **Integrating Projects.** Integrating projects are designed to reflect real-world graphic-design jobs, drawing on the skills you have learned throughout this book.

TASK GUIDE

Task	Macintosh	Windows
Managing the Workspace		
CONTROL THE SCREEN MODE		
Toggle between Standard screen, Full screen, and Full screen with menu bar	F	F
Toggle between Standard and Quick mask mode	Q	Q
Cycle through open documents	Control-Tab	Control-Tab
NAVIGATE IMAGES		
Fit image in window	Double-click Hand tool	Double-click Hand tool
Magnify 100%	Double-click Zoom tool	Double-click Zoom tool
Scroll up 1 screen	Page Up	Page Up
Scroll down 1 screen	Page Down	Page Down
Scroll left 1 screen	Command-Page Up	Control-Page Up
Scroll right 1 screen	Command-Page Down	Control-Page Down
Scroll up 10 units	Shift-Page Up	Shift-Page Up
Scroll down 10 units	Shift-Page Down	Shift-Page Down
Scroll left 10 units	Command-Shift-Page Up	Control-Shift-Page Up
Scroll right 10 units	Command-Shift-Page Down	Control-Shift-Page Down
Move view to upper-left corner	Home	Home
Move view to lower-right corner	End	End
Move marquee while dragging with Zoom tool	Spacebar-drag	Spacebar-drag
Apply and keep zoom percentage field active (Navigator palette)	Shift-Return	Shift-Enter
Zoom in on specified area (Navigator palette)	Command-drag over preview	Control-drag over preview
ACCESS PALETTES		
Show/Hide Brushes palette	F5	F5
Show/Hide Color palette	F6	F6
Show/Hide Layers palette	F7	F7
Show/Hide Info palette	F8	F8
Show/Hide Actions palette	Option-F9	F9
Show/Hide all palettes	Tab	Tab
Show/Hide all except Toolbox and Options bar	Shift-Tab	Shift-Tab
Highlight Options bar	Select tool and press Return	Select tool and press Enter

Task Guides. These charts, found at the end of each book, list alternative ways to complete common procedures and provide a handy reference tool. ▶

STUDENT INFORMATION AND RESOURCES

Companion Web Site (www.prenhall.com/essentials). This text-specific Web site provides students with additional information and exercises to reinforce their learning. Features include: additional end-of-project reinforcement material, online Study Guide, easy access to *all* resource files, and much, much more!

Before completing the projects within this text, you need to download the Resource Files from the Prentice Hall Companion Web site. Check with your instructor for the best way to gain access to these files or simply follow these instructions:

1. From an open Web browser, go to http://www.prenhall.com/essentials.

2. Select your textbook or series to access the Companion Web site. We suggest you bookmark this page, as it has links to additional Prentice Hall resources that you may use in class.

3. Click the Student Resources link. All files in the Student Resources area are provided as .sea files for Macintosh users and .exe files for those using the Windows operating system. These files do not require any additional software to open.

4. Click the Start Here link for the platform you are using (Macintosh or Windows).

5. Once you have downloaded the proper file, double-click that file to begin the self-extraction process. You will be prompted to select a folder location specific for your book; you may extract the file to your hard drive or to a removable disk/drive.

   The Start Here file contains three folders:

   ■ **Fonts.**

   ■ **RF_Photoshop_L1.** You can place this folder on your hard drive, or on a removable disk/drive.

   ■ **Work_In_Progress.** You can place this folder on your hard drive, or on a removable disk/drive.

6. Locate the project files you need from the list of available resources and click the active link to download. There is a separate file for each project in this book (e.g., Project_01, Project_02, etc.).

7. Once you have downloaded the proper file, double-click that file to begin the self-extraction process. You will be prompted to select a folder location specific to your book; you should extract the project-specific folders into the RF_Photoshop_L1 folder that was extracted from the Start Here file.

Resource CD. If you are using a Resource CD, all the fonts and files you need are provided on the CD. Resource files are organized in project-specific folders (e.g., Project_01, Project_02, etc.), which are contained in the RF_Photoshop_L1 folder. You can either work directly from the CD, or copy the files onto your hard drive before beginning the exercises.

Before you begin working on the projects or lessons in this book, you should copy the Work_In_Progress folder from the Resource CD onto your hard drive or a removable disk/drive.

Fonts. You must install the ATC fonts to ensure that your exercises and projects will work as described in the book. Specific instructions for installing fonts are provided in the documentation that came with your computer.

If you have an older version (pre-2004) of the ATC fonts installed, replace them with the fonts in this folder.

Resource Files. Resource files are organized in project-specific folders, and are named to facilitate cross-platform compatibility. Words are separated by an underscore, and all file names include a lowercase three-letter extension. For example, if you are directed to open the file "graphics.eps" in Project 2, the file can be found in the RF_Photoshop_L1> Project_02 folder. We repeat these directions frequently in the early projects.

The Work In Progress Folder. This folder contains individual folders for each project in the book (e.g., WIP_01, WIP_02, etc.). When an exercise directs you to save a file, you should save it to the appropriate folder for the project in which you are working.

The exercises in this book frequently build upon work that you have already completed. At the end of each exercise, you will be directed to save your work and either close the file or continue to the next exercise. If you are directed to continue but your time is limited, you can stop at a logical point, save the file, and later return to the point at which you stopped. In this case, you will need to open the file from the appropriate WIP folder and continue working on the same file.

Typeface Conventions. Computer programming code appears in a monospace font that `looks like this`. In many cases, you only need to change or enter specific pieces of code; in these instances, the code you need to type or change appears in a second color and `looks like this`.

INSTRUCTOR'S RESOURCES

Customize Your Book (www.prenhall.com/customphit).   The Prentice Hall Information Technology Custom PHIT Program gives professors the power to control and customize their books to suit their course needs. The best part is that it is done completely online using a simple interface.

Professors choose exactly what projects they need in the *Essentials for Design* series, and in what order they appear. The program also enables professors to add their own material anywhere in the text's presentation, and the final product will arrive at each professor's bookstore as a professionally formatted text.

To learn more about this new system for creating the perfect textbook, go to www.prenhall.com/customphit, where the online walk-through demonstrates how to create a book.

Instructor's Resource Center.   This CD-ROM includes the entire Instructor's Manual for each application in Microsoft Word format. Student data files and completed solutions files are also on this CD-ROM. The Instructor's Manual contains a reference guide of these files for the instructor's convenience. PowerPoint slides with more information about each project are also available for classroom use.

Companion Web site (www.prenhall.com/essentials).   Instructors will find all of the resources available on the Instructor's Resource CD-ROM available for download from the Companion Web site.

TestGen Software.   TestGen is a test generator program that lets you view and easily edit test bank questions, transfer them to tests, and print the tests in a variety of formats suitable to your teaching situation. The program also offers many options for organizing and displaying test banks and tests. A built-in random number and text generator makes it ideal for creating multiple versions of tests. Powerful search and sort functions let you easily locate questions and arrange them in the order you prefer.

QuizMaster, also included in this package, enables students to take tests created with TestGen on a local area network. The QuizMaster utility built into TestGen lets instructors view student records and print a variety of reports. Building tests is easy with TestGen, and exams can be easily uploaded into WebCT, Blackboard, and CourseCompass.

Prentice Hall has formed close alliances with each of the leading online platform providers: WebCT, Blackboard, and our own Pearson CourseCompass.

OneKey. OneKey lets you in to the best teaching and learning resources all in one place. OneKey for *Essentials for Design* is all your students need for out-of-class work conveniently organized by chapter to reinforce and apply what they've learned in  class and from the text. OneKey is all you need to plan and administer your course. All your instructor resources are in one place to maximize your effectiveness and minimize your time and effort. OneKey for convenience, simplicity, and success.

WebCT and Blackboard. Each of these custom-built distance-learning courses features exercises, sample quizzes, and tests in a course management system that provides class administration tools as well as the ability to customize this material at the instructor's discretion.

CourseCompass. CourseCompass is a dynamic, interactive online course management tool powered by  Blackboard. It lets professors create their own courses in 15 minutes or less with preloaded quality content that can include quizzes, tests, lecture materials, and interactive exercises.

Performance-Based Training and Assessment: Train & Assess IT. Prentice Hall offers performance-based training and assessment in one product — Train & Assess IT.

The Training component offers computer-based instruction that a student can use to preview, learn, and review graphic design application skills. Delivered via Web or CD-ROM, Train IT offers interactive multimedia, and computer-based training to augment classroom learning. Built-in prescriptive testing suggests a study path based not only on student test results but also on the specific textbook chosen for the course.

The Assessment component offers computer-based testing that shares the same user interface as Train IT and is used to evaluate a student's knowledge about specific topics in software including Photoshop, InDesign, Illustrator, Flash, and Dreamweaver. It does this in a task-oriented, performance-based environment to demonstrate students' proficiency and comprehension of the topics. More extensive than the testing in Train IT, Assess IT offers more administrative features for the instructor and additional questions for the student. Assess IT also enables professors to test students out of a course, place students in appropriate courses, and evaluate skill sets.

INTRODUCTION

Adobe's Photoshop, originally introduced to the market in 1987, has become the leading image-editing and painting application in the world. While other programs claim to offer similar or better features and functionality, Photoshop — and its companion Web-imaging application, ImageReady — stand alone in their field.

From the earliest versions of the software, Photoshop has provided functionality that photographers, color-correction professionals, designers, and Web developers only dreamt about a few short years before the program's introduction and widespread adoption.

Photoshop CS expands on the established interface, providing even more tools and utilities to facilitate image modification and creation, as well as improve digital workflows. Photoshop CS and ImageReady also include many tools that make the transition from print to the Web to PDF far easier than ever before.

This book is designed to introduce the tools, utilities, and features that are built into Photoshop CS, and provide hands-on practice so you can apply the skills to your own design projects. We define many of the terms and concepts that you need to understand when working in the commercial graphic design and imaging fields, and explain how those ideas relate to Photoshop projects.

Our goal in creating these exercises and projects was to show you how to use the software's features to implement your creative ideas. The skills you learn throughout this book can be applied to any image, whether a family portrait or the graphic assets required for a 200-page catalog. We encourage you to consider the bigger picture of digital imaging.

This book is targeted toward design and imaging techniques. It shows you how to create documents that can be printed from your desktop, or migrated into digital document creation, where your pictures become components in magazines, books, catalogs, and more. Furthermore, this book teaches you how to produce Web-compliant graphics, ensuring that the images you create in Photoshop will work wherever and whenever they are used.

P R O J E C T **1**

Taking a Tour of Photoshop CS

O B J E C T I V E S

In this project, you learn how to

- Open and save an image

- Identify the different parts of the Photoshop working environment

- Learn to use the File Browser to organize your images

- Recognize different tools in the Photoshop Toolbox

- Use a selection tool to isolate part of an image

- Modify an existing image using painting tools

- Move around an image

- Select different viewing options

WHY WOULD I DO THIS?

Adobe Photoshop is the world's most popular photo- and image-editing program – and with good cause. Photoshop offers a vast array of tools, functions, and methods for creating, editing, capturing, repairing, resizing, and enhancing digital images. The power and elegance of the program has made it the favorite of professionals in a wide variety of job functions within the graphic and visual arts. Whether you're a designer, photographer, graphic artist, creative director, advertising professional, marketing guru, or simply want to work with your own personal images, Photoshop has something for you.

The first step in learning to use any tool — even one as powerful and complex as Photoshop — is to gain an understanding of the program's working environment. Taking this approach allows you to see how the various tools and palettes are organized, what functions are available, and what you're going to learn as you develop proficiency with the application.

VISUAL SUMMARY

Let's begin by getting a basic feel for the Photoshop interface. An ***interface*** is comprised of the windows, palettes, tools, and other components that make up a program. As is the case with any industrial-strength program such as Photoshop, there is much on-screen activity when you first start the program. For now, however, all you need to do is become comfortable moving around the interface, and opening and saving image files. Take a few moments to review the location of the different palettes and menus. You use each of them in this and upcoming projects.

FIGURE 1.1

LESSON 1   Opening and Saving Images

Opening images is quite simple; saving files, however, can be a complex procedure since Photoshop supports so many file formats. Photoshop was originally designed to be a file conversion application; the tools and image-editing functions were added later. As you learn more about the application, you'll work with many different file formats. For now, it's important that you become familiar and comfortable with the most common formats you'll use initially.

In the following exercise, you open and save an image. After that, you learn how to recognize and use the important interface components. Remember, an interface is the collection of toolbars, palettes, information boxes, fields, and other elements that determine how a program looks and operates.

Start Photoshop

1   **Launch the Photoshop application.**

The Welcome Screen appears.

If you're on a Macintosh, open the Applications folder and look for the application icon. Double-click the icon when you find it.

If you're on a Windows system, click the Start button and then choose Programs>Adobe to view the Adobe folder, where you will find application.

? If you have problems...

When developing Photoshop Essentials, we used a Macintosh G4 running OS X Panther. We used that operating system to create the screen captures. If you're working on a Windows system, the exercises will work exactly as written. You might, however, see some minor discrepancies between the Macintosh and Windows screen images. These differences are purely cosmetic, and will not affect the functionality of the lessons, hands-on activities, or other activities in this book.

Key commands (shortcuts) are slightly different, however, and we provide all such commands for both operating systems. For example, if we include the shortcut Command/Control-S, Macintosh users should press Command-S, and Windows users should press Control-S — the Macintosh shortcut is always presented first.

2 Take a moment to look at the Welcome Screen.

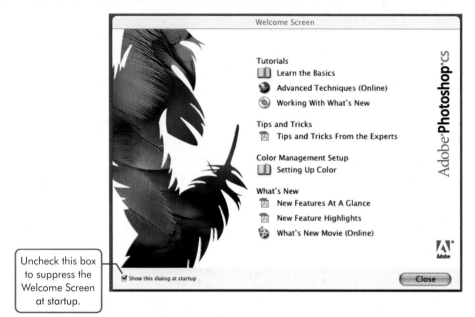

Uncheck this box to suppress the Welcome Screen at startup.

FIGURE 1.2

3 Uncheck the "Show this dialog at startup" check box in the lower left of the dialog box.

The next time you launch Photoshop, this screen will not display.

4 Click the Close button to close the Welcome Screen.

5 Keep Photoshop running for the next exercise.

You will work with the Help features as you develop your skills and become more comfortable using Photoshop. For now, however, it's best to keep this feature turned off so you don't have to close it every time you launch the application.

To Extend Your Knowledge...

RESOURCE FOLDERS

Throughout the book, you will be asked to open existing images that were created specifically for the exercises contained within each lesson. These images are organized according to the project in which they're used (and in some cases, within folders according to a specific lesson within a project). The main folder is named RF_Photoshop_L1; it contains nine folders named Project_01, Project_02, and so on through Project_08, plus the WIP_IP folder for the Integrating Project. Whenever you're asked to open a file, you can find it in the appropriate Project_0x folder. This way, we do not have to include the entire path name every time we ask you to find and open an image.

Open and Save an Image

In this exercise, you open an image and save it into another location.

1   **Choose Open from the File menu.**

2   **Navigate to the RF_Photoshop_L1>Project_01 folder.**

3   **Double-click the strand_keywest.psd image.**

You see a picture of the Strand Theater in Key West, Florida.

FIGURE 1.3

To Extend Your Knowledge...

USING DIFFERENT FILE FORMATS

Since Photoshop supports so many file formats, they're presented in a pop-up menu accessible from the Save or Save As dialog boxes. To access the menu, click and hold the small arrow on the right side of the Format field, and all the available choices are displayed. If you want to save your image in a different format, you can choose the appropriate selection from the list.

You use several different formats as you move forward with your lessons. Some of the selections aren't used very often, or are used only in specialized situations and environments. The most popular and useful formats include: PSD, or native Photoshop format; GIF, which is the most commonly used format for Web graphics; JPEG, another Web-compliant format used for displaying photographs on Web sites; RAW, an increasingly popular format for digital camera images; and TIF, Tagged Image Format, which is the format of choice when images are going to be printed.

4   **Choose File>Save As.**

The Save dialog box appears. Depending on the system you're using, it might look a little different than the one you see here, but all the features work the same.

5   **Click and hold the Format pop-up menu.**

This menu provides a list of the file formats available to you when you're saving a Photoshop image. The appropriate file format for a piece of work is determined by the ultimate use of the picture. When you're working on a file, it's best to keep it in its ***native format***, which is the format specific to a particular program. The extension for native Photoshop images is ***.psd***, which stands for Photoshop Document.

FIGURE 1.4

6   **Navigate to your Work_In_Progress folder. Navigate one level down to the WIP_01 folder. Name the file "my_strand.psd".**

7   **Click the Save button to complete the process.**

FIGURE 1.5

8   **Keep the file open for the next exercise.**

LESSON 2   Exploring the Photoshop Environment

When you first see Photoshop, it can appear somewhat intimidating; there are dozens of interface components, including a Toolbox, tool palettes, tool preferences, an application-specific menu bar, measurement devices, and more.

In the following exercise, you explore the various palettes, menus, and tools while you work on your images.

Reset Default Palette Locations

1   **If necessary, open the my_strand.psd image you saved in the previous exercise.**

The image was saved into the Work_In_Progress>WIP_01 folder.

2   **Choose Window>Workspace>Reset Palette Locations to restore all the palettes to their original "factory" settings.**

FIGURE 1.6

Whenever you use Photoshop, the program remembers the settings from your previous session. This means that if you already used the program (or someone else used the machine before you did), the program's settings might not be what you expect — or as they're shown in these exercises.

3   **Leave the file open for the next exercise.**

To Extend Your Knowledge...

BUILDING KNOWLEDGE

Even though Photoshop might seem intimidating at first, you don't need to know every available command, tool, and technique before you start using the program. Your knowledge of the program will grow as you use it. Even the most experienced users learn a new feature or technique when they work on new projects; the same will undoubtedly be true for you.

LESSON 3 Managing Palettes

Since Photoshop has so many different tool sets, they're organized into interface components known as palettes. **Palettes** are floating windows that provide access to program features such as layers, brushes, color swatches, actions (which allow you to automate the software to reduce the time it takes to perform repetitive tasks), and more. **Pop-up palettes** are associated with specific tools and functions; they pop up to provide access to additional features not visible when the pop-up palette is closed.

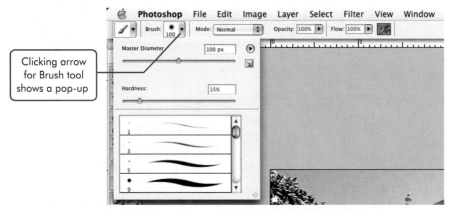

FIGURE 1.7

To accommodate unique workflows, palettes can be organized in many different ways, and their current "state" saved and recalled later. That way, you can set up the Photoshop interface to meet the requirements of different kinds of assignments.

You can do several other things with docked palettes. For example, you can minimize a palette by double-clicking the solid bar at the top. Doing so reduces the palette to a small strip showing only the name tab. Other palettes, such as the Layers palette, can be resized as well; simply drag the lower-right corner until it reaches the size you prefer.

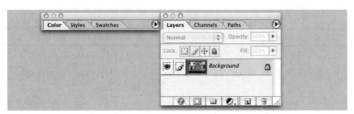

FIGURE 1.8

Manage and Organize Palettes

1   **In the open file, click the palette containing the Color tab. Drag it onto the center of the working area.**

The palette actually contains three different feature sets. The first is Color, the second is named Swatches, and the third contains Styles. This collection of palettes represents a function called docking. **Docking** allows you to combine (or separate) palettes to better suit the way you use the program.

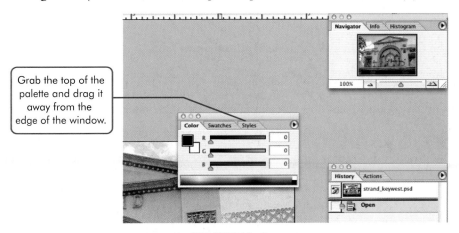

Grab the top of the palette and drag it away from the edge of the window.

FIGURE 1.9

2   **Click the Swatches tab.**

Clicking the tab of a specific palette brings it to the front of the stack; it then becomes active, and you can access its features.

FIGURE 1.10

3   **Click the Swatches tab. Drag it away from the Color and Styles palettes.**

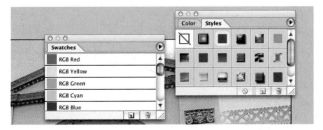

FIGURE 1.11

Dragging the Swatches tab away from the other palettes separates it from the other palettes, and allows it to float by itself. You can position the Swatches palette anywhere you want simply by dragging it to where you want it to appear.

4   **Click the Styles tab. Drag it away from the Color palette.**

Each individual palette can stand alone, but it's best to dock palettes so they are organized according to their primary functions — which is why the Color, Swatches, and Styles palettes are docked together by default.

5   **Drag the Color, Swatches, and Styles tabs onto one another.**

Dragging a palette's tab onto another palette docks (connects) the palettes. Docking palettes is an excellent way to customize your workspace to achieve maximum productivity.

6   **Click the Color tab. Click the Palette Options menu icon.**

Don't choose anything from the menu right now; you'll learn much more about the options available for each of the program's many palettes. The Options menu icon exists on any palette that offers additional features or functions. Most palettes have a Palette Options menu icon.

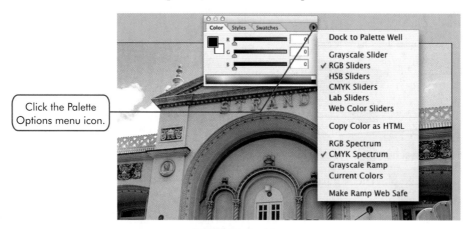

FIGURE 1.12

7   **Click anywhere outside the pop-up menu to close it.**

8   **Leave the file open for the next exercise.**

To Extend Your Knowledge...

MAGNETIC PALETTES

Photoshop's palettes all have a magnetic feature called **Snap-to Palettes**; if you drag a palette close to the edge of the working environment (right, left, top, or bottom), you'll notice that they "stick" in place. This helps you to organize your workspace by ensuring your palettes are all properly aligned. This might not seem important right now, but as you work on increasingly complex documents, the screen will become quite cluttered, and you will find this feature is very helpful.

LESSON 4 Establishing Personal Preferences

Almost all commercial-grade programs can be personalized to some extent, and Photoshop is no exception. Personalization can be achieved in several ways. First, you can save and restore the current state of your palettes; secondly, you can create a collection of what are known as tool presets; and you can change a collection of related settings known as the program preferences.

Tool presets are stored values relative to a specific tool, such as brush size, softness, shape, marquee size, tolerance for the Magic Wand, and others. Almost every tool can be assigned any number of presets, allowing you to rapidly assign complex settings before using a tool.

Program preferences are the fundamental settings that control the overall behavior of an application. In the case of Photoshop, this includes how painting tools appear, file format preferences, and many others. You work with preference settings throughout this book.

In this lesson, you learn how to save your workspace and begin to explore the program's preference settings. As you learn more about the software, you'll become comfortable establishing tool presets and the more advanced preference settings.

Set Preferences

1 **Continue in the open file. If you are using a Macintosh, choose Photoshop>Preferences>General; Windows users should choose Edit>Preferences>General.**

A dialog box appears that shows a collection of pop-up menus, check boxes, and other options related to the general functionality of the program. Included among the choices is Show Tool Tips. It is probably already turned on, displaying a checkmark in the box to the left of the selection. If it's not activated, click the box now to turn it on. When this option is active, Photoshop displays tool names, and in some cases tips about the use of the tool, when you place the mouse pointer over a tool's icon.

FIGURE 1.13

2   **Click the Next button to go to the next Preferences dialog box.**

Nine different windows provide control over a wide array of program preferences. The File Handling dialog box, shown in Figure 1.14, contains the settings related to how Photoshop saves images. You work with these functions later in the book.

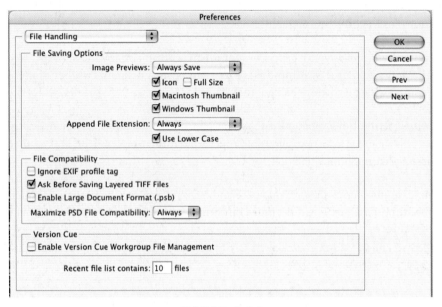

FIGURE 1.14

3   **Click Next to move to the Display & Cursors Preferences dialog box.**

4   **Change Painting Cursors to Brush Size by clicking the appropriate radio button.**

When you begin to use painting tools, you'll see the advantage of setting the Painting Cursors' display to Brush Size. For one thing, changing the size of your painting brushes is very important; if you use the default preference of "standard," you won't be able to see the size of the brush while you paint. In other cases, you'll need to match the size of the brush to a specific detail in an image (particularly when *retouching* an image, which includes correcting flaws, removing artifacts and other unsightly objects, and merging one image into another). You can see the preference being set correctly in Figure 1.15.

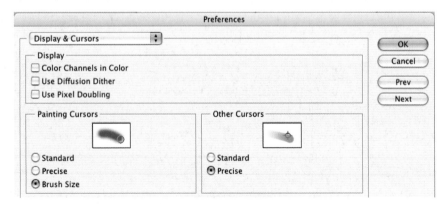

FIGURE 1.15

5 | **Continue clicking the Next button to see the rest of the Preferences dialog boxes.**

For now, leave the remaining preferences at their default settings. You'll have ample opportunity to work with the various Preferences dialogs as you become more familiar with the program.

6 | **Take some time to review the available options.**

7 | **Click Cancel or OK to close the Preferences dialog box.**

8 | **Close the file.**

To Extend Your Knowledge...

SAVING YOUR WORKSPACE

As you develop skills with Photoshop's diverse tools, techniques, and methods, you'll learn that some palettes are more useful than others. This varies, of course, depending on what you're trying to accomplish. For example, if you have multiple images that must be converted from color to black and white, having the Actions palette available would allow you to apply a series of repetitive tasks with a single mouse click. If you're retouching an image or creating new artwork, the Actions palette wouldn't be quite as useful.

To save your palette configurations, including their on-screen locations, choose Window>Workspace> Save Workspace. Simply type in the name you want to use for the specific configuration, and click Save. Workspaces saved in this manner appear in a list at the bottom of the Workspace submenu. You can see the Save Workspace dialog box being used in Figure 1.16.

FIGURE 1.16

LESSON 5 Using the File Browser

The File Browser is a relatively new feature in Photoshop. It provides an excellent method for organizing and managing large numbers of images. You can sort images, select from a number of different views, load images, apply automated functions, and much more. The *File Browser* is essentially an *image database* that allows you to assign keywords, search your image library for specific images, place images into categories, and store information about the image itself. This information, called *metadata*, is divided into three categories: one for the file information, another about the usage of the image (writer, creative director, and more), and a third that incorporates information about the camera equipment used to capture the image.

In the following exercise, you work with the File Browser to organize and manage a number of related images. To get ready, open the RF_Photoshop_L1>Project_01 folder and drag the cook book pics folder into your WIP_01 folder.

Use the File Browser

1 Choose File>Browse.

2 In the upper-left corner of the window, navigate to the RF_Photoshop_L1>WIP_01 folder.

3 Single-click the cook book pics folder.

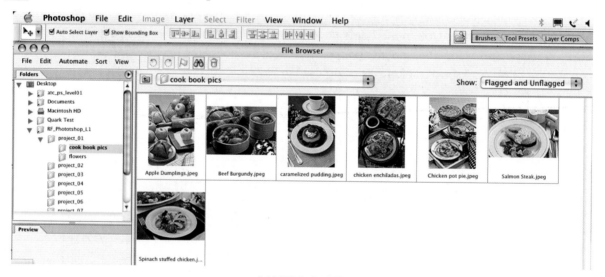

FIGURE 1.17

This selects the folder. When you select a folder within the File Browser, its content is displayed on the right side of the Browser window.

4 From the File Browser menu, choose View>Small Thumbnails.

Figure 1.18 shows one of the alternative views available in the File Browser called Small Thumbnails, which lists files vertically. The selection displays just enough of a thumbnail for you to identify the content of the file. Used for image files, a *thumbnail* is a small icon that represents the actual picture.

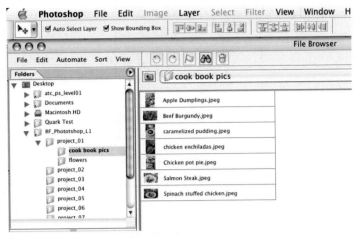

FIGURE 1.18

5 Collapse the three existing keyword set folders in the Keywords palette by clicking the arrows to the left of the category names.

FIGURE 1.19

6 Click the New Keyword Set icon. Name the new keyword set "Food".

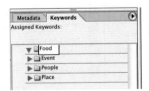

FIGURE 1.20

7 Select the Food set. Click the New Keyword icon. Name the new keyword "Chicken".

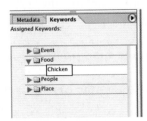

FIGURE 1.21

8   Add two more keywords to the Food set, one called "Beef" and the other called "Desserts".

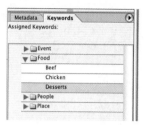

FIGURE 1.22

❓ If you have problems...

Whenever you want to add a new keyword to a keyword set, make sure that you first select the set in which you want the new keyword to appear; otherwise, the new keyword will be created at the same level as existing sets rather than being contained within a set. If this happens, you can't use Undo to reverse the error; you have to click the trash can icon to delete the entry and start over — this time placing the new keyword into its proper set.

9   Select the Apple Dumplings.jpeg image and check the box next to Desserts in the Keywords palette.

FIGURE 1.23

Apple Dumplings.jpeg is assigned a Desserts keyword. You can select multiple images at the same time and assign them all the same keyword by holding down the Command/Control key as you make your selections in the File Browser window.

10   Use the same technique to assign the appropriate keywords to the rest of the images.

11   Click the Palette Options menu icon on the Keywords palette. Select the Search option.

12   Use the Search Criteria pop-up menus to select "Keywords contains". Enter "chicken" in the Search text field.

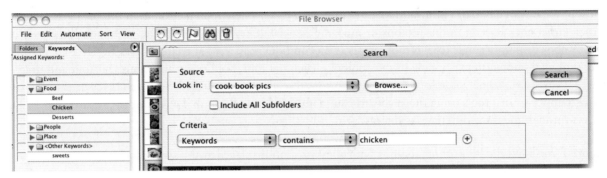

FIGURE 1.24

13   Click the Search button.

FIGURE 1.25

14   Click the Search Results pop-up menu. Navigate to the cook book pics folder to display all the images again.

15   Click the Close button on the File Browser window.

You can see how the File Browser provides a method to collect images into related keyword sets, as well as allow you to search and isolate specific images based on the keyword(s) you assigned to each. This feature is quite powerful, and can result in significant timesavings when you're working on a project containing multiple graphics. Many projects require so many images that simply organizing them on your hard drive becomes quite cumbersome. Examples of such projects include Web sites that can contain hundreds of images.

16   Leave the file open for the next exercise.

LESSON 6   Understanding the Photoshop Toolbox

Most of the work you do in Photoshop requires the use of tools. These tools are found in the Toolbox. To select a tool, either click its icon in the Toolbox or press the associated keyboard equivalent. Although each space on the Toolbox displays a single icon, a tool can also be a component in a set of related tools. To select an alternate tool (one that's not currently visible in the Toolbox), click the tool, hold down the mouse button, and drag to the tool you need. When you release the mouse button, the new tool is selected. You can also cycle through certain groups of similar tools using the keyboard command for that tool group. For example, pressing the "L" key moves through the three different lasso tools.

Figure 1.26 shows the Photoshop Toolbox with all of its tools displayed at the same time.

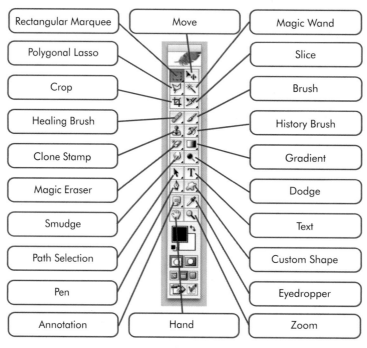

Rectangular Marquee   Move   Magic Wand

Polygonal Lasso   Slice

Crop   Brush

Healing Brush   History Brush

Clone Stamp   Gradient

Magic Eraser   Dodge

Smudge   Text

Path Selection   Custom Shape

Pen   Eyedropper

Annotation   Hand   Zoom

FIGURE 1.26

View Alternate Tools in the Toolbox

1   **In the open file, click and hold the Selection tool in the upper left of the Toolbox.**

A collection of alternate tools appears. All of the tools you see perform the same function — selecting an area of an image. Their names are self-explanatory; the first one selects rectangles and squares, the second ovals and circles, and the last two are used to select single rows or columns of pixels.

FIGURE 1.27

2   **One at a time, select each of the tools and repeat the process in Step 1.**

As you familiarize yourself with the Toolbox, notice that alternate tools are available only for those icons that display a small triangle. Some tools come in only one "flavor" and do not display the black triangle.

3   **Close the file.**

To Extend Your Knowledge...

TOOL CATEGORIES

Although there are quite a few tools contained in the Photoshop Toolbox — especially when you take alternate tools into consideration — they're quite simple to understand once you get a feel for what they're designed to do. Tools are broken into three major categories: selection tools, which are used to select parts of an image; painting and drawing tools, which are used to create shapes, apply colors or tones, and manage type elements; and information tools, used to analyze images. In addition to these three primary categories, there are tools that simplify zooming in and out and viewing images.

LESSON 7   Exploring Selection Tools

As we mentioned above, selection tools are designed to select, isolate, protect, move, copy, or paste portions of an image. The ability to effectively use Photoshop's selection tools is among the most important skills the artist and designer can develop; a large majority of the work you'll do with the program requires sophisticated selection techniques. As your mastery of the application grows, this fact will become increasingly evident.

TABLE 1.1: SELECTION TOOLS

Rectangular Marquee Tool M Elliptical Marquee Tool M Single Row Marquee Tool Single Column Marquee Tool	Marquee Tools	These tools allow you to select areas of an image within its boundaries. A marquee may be elliptical, rectangular, or a single row of pixels.
	Move Tool	This tool allows you to move a selection or layer within the boundaries of the Document window.
Lasso Tool L Polygonal Lasso Tool L Magnetic Lasso Tool L	Lasso, Polygon Lasso, and Magnetic Lasso Tools	These tools allow you to draw freehand marquees, capturing an image area within its boundary. The Lasso is used to draw a freehand marquee that encircles parts of the image; the Polygon Lasso tool uses straight lines created by point-to-point clicking; the Magnetic Lasso tool traces an edge on the basis of the color of the pixels and the tolerances you set for the tool.
	Magic Wand	This tool allows you to capture contiguous or noncontiguous pixels that are similar to the initial pixel upon which you clicked. The range of pixels selected is determined by the Tolerance setting on the Magic Wand Options palette.
	Crop Tool	This tool allows you to permanently cut off (crop) parts of an image.
Slice Tool K Slice Select Tool K	Slice and Slice Select Tools	These tools allow you to create user-defined slices of an image for creation of Web graphics.

Selection tools are so important, in fact, that you'll find an entire project devoted solely to their use. For now, let's see how powerful the selection tools can be — and how practical application of the tools comes into play in a wide variety of functions.

Use Selection Tools

1 | Open the file named red_hat.tif from your RF_Photoshop_L1>Project_01 folder.

2 | Select the Magic Wand tool from the Toolbox.

Note the tool settings at the top of the workspace.

FIGURE 1.28

3 | Among the settings available for the Magic Wand is a field titled Tolerance. Click in the field and enter "32".

The Tolerance setting of the Magic Wand controls how close in values specific pixels must be in order to become selected. If it's set very low — at 8 or 12, for example — only a very few red pixels will become selected. Set it too high, and too much of the image will become selected. Your goal in this exercise is to select only the red hat — not the entire picture.

4 | Click the Magic Wand tool on the baby's red hat.

You can see that a portion of the hat is selected, but not all of it. The selection itself is identified by a flashing dotted border. This selection outline is often called *marching ants* because it resembles tiny insects moving around the region.

FIGURE 1.29

5   **Press Command/Control-D.**

This command deselects the area.

6   **Click in the Tolerance field again and enter "96". Click the hat again.**

FIGURE 1.30

7   **Press Command/Control-H to hide the selection region.**

This command doesn't deselect the area you just picked; it simply hides the selection outline. This makes it easier to see the result of the change in the Tolerance setting.

8   **Choose Image>Adjustment>Hue/Saturation. Click the Colorize box in the lower-right corner of the dialog box.**

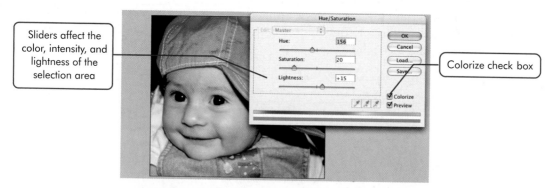

Sliders affect the color, intensity, and lightness of the selection area

Colorize check box

FIGURE 1.31

To Extend Your Knowledge...

SELECTION MASKS

The previous exercise shows something more than how to make a selection using the Magic Wand; it shows the effect of what are known as selection masks. **Selection masks** (or simply **masks**) act like holes in a piece of clear plastic, where the marching ants define the edge of the hole, and areas covered by the plastic are protected from change. You probably noticed that when you adjusted the sliders controlling hue, saturation, and lightness, only the hat changed color — the baby's skin tones and clothes weren't affected. This is the result of the selection; only areas within the selected region were affected by changes made to the image. This is true when you're painting, applying filters, and a host of other techniques. The area outside the selection area is protected (masked) by the selection region. This concept will become much more familiar as you move forward in the book.

9   **Move the dialog box out of the way. Move the Hue slider to the right and left to change the color of the baby's hat.**

The term *hue* refers to the actual color you see: red, blue, green, brown. *Saturation* values determine how rich or intense a color is: pink vs. red, lime vs. forest green, or sky blue vs. deep blue. *Lightness* controls the relative strength of a specific hue.

10   **Work with the Saturation and Lightness sliders to further modify the color of the hat.**

11   **When you're done, close the file without saving your changes.**

LESSON 8   Working with Painting Tools

Painting tools comprise the second major category in the Photoshop Toolbox. As was the case in the previous lesson, you only need to get a feel for how the tools work. As you gain experience with the program, you'll become comfortable using the entire spectrum of the drawing, painting, and selection tools.

Painting tools are used to apply color or tones to an image. There are brushes, stamps, patterns, and a host of other tools you can use to modify and repair existing images, and create new images from scratch.

In the following exercises, you will only use a tiny percentage of the available painting tools, which are described in Table 1.2.

TABLE 1.2: PAINTING TOOLS

Icon	Tool	Description
	Brush Tool	This tool allows you to apply color to an image. The brush you select from the Brushes palette determines the width of the stroke.
	Pencil Tool	The Pencil tool creates hard-edged lines. Generally, this tool is useful only when working with bitmapped images, which are hard-edged by nature.
	Healing Brush Patch Tools Color Replacement Tool	These tools are used primarily to repair and retouch images to remove damage, hide wrinkles, remove offending components, and other similar editing functions.
	Clone Stamp Pattern Stamp	The Clone Stamp tool duplicates one part of the image to another from a reference point on the image; each stroke paints more of the image. The Pattern Stamp tool uses the rectangular selection marquee to select part of the image as a pattern. The Pattern Maker filter then defines the pattern. It paints over designated parts of the image with that repetitive pattern.
	History Brush Art History Brush	The History Brush repaints parts of an image based on a "snapshot" in the History palette. The Art History Brush paints with stylized strokes to any selected state or snapshot in the History palette.
Eraser Tool E Background Eraser Tool E Magic Eraser Tool E	Eraser Tool Background Eraser Tool Magic Eraser Tool	The Eraser tool removes pixels and replaces them with the foreground color. The Background Eraser tool erases pixels to transparency. The Magic Eraser tool converts solid colors to transparency with a single click.
Gradient Tool G Paint Bucket Tool G	Gradient Tool Paint Bucket Tool	The Gradient tool creates smooth blends between shades of a single color, between two colors, or as a mixture of several colors and transparent areas. Linear gradients are smooth gradations in tone in a straight line. Radial and diamond gradients begin at a center point and radiate in concentric circles or diamonds from one color to another. The angular gradient creates shades in a counterclockwise sweep around the beginning point of a blended area. The Paint Bucket tool fills areas of similar color with the foreground color or a pattern.
Pen Tool P Freeform Pen Tool P Add Anchor Point Tool Delete Anchor Point Tool Convert Point Tool	Pen Tools	There are tools for selecting, creating, and editing paths. Paths may be created directly in Photoshop or pasted from the clipboard from Adobe Illustrator.
Rectangle Tool U Rounded Rectangle Tool U Ellipse Tool U Polygon Tool U Line Tool U Custom Shape Tool U	Shape Tools	These tools include the Rectangle, Rounded Rectangle, Ellipse, Polygon, Line, and Custom Shape tools.

Use Painting Tools

1   Open the image named sailboat_beach.tif from your Project_01 folder.

2   Select the Paintbrush tool from the Toolbox.

3   If it's not visible, choose Window>Swatches to activate the Swatches palette.

4   Click the Paintbrush tool on a bright yellow color on the Swatches palette.

FIGURE 1.32

5   Use the brush to draw some shapes on the sky.

6   Choose File>Step Backward to remove the shapes you just drew.

You can press Command/Option-Z (Macintosh) or Control/Alt-Z (Windows) to undo (remove) the shapes one at a time.

7   Press the "]" key to enlarge the brush size.

When you want to reduce the brush size, press the "[" key.

8   Draw a sun in the sky.

Increase your brush size so you can draw a believable sun in the sky.

FIGURE 1.33

9   Select Undo Brush Tool to remove the sun.

10 **Choose the Clone Stamp tool from the Toolbox.**

11 **Option/Alt-click the striped sail on the sailboat.**

This sets the striped sail as the source of the clone.

12 **Click in the middle of the image and begin to paint. A clone of the original boat appears where you stroke the brush.**

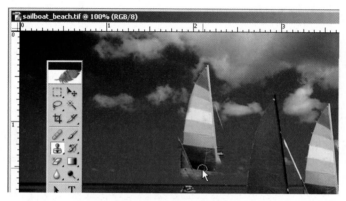

FIGURE 1.34

13 **Continue to work with the various painting tools until you are comfortable with them. When you're done, close the image without saving.**

LESSON 9 Moving Around an Image

In almost all cases, with very few exceptions, you must move around an image (*navigate*) while you're working on it. One example of navigation is zooming into a specific area of a picture so you can fix a problem; another is zooming out so you can see the entire image at once. Sometimes you'll want to use every available inch of your monitor; other times you might want Photoshop on half your monitor and Illustrator on the remainder. How you set up your workspace depends on what you're doing at that particular moment.

Navigate an Image

1 **Open my_strand.psd from your Work_In_Progress>WIP_01 folder.**

You opened this file earlier in the project. This time, you're going to open it from the Work_In_Progress>WIP_01 folder where you saved it earlier.

2 **Activate the Navigator palette (Window>Navigator).**

The small slider on the Navigator palette can be used to change the viewing percentage.

3 **Move the slider all the way to the left.**

You zoom all the way out of the image. Notice the small red rectangle on the preview in the palette. It represents how much of the image you see.

4   **Move the slider to the right.**

You zoom into the image and the red rectangle shrinks accordingly.

As you move the slider, the red rectangle indicates the view location.

FIGURE 1.35

5   **Click in the field on the lower left of the palette and enter "300".**

6   **Choose the Hand tool from the Toolbox (if it's not already active).**

7   **Place the Hand tool on the image and try pushing the picture around the monitor.**

Notice that the red rectangle in the Navigator palette moves at the same time.

8   **Choose View>Fit on Screen.**

An alternate method of fitting an image into the window is to press Command/Control-0 (zero). The result is the same — the image resizes to fill the available space.

9   **Look at the Navigator palette or the Title bar to see the current view percentage.**

FIGURE 1.36

10   **Change the viewing mode by choosing View>Screen Mode>Full Screen with Menu Bar.**

An alternate method of changing the viewing mode (probably the best way) is to press the "F" key.

11   **Press the "F" key.**

The first time you press it, Photoshop takes over the entire monitor — neither other menus, nor the desktop, are visible.

12   **Press the "F" key again.**

The image appears on a black background. This is the preferred view for color retouching and painting assignments because it's the least distracting.

FIGURE 1.37

13   **Close the file without saving.**

To Extend Your Knowledge...

KEYBOARD NAVIGATION

As you learn Photoshop, you'll find there are many different ways to perform similar tasks. For example, you can select the Zoom tool by clicking it in the Toolbox or by pressing the "Z" key. In addition, you can zoom by:

- Selecting Zoom In or Zoom Out from the View menu
- Pressing Command/Control-plus (+) or Command/Control-minus (-)
- Pressing Command/Control-Spacebar or Option/Alt-Spacebar to temporarily toggle the Zoom tool in or out
- Changing the view percentage in the lower-left corner of the window
- Changing the scale factor on the Navigator palette

All of these options work; but for novice Photoshop users, it is easiest to concentrate on a few shortcuts that work for the widest variety of tasks. You will gradually learn the rest of the shortcuts as you become more familiar with the program. From the list above, the two best zoom choices are Command/Control-Spacebar and the Navigator palette.

When dialog boxes are open, the items in the Toolbox are not available; the character sequence Command/Control-Spacebar temporarily activates the Zoom tool from nearly any dialog box, as well as when working on a document with another tool. The Navigator palette combines the functionality of both the Zoom and Hand tools in a visual format; using this palette allows you to navigate your document quickly and easily.

C A R E E R S   I N   D E S I G N

UNDERSTANDING IMAGES AND GRAPHICS

Images brought into Photoshop come from two primary sources. A ***digital image*** is one that already exists in electronic form, such as: a CD image; an image that originated in a painting or drawing program, such as Adobe Illustrator or Macromedia FreeHand; or the image may have originated on a digital camera. An ***analog image*** begins its life as a physical object — a photograph, illustration, or painting. In order to work with an analog image in Photoshop, it must first be digitized using a scanner or similar digital-capture device.

Analog Images

The most common type of image used in today's publications is photographic (prints or transparencies), although the increasing capabilities and popularity of digital cameras is resulting in an expanding reliance on digital originals. The color, contrast, density, and sharpness of each photo varies, depending on many factors, including the camera, type of film, lighting, and, of course, the ability of the photographer. Other analog image sources include paintings, pastels, charcoals, and pencil drawings. All these images are called ***continuous tone*** images because the colors or shades blend smoothly from one to another. Black-and-white photographs and certain types of charcoal or pencil illustrations — ones containing intermediate shades of gray — are referred to as ***grayscale*** images.

Another category is ***line art***, which contains only black and white; examples include logos, pen-and-ink drawings, and other graphics that don't contain any shades or tones. ***Flat*** artwork contains only solid colors; examples include icons, certain logos, and simple cartoons.

The image on the left is a scanned photograph. The image on the right is an icon created in Adobe Illustrator and opened in Photoshop; it's considered flat art because it contains only solid colors.

FIGURE 1.38

Digital Images

In addition to analog images that are converted to digital form, many images are readily available as digital data. Photo images are available for downloading from online sources, or may be purchased on CD from stock photo houses. Digital cameras produce images ranging in quality comparable to those from professional large-format cameras, to the quality available from an inexpensive consumer camera. Video-capture equipment provides similar capabilities.

C A R E E R S   I N   D E S I G N

Photographs comprise the majority of images brought into Photoshop for manipulation, although original artwork created in drawing and painting programs plays a role, as well. It is often easier to adjust these images in their originating programs, but images from dissimilar sources are often merged in Photoshop to create composite images.

Digital Cameras. Digital cameras have come a long way since the first models were introduced. Where they once were suitable solely for Web use or lower-quality printing projects, they're now found in the most demanding applications — in many cases, for high-end product and fashion photography.

Digital Art. Digital art is usually defined as artwork created in Photoshop or other image-editing applications (you can also import a wide variety of file formats into Photoshop). Within the Adobe family of graphic applications, Illustrator, Dimensions, Atmosphere, and Premiere can also produce images that are compatible with Photoshop.

Stock Photography. We remember spending endless hours looking through *stock books* — four-color catalogs of available images sold through businesses known as *stock houses*. These companies maintained the rights to a wide variety of photographic and artistic copyrights, and managed the licensing of those images for the original creators. If an ad agency, for example, wanted to use a photograph of jazz great Dizzy Gillespie, or a photograph of Elvis Presley, or a picture from the Ufizzi museum in Florence, Italy, they paid a fee to the stock house that offered the photograph. In turn, the stock house took its percentage of the fee, and paid the balance to actual copyright owner.

Using stock photography had many advantages. Even though costs for one-time usage (the most common type of license available for stock imagery) can be expensive, setting up a physical camera shoot to create the images envisioned by the designer can be even more so.

In recent years, largely due to the explosion in digital imaging technology, a new form of stock image has emerged. Many of the images used in our books, for example, come from a stock house called Photospin (www.photospin.com). For a small annual fee, an artist can gain access to thousands of photographs, already organized into logical categories, and available directly from the company's Web site.

Scanners. Once original source photographic film is processed (making the image visible and permanent), the image can be scanned — that is, digitized and recorded on a variety of media — and then manipulated on a computer. Before the advent of digital cameras, scanners provided the only way to create a digital image from an analog source. They're still very popular. Seven or eight years ago, a decent scanner cost more than $2,500; today, they're available for under $100.

There are many types of scanners. They differ in their methods of collecting the image data, the type of media they can scan, and how accurately they reproduce the image in digital form. All scanners share the same principle of operation: they convert images into a pattern of squares called pixels (stands for picture elements). A *pixel* is the smallest distinct unit of an image that can be recorded or displayed by a digital device at any given resolution.

SUMMARY

In Project 1, you began your exploration of the Photoshop interface, which we refer to as the working environment. You learned about the various palettes available to you, and how they can be managed using a combination of techniques, including separating them and docking them.

You learned about the Photoshop Toolbox and how it's split into three primary categories: selection tools, painting and drawing tools, and tools that provide information about the images you're working with. While analyzing the Toolbox, you found that many tools offer alternates that are displayed on pop-up menus.

You began to work with several different navigation methods, which, as you work on increasingly complex tasks, become critical skills. While these techniques are not as important as selection and layer management, being able to effectively manage the amount of available onscreen "real estate" saves a lot of time.

KEY TERMS

Analog image	Line art	Save As
Continuous tone	Marching ants	Selection mask
Digital Image	Mask	Selection tools
Docking	Metadata	Snap-to-palette
File Browser	Native format	Stock books
File format	Navigation	Stock houses
Flat color	Open	Thumbnail
Grayscale	Painting tools	Tolerance
Hue	Palette	Toolbox
Image database	Preferences	Tool preset
Interface	.psd	Workspace
Keyword	Retouching	Zoom percentage
Lightness	Saturation	

CHECKING CONCEPTS AND TERMS

SCREEN ID

Name the following items.

a. _____

b. _____

c. _____

d. _____

e. _____

f. _____

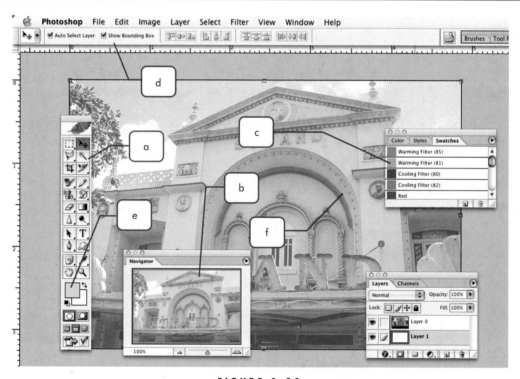

FIGURE 1.38

MULTIPLE CHOICE

Circle the letter of the correct answer for each of the following questions.

1. Which of the following is not a painting tool?
   a. Clone Stamp tool
   b. History Brush tool
   c. Healing Brush tool
   d. Slice tool
   e. a through d are all painting tools

2. A selection mask _____.
   a. protects the image within the selection area
   b. protects the image outside the selection area
   c. is created using the Clone Stamp tool
   d. is only active when visible

3. Connecting related palettes is called _____.
   a. tabbing
   b. linking
   c. docking
   d. activating
   e. welling

4. The sensitivity of a tool such as the Magic Wand is referred to as its _____.
   a. softness
   b. hardness
   c. tolerance
   d. transparency

5. Factory settings are also known as _____.
   a. reset workspace
   b. preferences
   c. General preferences
   d. defaults
   e. All of the above.
   f. None of the above.

6. Displays & Cursors is a _____.
   a. tool palette
   b. preference dialog box
   c. factory setting
   d. Toolbox component
   e. All of the above.

7. You can step backward through a series of steps by pressing _____.
   a. Command/Control-Z
   b. Command/Control-X
   c. Command/Control-Alt-S
   d. Command/Control-Alt-P
   e. None of the above.

8. The Type tool is considered a _____.
   a. painting tool
   b. shape tool
   c. selection tool
   d. masking tool
   e. a, b, and d
   f. b, c, and d
   g. All of the above.

9. You can make a brush larger and smaller by pressing the _____ keys.
   a. { and }
   b. < and >
   c. [and]
   d. - and +

10. The _____ palette allows you to select colors from predefined chips.
    a. Color
    b. Brushes
    c. Gradient
    d. Swatches
    e. a and c
    f. a and d

DISCUSSION QUESTIONS

1. Identify four different ways you can use the Photoshop interface to zoom into and out of an image.

2. What is one of the most critically important skills you need to develop to become a competent Photoshop user, and why?

3. Why is the File Browser useful, and of what significance are keywords and search capacity when managing large, complex projects?

SKILL DRILL

Skill Drills reinforce project skills. Each skill reinforced is the same, or nearly the same, as a skill presented in the project. Detailed instructions are provided in a step-by-step format. You should work through the exercises in the order provided.

1. Create Browser Sets for Your Resource Folder

You're working in this classroom as a teacher's assistant. The teacher asked you to use the File Browser to create categories for each of the eight projects found in this Photoshop Level 1 book.

1. Choose File>Browse to activate the File Browser.

   You can also press Shift-Command/Control-O, or click the Browser icon on the upper-right side of the workspace.

2. Using the Keywords palette in the Browser, create eight new sets named WIP_01 through WIP_08.

3. Using the Browser, navigate within the RF_Photoshop_L1 folder until you find the WIP_01 folder. Select the WIP_01 folder.

4. Create a keyword named "WIP1" within the WIP_01 set.

5. Assign the keyword to every image within the folder.

6. Repeat the process for the next three projects.

   Be sure to accommodate the subfolders in several of the projects. You should also consider creating a single master keyword named Photoshop_01 and assign it to every image. This way, they can be differentiated from similar resource files used in other Essentials series books.

7. Leave the file open for the next exercise.

2. Create Personalized Workspaces

In this drill, you create a personalized palette configuration using the Save Workspace command.

1. In the open file, choose Window>Workspace>Reset Palette Locations.

2. Close the Navigator palette by clicking the palette's Close box.

3. Separate the Styles palette from the Color palette.

4. Close the Styles palette.

5. Close the palette containing Actions.

6. Position the two palette sets in the upper-right corner of the workspace.

7. Choose Window>Save Workspace and name the workspace "Retouching".

8. From the Window menu, choose Workspace>Reset Palette Locations to return to the default settings.

9. Load your new workspace by choosing Window>Workspace>Retouching.

10. Close the file.

3. Fix a Washed-Out Image

The term "washed out" is used when a photograph was taken at the wrong exposure — a technical term for incorrect lens settings and too much light. As you go through the lessons, you're going to learn a great deal more about repairing images, but you already know about a technique commonly used in the image-repair field. That technique involves using the Hue/Saturation settings to change the color in a specific portion of an image.

In this exercise, you darken the sky and make it bluer.

1. Open the image named clouds.psd from the RF_Photoshop_L1 folder.

2. Select the Magic Wand tool.

3. Set the Tolerance value to "128".

4. Click the sky.

5. Change the Tolerance setting to "64" and click the sky again.

6. Continue to experiment with Tolerance values until you're able to select the sky perfectly.

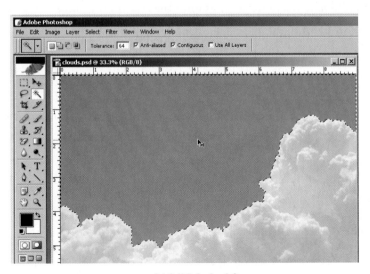

FIGURE 1.40

7. Choose Image>Adjustments>Hue/Saturation.

8. Adjust the three sliders on the dialog box.

   Leave the Colorize option unchecked. Move the Hue slider with restraint; you want the color of the sky to remain natural. Always keep the natural world in mind when you're repairing images. Otherwise, your repairs will be apparent — the exact opposite of your goal.

9. When you're satisfied with the result, choose File>Save As and save the file as "fixed_sky.psd" in your Work_In_Progress>WIP_01 folder.

   You should always consider saving copies of the important images you work on, just in case you want to start over again. Although Photoshop provides many options for restoring an image to its original state, having a true original is always a good idea.

CHALLENGE

Challenge exercises expand on, or are somewhat related to, skills presented in the lessons. Each exercise provides a brief introduction, followed by instructions presented in a numbered-step format that are not as detailed as those in the Skill Drill exercises. You can work through one or more exercises in any order.

1. Create Multiple Client Versions

Your company was hired by a New England-based conservation group to paint a series of covered bridges in their region. Although many of the client's members feel the old-fashioned red color already in place is the only choice, some of the more adventurous members want to see some ideas for different colors.

1. Open the image named bridge start.psd from your RF_Photoshop_L1 folder.

2. Choose the Magic Wand tool.

3. Select the bridge using the current Tolerance setting.

4. Experiment with different Tolerance settings until the selection accurately encloses all the red boards.

5. Press Command/Control-H to hide the selection marquee.

6. Choose Image>Adjustments>Hue/Saturation.

7. Check the Colorize box.

8. Use the three sliders to adjust the Hue, Saturation, and Brightness settings and select another color for the bridge.

9. Save the image as "sample_bridge_01.psd" into your WIP_01 folder.

10. Repeat the process and create another colored version of the bridge.

11. Save this second sample as "sample_bridge_02.psd" into your WIP_01 folder.

12. Repeat the process, naming each version sequentially until you have six samples.

13. Open each of the six samples at the same time.

14. Choose Window>Arrange>Tile to view all six at the same time.

15. Close the files when you're done reviewing them.

2. Create a Floral Catalog

Your local neighborhood beautification committee is having a flower sale to raise money for a new entrance planting. Several of the members grow orchids as a hobby and have kindly volunteered to donate some plants for the event.

1. Start Photoshop (if it is not already running).

2. Choose File>Browser or click the File Browser icon to activate the File Browser.

3. Navigate to the RF_Photoshop_L1>WIP_01 folder.

4. Select the Flowers folder.

5. Set the View to Large Thumbnails so you can view the images.

6. Create a new keyword set named "orchids".

7. Create a new keyword named "flowers".

8. Create a new keyword named "orchid".

9. Assign both keywords to each of the images in the keyword set.

10. Assign a Color keyword to each image, using their approximate color values as the keyword for each set.

11. Choose Automate>Contact Sheet II. Click OK in the dialog box that appears after you invoke the command.

12. If you have access to a color printer, choose File>Print to generate a colored contact sheet of all the images in the folder.

PORTFOLIO BUILDER

Interview Professionals

The best way to begin a solid portfolio of your work — particularly when it comes to using Photoshop in a design and creative capacity — is to find out what other people are doing.

Your assignment is to call local advertising agencies and design studios and set up brief interviews with creative directors and/or staff artists who use Photoshop on a regular basis. Ask them the following questions during the interviews:

1. What is the primary use of Photoshop at your company?

2. What version of Photoshop are you using?

3. What happens to your images once you're done with them?

4. Do you only work with your own original images, or do you work with client images?

5. Do you customize Photoshop to make it easier to work with? If so, how? Do you save custom workspaces? Do you keep the most important palettes connected, while others are usually put away?

PROJECT 2

Learning Selection Techniques

OBJECTIVES

In this project, you learn how to

- Create elliptical and rectangular selections

- Work with the lasso tools

- Select and isolate specific colors and tones

- Combine selections

- Remove portions of a selection

- Copy selections

- Save and load selections

- Use selections to enhance your images

WHY WOULD I DO THIS?

There are many instances when you must make changes to an entire image (sometimes called making *global changes*). These modifications and enhancements might include correcting a noticeable *color cast* (an obvious and unnatural tint that appears in a photograph or digital image), sharpening the details of a picture, or changing a color image into a black-and-white version. On the other hand, the large majority of the work you'll do with Photoshop will be applied only to a portion of the image; the balance of the image will remain unchanged.

To make things even more interesting, you'll need to protect the areas of an image that you don't want to be affected by your changes. This is where selection techniques come into play. Photoshop offers many ways to select and protect portions of an image. It's very important to master Photoshop selection techniques; the more comfortable you become with making complex selections using a variety of methods, the more success you'll enjoy with the rest of the program.

VISUAL SUMMARY

Photoshop includes many tools that can be used to modify an entire image. For example, a blur filter can be applied to the whole image, or the intensity of a yellow cast can be reduced globally using the Curves control.

If you wanted to change the color of a model's sweater from red to blue, you would first make a careful selection of the pixels that comprise the sweater portion of the image. You would then change the *hue* (color) of only those selected pixels. As another example, a photograph of a model home was taken on an overcast day. You feel the image would be much more effective with a blue sky. To make this modification, you would select the pixels that make up the sky and apply the File>Paste Into command to replace the gray area with a bright blue sky.

FIGURE 2.1

Selections can be made using selection tools or by activating layers that contain individual components of the image in Photoshop. There are many different ways to use the selection tools on specific pixels in an image. We'll explore several methods in this project.

The selection tools, layers, masks and channels, and the painting tools are designed so they may be used in concert with one another. For this reason, some aspects of each of these tools are introduced using real-life scenarios. Each deserves, and will receive, its own project to fully explore the role each tool plays in producing professional-quality documents.

Selection tools — similar to most tools in Photoshop — exhibit specific behaviors. The ***behavior*** of a tool depends on what you need it to do. For example, if you want to remove a portion of a selection, you would apply settings that result in that particular behavior. Another behavior might be setting a selection tool so it adds to a selection instead of removing a portion from the selection. These behaviors are controlled from the Selection Tool Options palette, which appears at the top of the workspace when you choose a selection tool.

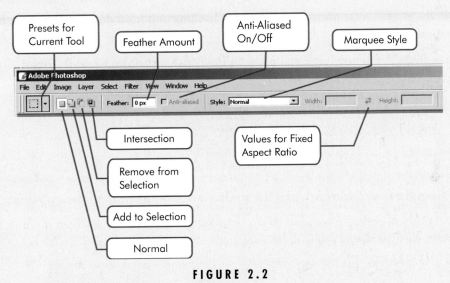

FIGURE 2.2

LESSON 1   Creating Elliptical and Rectangular Selections

As you learned in Project 1, the simplest type of selection is a marquee. You can use four of the selection tools to make marquees: the Elliptical Marquee and Rectangular Marquee tools, and the two Column Selection tools. You won't use the Column Selection tools very often; you will, however, make extensive use of the Elliptical Marquee and Rectangular Marquee tools. As you make increasingly complex selections, you'll use combinations of selection tools that allow you to refine selections until they're perfect.

In the following exercise, you work with the two primary marquee tools to make elliptical and rectangular selections. To get ready for this exercise, launch Photoshop.

Use the Rectangular and Elliptical Marquee Tools

1 Open the file named bigmean.psd from the Project_02 resource folder.

2 Access the Screen Mode icon at the bottom of the Toolbox to change to Full Screen with Menus mode.

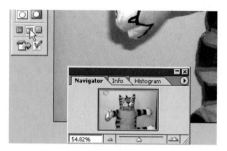

FIGURE 2.3

3 Choose the Rectangular Marquee tool in the Toolbox and hold down your mouse button for a moment.

Holding down the mouse button displays all four of the marquee tools. If it's not already selected, choose the Rectangular Marquee tool.

FIGURE 2.4

4 Hold down the mouse button and draw a selection marquee around the cat's head.

The selection you created is outlined by the "marching ants" you learned about in Project 1. In its current mode, the tool allows you to draw a rectangle of any size or shape.

FIGURE 2.5

5 From the tool Options bar at the top of the workspace, change the Style of the tool to Fixed Aspect Ratio.

6 **If necessary, enter "1" in both the Width and Height fields.**

This setting causes the tool to draw a perfect square. You can achieve the same result by holding down the Shift key while you use the tool.

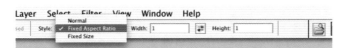

FIGURE 2.6

7 **With the Style still set to Fixed Aspect Ratio, change the ratio to 3:1; enter "3" in the Width field, and leave the Height field set to 1.**

With the mode set to Fixed Aspect Ratio, the next selection you make will automatically match the values in the Width and Height fields. This also works when you're using the Elliptical Marquee tool.

FIGURE 2.7

8 **Use the same pop-up menu to set the Style of the Rectangular Marquee tool to Fixed Size. Enter "64 px" for the Width and "72 px" for the Height.**

This mode is often used when designers want to grab a piece of an image for use in a predefined layout. This often occurs when you need graphics for a Web site. Click the tool on the image to see exactly what we mean.

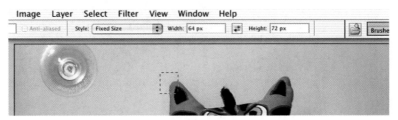

FIGURE 2.8

9 **Choose the Elliptical Marquee tool from the Toolbox.**

10 **Repeat Steps 4–8 using the Elliptical Marquee tool.**

You can see that the Elliptical and Rectangular Marquee tools work exactly the same way — they just draw different shapes.

11 **Keep the file open for the next exercise.**

LESSON 2 Adding and Removing Parts of a Selection

The marquee tools allow you to make rough selections. They don't provide the power you need to make complex selections. The marquee tools are considered very limited when compared to the full range of selection methods that are at your disposal.

The ability to add and remove portions of a selection is a critical skill for the graphic designer. When you begin working with increasingly complex selections, you will need to use more than one tool to accomplish the task, and you will most likely need to add and remove portions of the selection while you work.

Add and Remove Portions of a Selection

1   **In the open bigmean.psd file, choose the Rectangular Marquee tool from the Toolbox.**

2   **Set the Style to Normal.**

3   **Make a selection that surrounds the cat's head.**

4   **From the Options palette, change the behavior of the tool to Add to Selection.**

You can apply three behaviors to a selection tool. The first is Normal, which is the behavior you've been using. The second is the Add to Selection behavior.

FIGURE 2.9

5   **Zoom out of the image so you can see the entire cat.**

6   **Use the Rectangular Marquee tool to add to the selection so it includes the cat's arms and paws.**

Instead of drawing a new marquee that replaces the one that was already on the image, the original selection remains intact and the new selection is added to it.

FIGURE 2.10

7   **Choose the Elliptical Marquee tool from the Toolbox. Change its Behavior to Remove from Selection.**

8   **Use the tool to remove two half-circles from the side of the cat's head.**

You can see how the behavior of the tool allows you to build a selection one piece at a time. This will become even more apparent when you make increasingly complex selections.

FIGURE 2.11

9   **Choose Select>Deselect to eliminate the selection.**

10   If necessary, choose the Elliptical Marquee tool and set its behavior to Add to Selection.

11   Draw a series of circles and ovals on the image.

12   Choose Edit>Clear or press the Delete/Backspace key.

The selection areas are removed from the image.

FIGURE 2.12

13   Choose Edit>Undo Clear to restore the image.

14   From the Select menu, choose Inverse to turn the selection area inside out.

15   Choose Edit>Clear or press the Delete/Backspace key again.

In Project 1, you learned that selections can be used to isolate changes you make to an image. In this example, you can see this happen. Turning a selection area inside out (inverse) is a very useful technique that you will use often.

FIGURE 2.13

16   Close the file without saving your changes.

To Extend Your Knowledge...

CONSTRAINING A SELECTION TOOL

Holding down the Shift key while using the marquee tools — both the Rectangular and Elliptical Marquee tools — constrains the shapes to perfect squares or circles. This is the same as setting the tool's operating mode to Fixed Aspect Ratio and entering equal values in both the Height and Width fields.

LESSON 3 Feathering a Selection

Up until now, your selections have all had well-defined edges. *Feathering* is a technique that softens the edges of your selections. Feathering is a commonly used method of creating special effects, and is often used when two or more images are combined into a single graphic.

A field on the selection tool Options bar allows you to enter a Feather value. If feathering is set to zero (0), selections have hard edges; as you increase the feathering amount, the edges become increasingly fuzzy.

In the following exercise, you experiment with feathering to better understand its effects and how it can be used to enhance your images.

Create Feathered Selections

1 Open the file named flower_trays.tif from the Project_02 resource folder.

2 Save the image into the WIP_02 folder.

3 Change the View to Full Screen with Menu Bar.

You can do this in several different ways; the easiest is to press the "F" key. You can also click the appropriate icon on the bottom of the Toolbox, or choose View>Screen Mode and select the appropriate mode from the submenu.

4 Choose the Rectangular Marquee tool in the Toolbox. Set the Style to Normal.

5 Draw a selection around the long tray of plants on the right side of the image.

FIGURE 2.14

6   **Invert the selection (Select>Inverse) and then clear it (Edit>Clear).**

Examine the edges of the remaining image; you can see that they're very well defined.

7   **Choose Edit>Undo Clear to restore the image.**

8   **Deselect the area.**

9   **Enter "12 px" into the Feather field on the tool Options bar.**

10   **Repeat the process: draw the marquee, inverse it, and clear the area.**

You can see the effect of the value you entered into the Feather field. Rather than ending exactly where you created the selection marquee, the edge of the selection is soft. In fact, the fade spans the 12-pixel value you entered in the Feather field.

FIGURE 2.15

11   **Choose Edit>Step Backward and continue to experiment with different feathering values.**

12   **When you're done experimenting, save and close the file.**

To Extend Your Knowledge...

USING THE KEYBOARD

You can use many keyboard shortcuts to speed up your workflow. Here are a few you can use when working with selections:

Pressing the "M" key switches (toggles) back and forth between the Rectangular Marquee tool and the Elliptical Marquee tool. To turn a selection inside out (inverse) press Shift-Command/Control-I. To deselect a region, press Command/Control-D. To hide a selection border, press Command/Control-H.

LESSON 4 Creating Polygonal Selections

While convenient, the marquee tools can't handle every selection situation. The lasso tools provide a much more flexible method of isolating a portion of an image. There are three lasso tools: the ***Polygonal Lasso tool*** is used to create selections around objects by clicking at points around the object's edge; the ***Magnetic Lasso tool*** tracks the edge of an object based on shifts in color or tone; and the ***Lasso tool*** is a freehand tracing tool that allows you to draw selections.

In the following exercise, you use the Polygonal Lasso tool to select and isolate the sky from the buildings in the foreground of the image.

Use the Polygonal Lasso Tool

1   **Open the file named tall_buildings.tif from the Project_02 folder.**

The Polygonal Lasso tool is the perfect tool for this task; the regions you want to isolate are well defined and they have straight edges.

2   **Choose the Polygonal Lasso tool from the Toolbox.**

FIGURE 2.16

3   **To start your selection, click the tool at the lower-left corner of the left-most slice of the sky (1).**

FIGURE 2.17

4   **Click at point 2, then point 3, and finally click again at point 1 to complete the first part of the selection.**

5   **Hold down the Shift key and use the same tool to select the part of the sky that is visible at the upper right of the image.**

When you hold down the Shift key, it changes the behavior of any selection tool to Add to Selection. You can also click the Behavior icon in the tool's Options bar, but the Shift key modifier is much more efficient.

FIGURE 2.18

6   **Choose Edit>Clear to fill the selection with white.**

7   **Save the file into your WIP_02 folder and close it.**

To Extend Your Knowledge...

CHANGING BEHAVIORS WITH THE KEYBOARD

When you're using a selection tool, holding down the Shift key displays a small plus sign (+) next to the pointer; this lets you know that you'll add to the current selection. If you press the Option/Alt key, the icon changes to a minus sign (-), telling you the tool will subtract from the current selection.

LESSON 5   Working with the Magnetic Lasso Tool

The Magnetic Lasso tool is another one of the Lasso tools. It is used to make selections based on the natural variation of colors or tones that occur at the edges of objects. In some cases, edges are very well defined; in others, edges are less obvious. Learning which tool is appropriate for a specific task isn't as easy as it might seem; only through experience will tool selection and use become second nature.

In the following exercise, you work with the Magnetic Lasso tool to create a more complex selection than the ones you've drawn so far.

Use the Magnetic Lasso to Develop a Selection

1   Open the florence_hotel.psd image from your Project_02 folder.

?   # If you have problems...

When you start this exercise, you should be able to see the size of the Magnetic Lasso tool displayed as a round icon. If you can't, choose Edit>Preferences>Display & Cursors and make sure you have Painting Cursors set to Brush Size, and Other Cursors set to Precise. This will solve the problem.

2   Choose the Zoom tool (the magnifying glass) from the Toolbox. Zoom into the window on the right side of the image.

3   Choose the Magnetic Lasso tool from the Toolbox.

4   In the tool Options bar, set the Feather amount to "0 px", uncheck Anti-aliased, enter "30 px" for the Width, set the Edge Contrast to "10%", and set the Frequency to "20".

For a detailed explanation of these tool options, refer to the "To Extend Your Knowledge" at the end of this exercise.

5   Trace the edge of the window to create your selection.

Even though you're getting a feel for how the tool operates, it's highly likely that the selection isn't very accurate. This is due to the rather broad settings you applied to the tool in Step 4.

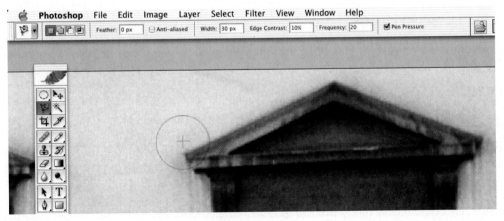

FIGURE 2.19

6   Discard the selection by choosing Select>Deselect.

It's much easier to deselect an existing selection by pressing Command/Control-D. Generally, the more experienced you are, the more you'll rely on keyboard commands instead of making menu selections; they're faster and require less use of the mouse.

7   Change the Width value to "8 px" to reduce the width of the tool.

8   Experiment with other settings for Edge Contrast and Frequency; try 6% or 8% for the Edge Contrast, and 40 or 50 for the Frequency setting.

Running the tool around the edge of the window with more appropriate settings results in a much more acceptable selection. Each image is unique, as is each selection; experimenting with different settings helps you develop a feel for which settings work best for different types of edges. When the settings are correct, you can develop complex selections quickly and easily.

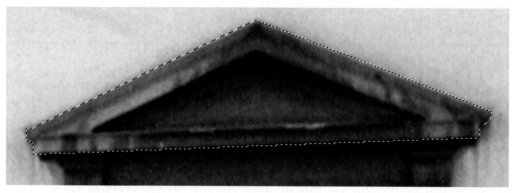

FIGURE 2.20

9   When you're done experimenting with the Magnetic Lasso tool, close the file without saving your changes.

To Extend Your Knowledge...

MAGNETIC LASSO SETTINGS

Several options are available to you when using the Magnetic Lasso tool; understanding these options makes the tool more effective.

Width determines how far to either side the tool looks for a change in tonal values. For well-defined edges, use a lower setting; for more subtle edges, try a wider (higher) value.

Edge Contrast determines how sensitive the tool is to the changes in tones that occur at the edge you're trying to trace. Lower settings work better for slight or soft edges, while higher settings can be used when the edge is well defined.

Frequency values define how many points the tool creates along the edge you're selecting. Lower values result in fewer points, while higher values result in a greater number of points.

LESSON 6 Transforming Selections

Transformation is a term that applies to several functions used to scale, rotate, skew, or otherwise modify a selection. You can apply the same concept to transform layers and imported objects. Photoshop provides several ways to apply transformations:

- *Scale* allows you to change the size of a selection.

- *Rotate* is used to spin a selection. The menu includes a number of rotations that are pre-set to 180 degrees, 90-degrees clockwise, and 90-degrees counterclockwise.

- *Skew* and *Distort* provide ways to stretch and pull a selection into a different shape.

- *Perspective* is the visual phenomenon that causes railroad tracks to appear to meet on the horizon, even though the distance between them remains constant. This transformation technique can be used to simulate that effect.

- *Flipping* a selection on its horizontal or vertical axis turns it over, either top-to-bottom (horizontal) or left-to-right (vertical). If you copy a selection and then flip it, you can create mirror images.

In the following exercise, you create a selection and then apply several different transformations to the selected region.

Transform a Selection

1   **Open plumbago.jpg from the Project_02 resource folder.**

2   **Choose the Lasso tool from the Toolbox. Enter "12 px" for the Feather value.**

3   **Draw a rough selection around the blue flowers.**

Make sure the selection is large enough to encompass all the flowers. You can always modify it later if it's too big.

FIGURE 2.21

4   **If the selection is too large, choose Select>Modify>Contract and enter "10" or "12" pixels.**

Before you can determine optimal settings for this tool, you must first gain some experience using it. You can always start with a small value and repeat the process to refine your selection.

FIGURE 2.22

5   **Choose the Move tool from the Toolbox. Hold down the Option/Alt key and drag the selected flower to the left.**

This process creates a *clone* (copy) of the selection.

FIGURE 2.23

6   **Choose Edit>Transform>Flip Horizontal.**

This command flips the selection on its horizontal axis. The flipped clone looks much more natural than if you had simply left the copy as an exact duplicate.

FIGURE 2.24

7 | **Use the same technique to create another clone of the selection.**

This time, drag the copy down and to the right of the original. You don't want them on top of each other.

8 | **Choose Edit>Transform>Scale.**

Control handles appear on the selection.

9 | **Hold down the Shift key and use the handles to reduce the size of the new clone.**

FIGURE 2.25

10 | **Press the Return/Enter key to commit the transformation.**

The transformation doesn't actually take place until you press the Return/Enter key. This allows you to change the size of the selection until you're satisfied with the result. You can also reposition the selection.

11 | **Experiment with different transformations.**

12 | **When you are done, close the file without saving your changes.**

To Extend Your Knowledge...

ENTERING FIELD VALUES

When entering values for tools such as the marquee selection tools, you can use "px" for pixels, "in" for inches, "mm" for millimeters, or "cm" for centimeters. Photoshop understands what you mean and adjusts the tool settings accordingly.

LESSON 7   Using Transformations to Create Artwork

Many designers and illustrators make extensive use of transformation techniques to create artwork that didn't exist in the natural world. Up until now, you've only worked with existing photographs; but as you progress through this book, you will work with existing artwork, as well as create new designs from scratch. In many cases, you will use transformation techniques to achieve effects that wouldn't otherwise be possible.

In the following brief exercise, you apply several transformation techniques to create a commonly used mirror effect for a type element.

Use Transformations to Generate Artwork

1   **Open the file named hike.psd from the Project_02 folder and save it into the WIP_01 folder.**

We already created this document for you; but once you learn a few tricks about textures and understand how to put type into your documents, you'll be able to quickly generate similar graphics.

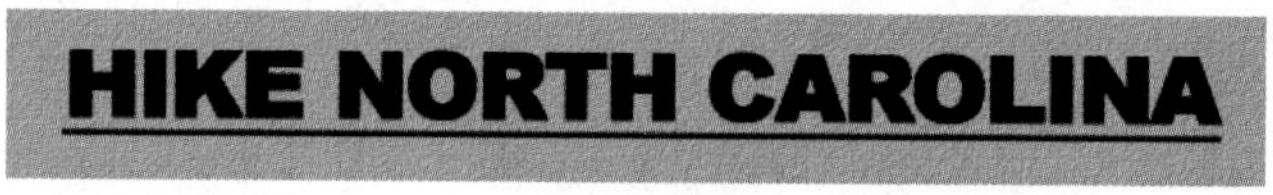

HIKE NORTH CAROLINA

FIGURE 2.26

2   **Choose the Rectangular Marquee tool. Set the Feathering to "0 px", and then draw a selection around the text.**

3   **Choose the Move tool. Press Command/Control-Option/Alt-drag to create a clone of the text.**

Since you want the copy to align directly below the original, hold down the Shift key while you create the clone; it keeps the copy aligned directly below the existing text.

FIGURE 2.27

4   **From the Edit menu, choose Transform>Flip Vertical.**

This transformation results in a mirroring effect. The new text turns over, but stays in its exact position relative to the text above it.

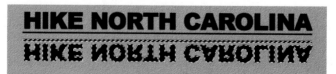

FIGURE 2.28

5 Hold down the Shift key while you use the Move tool to slide the mirrored type up until the two lines are perfectly aligned.

You can also use the Arrow keys to move selections 1 pixel at a time. Sometimes, this is a more accurate and effective method than using the Move tool.

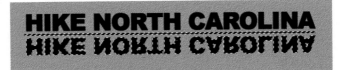

FIGURE 2.29

6 Choose Edit>Transform>Perspective. Drag the lower handles outward.

Handles appear at all four sides of the lower text. When you grab either one of the lower handles and pull it away from the center of the graphic, the element distorts to create a sense of perspective.

FIGURE 2.30

7 Press Return/Enter to commit the transformation, hide the outline, and view the result.

8 Save and close the file.

To Extend Your Knowledge...

USING FREE TRANSFORM

When you're performing a transformation, the Options bar doesn't limit you to a single function. If you're scaling an object, as you did in the previous exercise, you can also rotate, skew, or reposition a selection at the same time. Simply enter the appropriate values in the desired fields and Photoshop applies them all at once.

FIGURE 2.31

LESSON 8   Saving and Loading Selections

Imagine that you just completed a rather complex selection. What happens to your selection if you need to work on another job or it's time to go home? Photoshop's Select menu includes tools for saving and loading the selections you create.

Once selections are made, they can be saved. Any number of selections can be saved in a given image. The entire selection may be saved, or a new selection can add to, subtract from, or intersect with an existing selection.

Selections are saved as channels and/or masks (which are essentially the same thing). We explore the use of masks in more depth in a later project of this book. For now, let's focus on the mechanics of creating, saving, and loading selections.

Save and Restore Selections

1.   Open the file named stone_crabs.psd from the Project_02 resource folder.

2.   Save the file in your WIP_02 folder.

3.   Choose the Magnetic Lasso tool. Enter "10 px" for the Width, set the Edge Contrast to "6%", and set the Frequency to "50".

4.   Use the tool to draw a selection around the outside edge of the plate.

    If necessary, switch to the regular Lasso tool and use the Add to (or Remove from) Selection to refine the selection until it's perfect.

FIGURE 2.32

5 | **Choose Select>Save Selection. Name the selection "whole_platter" and click OK.**

If you look around the dialog box, you see that you can save selections into other documents or into existing channels.

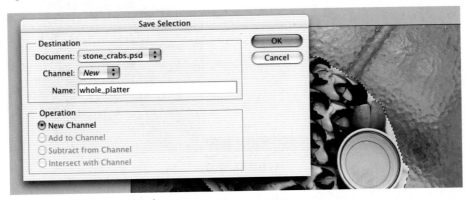

FIGURE 2.33

6 | **Choose Select>Deselect.**

You can also press Command/Control-D to deselect.

7 | **Create a selection for the small plate of butter. Save the selection as "small_plate".**

Now you have two selections stored in the document. It's a simple matter to load either one of them as needed, depending on the requirements of the project you're working on.

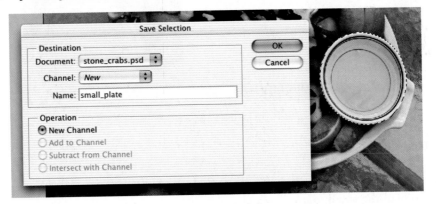

FIGURE 2.34

8 | **Save the file.**

Once you save the file, the selections that you preserved remain intact in the document. When you open the file to work on it later, the saved selections will be there; you won't have to redo them. This can be a tremendous advantage when you are working on complex projects.

9 | **Choose Select>Load Selection. Load the whole_platter channel from the pop-up menu.**

10 **Click the Invert check box, and then click OK.**

The selection is turned inside out — the same as when you apply the Select>Inverse menu option.

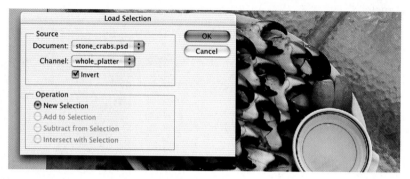

FIGURE 2.35

11 **Choose Edit>Fill and enter "60" in the Opacity field. Click OK.**

The Fill dialog box provides several options for filling a selection. You can apply the foreground color (in this case, black), the background color, or a pattern. For now, you're going to fill the background of the platter with a slightly transparent shade of black. The result will be a reduction of the background clutter and an emphasis on the tray of crab claws.

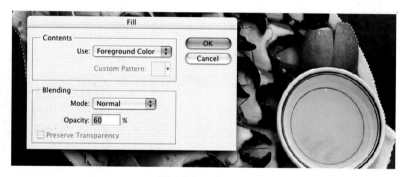

FIGURE 2.36

12 **Invert the selection again.**

13 **Choose Load Selection again, but this time, click the Subtract from Selection radio button before you load the small_plate channel.**

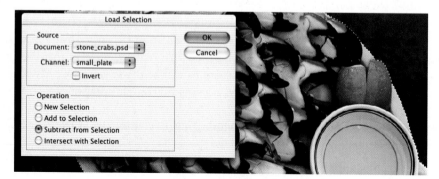

FIGURE 2.37

14 **Choose Filter>Artistic>Watercolor. Click OK to accept the default settings.**

Later in this book, an entire project is dedicated to filters. This step provides a small taste of what can be accomplished using filters in conjunction with effective selection techniques.

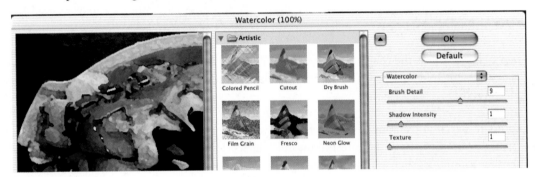

FIGURE 2.38

15 **Save and close the file.**

To Extend Your Knowledge...

CHANNELS

All Photoshop images — regardless of their file format or content — contain channels. A *channel* is a component of an image that contains specific image data.

A black-and-white image contains only one channel. This channel contains different shades of gray; each pixel has a value that ranges from 0 (white) to 256 (black). These 256 different tones (or shades) combine to produce the image that you see. Images containing only gray values are called *grayscale images*.

A typical color image contains three channels. The first channel contains 256 different red (R) values, the second channel 256 blue (B) values, and the third 256 green (G) values. The resultant combination of these three values generates what is known as an *RGB image*. This format is used for the Web and other electronic reproductions.

For print purposes, images are normally converted from three-channel RGB images into four-channel images containing colors related to printing. A color print image has one channel for cyan (C), one for magenta (M), one for yellow (Y), and a fourth for black (K) ink. These images are called *CMYK images*.

Later in the book, you will learn much more about RGB and different types of color and grayscale images. For now, it's only important that you understand what a channel is — because when you save or restore a selection, you are saving additional channels into what started out as a three-channel RGB image.

SUMMARY

In Project 2, you began to develop experience with what is arguably the most important technique available to you as a Photoshop designer. The ability to effectively develop complex selections will be used in the vast majority of your Photoshop projects.

You also had a chance to use the Magnetic Lasso, the Polygonal Lasso, and, of course, the freehand Lasso tools. You saw that different tolerance settings and width values can dramatically improve the effectiveness of the Magnetic Lasso tool.

When it comes to selection techniques, being able to develop complex selections efficiently isn't all you need to know — you also need to apply those techniques to real-world assignments. Saving and loading selections, along with other techniques such as filling and filtering, can result in dramatic graphics. You had a taste of what can be done with a few simple Photoshop techniques when you created a watercolor rendition of a photographic image.

KEY TERMS

Anti-aliasing	Edge contrast	Perspective
Behavior	Feathering	RGB image
Channel	Fixed Aspect Ratio	Rotate
Clone	Flipping	Scale
CMYK image	Global changes	Skew
Color cast	Grayscale image	Transformation
Contrast	Inverse	
Distort	Marquee	

CHECKING CONCEPTS AND TERMS

SCREEN ID

Define the following fields and provide a brief description of what they're used for.

a. _____

b. _____

c. _____

d. _____

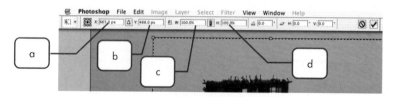

FIGURE 2.39

MULTIPLE CHOICE

Circle the letter of the correct answer for each of the following questions.

1. Which of the following is not a transformation technique?

   a. Fill

   b. Rotate

   c. Skew

   d. Perspective

   e. Scale

2. The tool's _____ determines whether a selection tool acts normally, adds to a selection, removes areas from a selection, or creates a selection from the intersection of two selections.

   a. style

   b. mode

   c. behavior

   d. aspect ratio

3. Define the following measurement values:

   a. mm = _____

   b. px = _____

   c. in = _____

   d. cm = _____

4. The higher the Feather value, the _____ the edge of the selection.

   a. tighter

   b. looser

   c. softer

   d. harder

5. If you had to create a selection around an irregular object with mostly straight sides, which tool would be best to use?

   a. Lasso tool

   b. Polygonal Lasso tool

   c. Magnetic Lasso tool

   d. Elliptical Marquee tool

6. Which tool/s would you use to create a selection that consisted of three ovals and a rectangle?

   a. Lasso tool

   b. Polygonal Lasso tool

   c. Magnetic Lasso tool

   d. Rectangular and Elliptical Marquee tools

7. A selection with a hard edge wasn't _____.

   a. selected

   b. feathered

   c. inversed

   d. Shift-clicked

8. To select tonal ranges, you would use the _____.

   a. Lasso tool

   b. Magic Wand tool

   c. Elliptical Marquee tool

   d. Magic Eraser

9. Increasing the _____ of the Magic Wand tool allows you to select a wider range of colors or tones.

   a. feathering

   b. tolerance

   c. foreground color

   d. background color

10. Decreasing the _____ value results in a harder edge.

    a. Edge Detection

    b. Skew

    c. Feathering

    d. Tolerance

DISCUSSION QUESTIONS

1. Define the term "feathering." What is the most common use for feathering?

2. Name two different ways you can change the behavior of a selection tool so it removes portions of a selection.

3. Why is it so important for today's graphic artists to be able to make accurate selections?

SKILL DRILL

Skill Drill exercises reinforce project skills. Each skill reinforced is the same, or nearly the same, as a skill presented in the project. Detailed instructions are provided in a step-by-step format. You can work through one or more exercises in any order.

1. Create Frames

1. Open the file named stilthouse.psd from the Project_02 resource folder.

2. Set the Feather value to "0". Draw a selection marquee around the house.

3. Choose Edit>Stroke. Enter "6" for the Width of the Stroke and click the Center radio button for the Location.

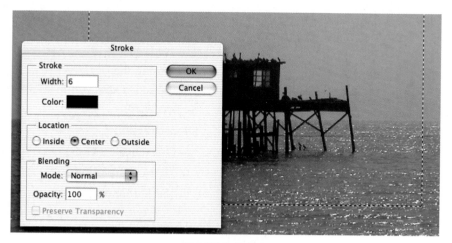

FIGURE 2.40

4. Invert the selection.

5. Choose Edit>Fill to fill the selection with 50% of the background color (white).

6. Save the file in your WIP_02 folder. Close it when you're done.

2. Paste Into

1. Open the file named capital.psd from the Project_02 folder.

2. Use the Magic Wand tool to make a very accurate selection of the sky.

FIGURE 2.41

3. Open the image named clouds.psd from the same folder.

4. From the Edit menu, choose Select All to select the entire image.

5. Choose Edit>Copy to copy the clouds to the pasteboard.

6. Switch back to the capital image.

7. Choose Edit>Paste Into to put the clouds into the sky behind the capital building.

8. Use the Move tool to position the clouds however you prefer.

    Remember that you can apply transformation techniques to the clouds once you've pasted them into the selection.

FIGURE 2.42

9. Save the file in your WIP_02 folder when you're done.

3. Modify Selections

1. Open the file named gull.tif from your Project_02 resource folder. Save it into your WIP_02 folder.

2. Use the Magic Wand tool to select the blue sky.

3. Invert the selection to select only the seagull.

4. Clone the seagull. Move the copy down and to the right of the original bird.

FIGURE 2.43

5. Scale the clone so it's smaller than the original seagull.

6. Choose Edit>Transform>Flip Horizontal to turn the clone on its horizontal axis.

FIGURE 2.44

7. Choose the Rectangular Marquee tool. Enter "36" for the Feather value. Draw a selection marquee around the two seagulls.

FIGURE 2.45

8. Invert the selection and clear it.

FIGURE 2.46

9. Change the Feather value to "0".

10. Create another selection around the seagulls.

11. Choose Select>Modify>Border. Enter "24" pixels for the border value.

This function — one of four on the Select>Modify submenu — is used to create borders around selections. The others are simple to understand and we encourage you to experiment with them on your own.

The Shrink function reduces the size of a selection by a specified number of pixels. The Grow function expands the selection. Smooth rounds and softens the edges of a selection. Border is the command you're using in this exercise.

FIGURE 2.47

12. Choose Edit>Fill to fill the border with black.

FIGURE 2.48

13. Choose the Crop tool.

The Crop tool is a specialized selection tool that only draws rectangular shapes. Once a selection is made, the areas outside the selected region are shaded, which indicates that they will be discarded when you press the Return/Enter key. You crop an image to change its size.

14. Draw a selection within the border you created in Step 11.

    You can use the handles that appear on the cropping selection to move the edges in or out until the selection fits properly.

FIGURE 2.49

15. Press the Return/Enter key.

    The image size is reduced to match the cropping rectangle you created in Step 14. Using only selection techniques, you created a new-and-improved image.

FIGURE 2.50

16. Save the file and close it.

CHALLENGE

Challenge exercises expand on, or are somewhat related to, skills presented in the lessons. Each exercise provides a brief introduction, followed by instructions presented in a numbered-step format that are not as detailed as those in the Skill Drill exercises. These Challenge exercises focus on using skills you learned; you should work through them in the order provided.

1. Repair the Sky

You took a photograph of the East River in New York City from the window of a friend's high-rise apartment. You're very pleased with the composition of the photo, but somewhat disappointed with the washed-out appearance of the sky. (*Washed-out* is a term that is used when an image lacks detail and saturated color.) You want to fix the image so the color of the sky more closely resembles the blue color you saw when you took the picture.

1. Open the image named east_river.psd from your Project_02 folder.

2. Select the Magic Wand tool.

3. Select the sky using the current Tolerance setting.

4. Experiment with different Tolerance settings until the selection accurately includes all the sky without the skyline.

5. Press Command/Control-H to hide the selection marquee.

6. Choose Image>Adjustments>Hue/Saturation.

7. Check the Colorize box.

8. Use the three sliders to adjust the Hue, Saturation, and Brightness settings, and then select another color for the sky.

9. Save the image as "fixed_nyc.psd" into your WIP_02 folder.

10. Keep the file open.

2. Add Some Life

Each time you prepare an image for a client, you like to add something to your personal signature that will later identify the image as yours. You can use formal techniques to do this; but in this Challenge, you add something totally unique — the image of a bird in flight. The effect must be subtle. It is something that you can always point to and say, "See? That's mine!"

1. Continue working in the open fixed_nyc.psd image.

2. Open the gull.tif image you used in the Skill Drills.

3. Create a selection around one of the seagulls that silhouettes him from the surrounding sky.

4. Press Command/Control-C to make a copy of the seagull.

5. Close the seagull image.

6. Select the fixed_nyc.psd image.

7. Choose Edit>Paste to bring the seagull image into the skyline image.
   Handles appear around the bird.

8. Grab the corner handle, hold down the Shift key, and reduce the size of the bird until it's barely noticeable.

9. Move the bird to an inconspicuous place in the image.

10. Press Return/Enter to finalize the pasting process.

11. Save and close the file when you're done.

3. Create a Panel Image

Whenever you copy an item to the clipboard, Photoshop automatically uses the dimensions of the copied element as the default values for any new documents you create. In this exercise, you use the size of the original stilthouse.psd image to automatically create a new document with the same dimensions.

1. Open the original stilthouse.psd image from the Project_02 resource folder.

2. Choose Edit>Select All.

3. Choose Edit>Copy.

4. From the File menu, choose New. Click OK to accept the defaults.

5. Select all, and then choose Edit>Fill to fill the new document with black.

6. Go to the original image. Choose the Rectangular Marquee tool.

7. Set the Mode of the tool to Fixed Size. The Width should be 64 pixels, the Height 800 pixels, and the Feathering value 16 pixels.

8. Choose Window>Arrange>Tile.

9. Click the Selection tool in the original image over the left side of the house.

10. Copy the selection.

11. Click the Rectangular Marquee tool in roughly the same location (on the left side of the house) on the new untitled image.

12.   Choose Edit>Paste.

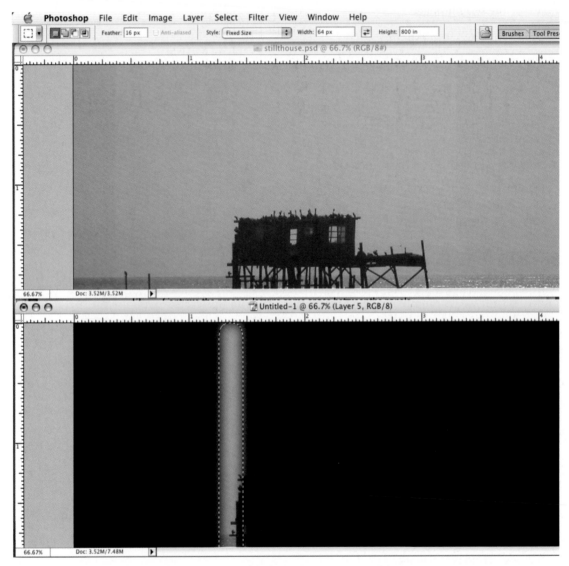

FIGURE 2.51

13. Create additional panels across the image, leaving some space between the panels.

FIGURE 2.52

14. Save the file into your WIP_02 folder as "shades.psd".

4. Look Through the Glasses

In this Challenge, you use what you've learned about selections — specifically what you know about reversing (inverting) a selection. Your task is to simulate the old-movie technique of looking through binoculars by creating two soft circular selections and masking the outside of the circles with black.

1. Open the File Browser. Review all the images in your resource folders. Select an image from one of the resource folders.

2. Choose the Elliptical Marquee tool in the Toolbox.

3. Draw a circle on the image that covers a little less than half of one side.

4. Look at the Options bar to determine the size of the circle.

5. Set the Mode to Fixed Size.

6. Hold down the Shift key and add another circle to the selection. The circles should slightly overlap at their centers.

7. Feather the combined selections between 6–10 pixels.

8. Invert the selection.

9. Fill the inverted selection with Black.

10. Save the image into your WIP_02 file as "binoculars.psd".

P O R T F O L I O   B U I L D E R

Anniversary Montage

Your best friend's parents are celebrating their twenty-fifth wedding anniversary. Since they have been like parents to you, too, you want to give them a special gift: a custom montage of images from their many happy years together as husband and wife. (This friend is fictitious, so you can make this a comedic experience.)

Collect an assortment of old images from a flea market, online (you might search for "public domain images"), or from your friends and family.

Scan all the images. Use your imagination to create interesting frames for the images using selection techniques. Vary the softness and width of the frames.

Once you have collected enough images, create one large image and fill it with a pattern. You can choose the Edit>Fill>Pattern command, and select from the preloaded patterns that come with Photoshop.

Select, copy, and paste the framed images into the large document. Use the Polygonal Lasso tool to create simulated tape to hold down the corners of each image. Use the tool to draw the shape of the tape and choose Edit>Fill to fill the selections with the color of yellowed Scotch tape.

Working with Layers

OBJECTIVES

In this project, you learn how to

- Recognize elements of the Layers palette

- Create new layers

- Use layers to merge multiple images

- Put type elements onto dedicated layers

- Utilize Photoshop's shape layers

- Connect and manage multiple layers

- Modify images using adjustment layers

- Use special effects layers

- Merge and simplify layers

- Export and save individual layers

WHY WOULD I DO THIS?

It would be impossible to overstate the usefulness of layers. In fact, if Photoshop didn't offer such powerful tools to manage and work with layers, the program wouldn't be nearly as valuable. As your overall Photoshop skills mature, the projects you work on become more complex, and you seek to master the advanced aspects of the program, you'll find many ways to apply layers in your day-to-day design activities.

Using layers, you can merge several images together to create *composite images*. You can use layers to correct color, apply special effects, colorize pictures, and repair damaged photographs, as well as change text elements, import line art, and much more. Almost as important as selection techniques, mastering the use and application of layers is fundamental in your Photoshop education.

Layers are also very important for developing structured, multi-component projects such as navigation bars or informational graphics destined for use on the Web. Sites can have dozens of buttons, text layers, graphics, and background images; using layers and layer sets allow you to efficiently organize and manage a large number of components.

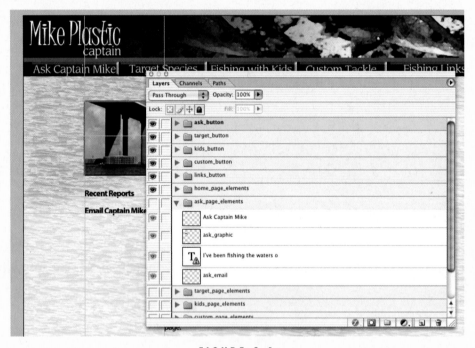

FIGURE 3.1

In simple terms, *layers* are separate images that are stacked on top of each other to form a final image. Layers can be *transparent* (see-through) or *opaque* (solid). Using the *Opacity* setting, you can control exactly how solid the objects on a specific layer appear.

Layers can contain text elements, **vector objects** (objects made with lines and points), photographs, or any other types of components you can create with the Photoshop tools. Unlike channels, layers can contain colors, and special types of layers can contain fills, masks, shapes, and color-correction adjustments. **Blending modes** provide control over how individual layers interact, and are routinely applied by professional artists and designers to achieve compelling results.

When you add a new layer to an image, it's created above the currently selected layer. The order in which layers are arranged is called the **stacking order**. To change the stacking order, you can simply drag a layer to a new position in the layer stack.

Think of layers as individual pieces of acetate that are stacked on top of one another. Depending on their individual opacity values, you can either see through layers to the other layers below, or the topmost layer obscures the rest of the layers in the stack. Opacity determines how solid a layer appears; a value of 100% opacity is solid; an opacity setting of 0% allows you to see right through a layer.

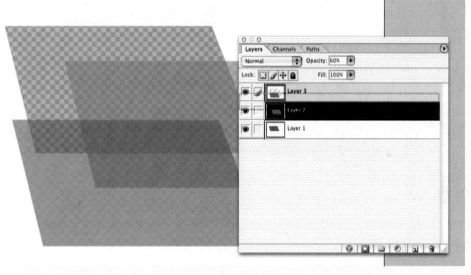

FIGURE 3.2

Layers remain intact until you flatten them. The process of **flattening** combines the elements on separate layers into a single layer.

V I S U A L   S U M M A R Y

The *Layers palette* provides a centralized location from which you can manage the layers in your documents. You can use the Layers palette to create a number of different types of layers, as well as lock, hide, link, or delete layers. You can also use the palette to organize related layers into *layer sets*, which are essentially folders within the Layers palette. You work with each of these features later in this book.

For now, it's important that you familiarize yourself with the Layers palette.

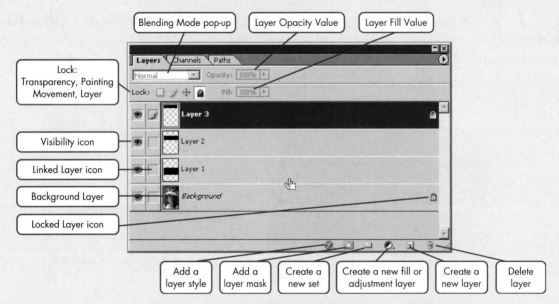

FIGURE 3.3

Take a few moments to review a few fundamental tasks you can accomplish from the Layers palette.

- **Locking and Unlocking Layers.** Using the Lock icon, you can lock and unlock the opacity, decide whether a layer can be painted on, set the position of a layer's content and where it is in the stacking order, or lock the entire layer.

- **Hiding and Showing Layers (Visibility).** Two check boxes are located to the left of each layer name. The first of these allows you to toggle the visibility of the layer. If the visibility icon (a small eye) is visible, so is the layer and all of its content (assuming that images on other layers aren't covering the layer). If you uncheck the icon, the layer becomes invisible (hidden). Hidden layers can be protected from changes affecting other layers.

- **Linking Layers.** The second check box is the Link check box. Linking two or more layers allows you to move them all at once, or align objects on all of them at once.

■ **Deleting Layers.** You can delete layers by dragging them to the trash can icon or selecting them and clicking the trash can.

■ **Adding Layers.** You can create a number of different types of layers. You can also create a layer by pasting content into an image from the clipboard, dragging layers from one image into another, creating text elements, and clicking the New Layer icon (for the appropriate type of layer you need).

■ **Copying Layers.** You can copy a layer by dragging it onto the New Layer icon, or by selecting the layer you want to duplicate, copying it, and pasting it back into the image.

LESSON 1   Working with Layers

Although layers are relatively simple to understand, their use is critical in the creation of complex artwork. Like any powerful feature, it takes time to truly master the use of layers. As we mentioned, they're used to hold imported type, contain color and tone adjustments, as well as completely different images dragged from one document to another.

In the following exercise, you open an existing document that already contains several layers and work with them to create a simple composite (merged) image.

Work with Layers

1 **Open banana_split.psd from the Project_03 resource folder.**

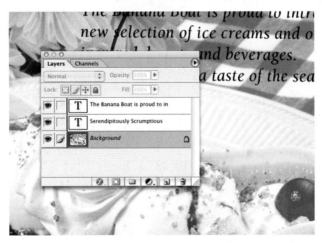

FIGURE 3.4

Take a moment to look at the Layers palette. (If you can't see it, choose Window>Layers). You'll see that it contains three layers: the Background layer, which contains the actual image; and two additional layers, each of which contains type elements (noted by the capital "T").

2 **Choose File>Place.**

3 Select and place ice_cream_shoppe.eps (from the Project_03 resource folder).

You see a new layer named ice_cream_shoppe.eps in the Layers palette.

4 Press Return/Enter to complete the Place process.

Placing a document into an existing Photoshop image automatically creates a new layer for the element — whether it's another Photoshop file, or, as is the case in this situation, a graphic created in another application. This image was created in Adobe Illustrator and saved as an EPS (Encapsulated Postscript) file.

? ## If you have problems...

Several of the exercises in this project require special fonts. **Fonts** are collections of individual typefaces. They are available to your system only after they have been properly installed.

The special fonts you need to complete the exercises in this project are included in this book; they are also available on the Essentials Series Web site at againsttheclock.com. If these fonts are not installed on your system, the exercises will not work as described.

If you have not already done so, please stop now and install these special fonts on your computer. For instructions on how to install fonts, refer to the information supplied for your specific computer, or use the Help feature built into the Macintosh or Windows operating systems.

---

5 Drag the logo graphic to the lower-left side of the image as shown below.

FIGURE 3.5

6 Temporarily hide the Background layer by clicking its visibility icon (the small eye on the left side of the palette).

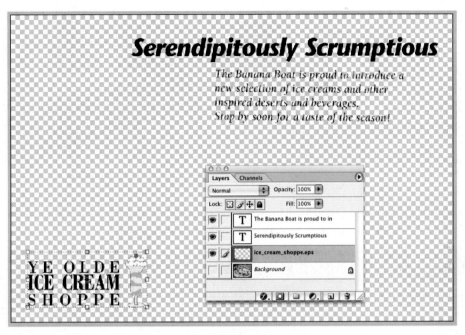

FIGURE 3.6

Now you can see the three transparent layers containing the type elements and the logo you just placed into the image.

7 Click the visibility icon again to show the Background layer, and then double-click it. Rename the Background layer "Photograph".

The Background layer is a special kind of layer; certain changes can't be made to a Background layer. When you rename a Background layer, however, it becomes a normal layer and it can be modified the same as any other layer.

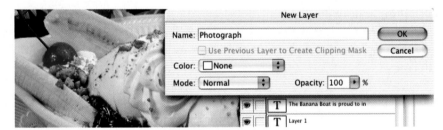

FIGURE 3.7

In the next step, you're going to make the type easier to read by lightening the area of the Photograph layer that lies behind the text.

8 With the Photograph layer still selected, draw a rectangular selection area around the paragraph of text.

FIGURE 3.8

9 Choose Image>Adjustments>Brightness/Contrast. Use the sliders on the Brightness/Contrast dialog box to set the Brightness to +30 and the Contrast to –60.

FIGURE 3.9

The result of this adjustment lightens the selected portion of the Photograph layer, but leaves the type layer intact. The text is now much easier to read. The ability to make changes to one layer, while protecting others, is only one of the many techniques available when you build your Photoshop document with layers.

10 Save the file in WIP_03 folder and close it.

To Extend Your Knowledge...

TYPES OF LAYERS

You can use several different types of layers to create or modify an image. Here's a short list of what you can expect to learn as you develop your skills with layers and the Layers palette.

Normal layers are "regular" layers that are added on top of the currently selected layer whenever you click the New Layer icon or choose Layer>New from the toolbar. As you develop your Photoshop skills, creating new layers and selecting appropriate options will become second nature.

Adjustment layers allow you to modify an image in a wide variety of ways without actually making any changes to the original data; the changes occur on the adjustment layer, not on the original image. In the previous exercise, you made a Brightness/Contrast adjustment, which is only one of dozens of adjustments available from the Adjustments menu. In most cases, adjustment layers are used for color and tonal correction.

Layer masks work in a similar manner to channel masks, but with the added advantage of protecting the original data that is being masked. When you use channels, they become part of the image; when you use layers to create masks, you can turn the layers on and off at will, and it is easy to discard the layers if they don't turn out the way you expect.

Shape layers contain shapes — a number of which are already built into the program. They include circles, squares, stars, and other objects commonly used in image development.

A *type layer* is a special shape layer that contains type elements. When you create type with Photoshop, it retains the quality of its edges, and therefore prints at the highest resolution available from your output device. You can turn type into a regular Photoshop object, and you can turn a type layer into a normal layer — but you cannot turn it back into a type layer once it has been changed to a normal layer.

LESSON 2 Creating Composite Images Using Layers

As we mentioned earlier, one of the most useful applications for layers within the Photoshop environment is the creation of a composite image — also referred to as a *montage*. A composite image is created by merging/combining two or more individual files. Since you have control over the stacking order, transparency, and many other attributes of each layer, the process of combining elements to create a new, original image is greatly simplified.

In the following exercise, you learn how to create a composite image using several pre-existing documents.

Use Layers to Combine Multiple Images

1 | **Open the file named picnic.tif from the Project_03 resource folder. Save it in your WIP_03 folder using the same name.**

Since the file is in TIF format, you will see several dialog boxes when you save the file. Click OK to accept the default TIF settings. Be sure to save the file with its layers intact.

2 | **Double-click the Background layer. Click OK to accept the default name (Layer 0).**

As you learned in the previous exercise, renaming the Background layer converts it from its special status into a normal layer. Only normal layers can contain transparent areas, which are necessary for the following steps.

FIGURE 3.10

3 | **Use the Rectangular Marquee tool to draw a selection around the two people in the image.**

Use the Zoom tool to enlarge the image on the screen so you can make an accurate selection.

FIGURE 3.11

4   **Choose Select>Modify>Smooth. Set the Sample Radius to 10 pixels. Click OK.**

The Smooth function softens the selection and creates rounded corners.

5   **From the Select menu, choose Feather and enter "10 pixels" for the Feather value. Click OK.**

6   **Invert the Selection (Select>Inverse). Press the Delete key to clear the area outside the selection.**

FIGURE 3.12

7   **Deselect the selection by pressing Command/Control-D.**

8   **Open bubbly.psd from the Project_03 folder. Choose Select>Load Selection to load the bubbly selection.**

This image already contains a saved selection. You learned how to create and save a selection in Project 2, so loading the selection shouldn't present a problem. If necessary, refer to Project 2 for detailed instructions.

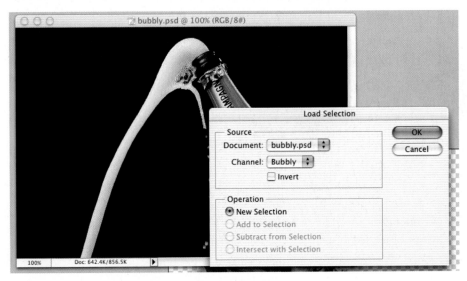

FIGURE 3.13

9   **Choose Edit>Copy to copy the selection to the clipboard. Close the bubbly.psd file.**

10   **Choose Edit>Paste to paste the bottle into the picnic image.**

Pasting the image of the champagne bottle into the picnic image automatically creates a new layer for the object. You can see this by looking at the Layers palette. By default, the new layer is named Layer 1, and it is created on top of the existing Layer 0.

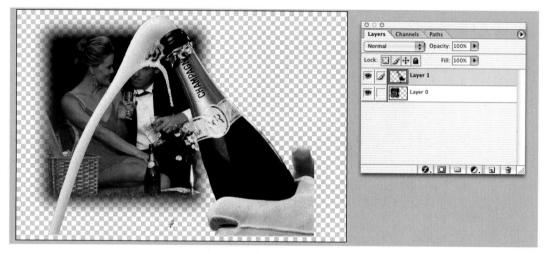

FIGURE 3.14

11   **Use the Move tool to position the champagne bottle on the lower-right side of the picture.**

12   **Create a new layer by clicking the New Layer icon in the Layers palette.**

The new layer is created at the top of the layer stack.

13   **Choose Edit>Fill to fill the layer with 100% white.**

Once you click OK, the new layer hides the two layers that already exist in the image. This is not what you want. Fixing the problem is simple, as you'll see in the next step.

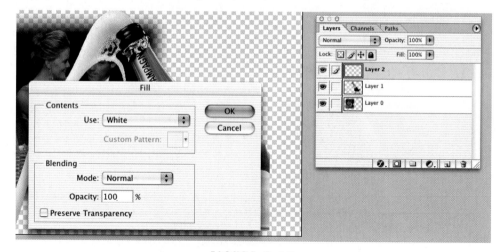

FIGURE 3.15

14 Drag Layer 2 to the bottom of the stack.

Changing the stacking order is as easy as dragging a layer to a new position.

FIGURE 3.16

15 Save your changes and keep the file open for the next exercise.

To Extend Your Knowledge...

LAYERS AND FILE FORMATS

Since not all file formats support layers, you need to make sure that the format you typically use during the development process is among those that do. The first and most common is the native Photoshop file format (PSD). Other file types can also support layers — most notably TIF files — but it's a good idea to keep your original layered files in PSD format and create a copy of the document in a format suitable for the intended distribution medium (either TIFF or EPS for print projects, and GIF or JPEG for use on the Web).

LESSON 3 | Moving Layers Between Documents

In the previous exercise, you created a new layer by copying and pasting an image from its original file into a composite image. This method works quite well, and is commonly used to combine elements from two or more documents. Another way to accomplish the same result is to drag a layer from one document into another. In the following exercise, you drag a layer containing a texture from an existing document into the picnic image.

Drag a Layer from one Document to Another

1 If it's not already open, open the picnic.tif image from the WIP_03 folder.

2 Open the picnic_texture.psd image from the Project_03 folder.

3   **Choose Window>Arrange>Tile to position the two images on your screen so you can see them both at the same time.**

If you select the picnic_texture.psd image, you'll see that it contains a single layer named cloth_texture.

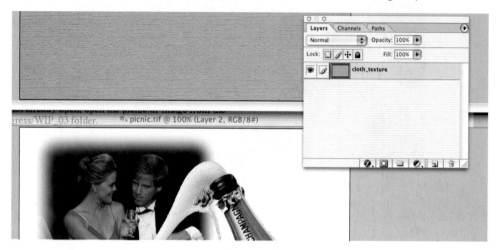

FIGURE 3.17

4   **Use the Move tool to grab the cloth_texture layer and drag it onto the picnic.tif image.**

When you drag a layer from one document to another, it automatically appears in the Layers palette and becomes part of the target document.

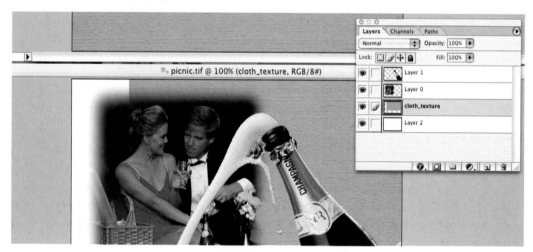

FIGURE 3.18

5   **Drag the layer and position it above Layer 2 (if necessary).**

You might not need to reposition the layer in the stacking order if Layer 2 was selected when you dragged it from the picnic_texture.psd image.

6   **Position the texture layer so it fits within the boundaries of the image.**

7 | Use the Opacity slider to experiment with different opacity values for individual layers.

You can see that each layer can be individually controlled — including the opacity values. Fading the texture and the bottle of champagne result in the following composite image.

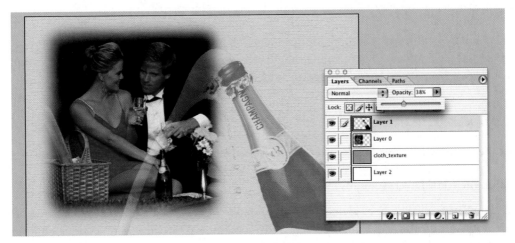

FIGURE 3.19

8 | Choose File>Save As. From the pop-up menu that appears, choose Photoshop as the Format, and name the file "picnic_composite.psd" in the Save As field. Click Save to complete the process.

20_PS_03.TIF FIGURE 3.20

9 | Keep the file open for the next exercise.

To Extend Your Knowledge...

LAYERS REQUIRE CONSIDERABLE RESOURCES

Layering is a powerful technique that allows flexibility in the design and modification of an image. If you're not careful, layers can quickly consume system resources. You should carefully plan your documents before you use layers because they can dramatically increase the size of an image and require additional memory, disk space, and scratch space.

LESSON 4 Flattening and Merging Layers

The greatest advantage of making opacity changes is that they're not permanently applied to the layer being modified; you can change opacity values at any time during development.

You can merge individual layers to simplify a document. *Merging* layers combines two or more layers into a single, normal layer. Flattening a file merges all the layers in a document and converts the layers into a single Background layer. Changes are not committed to a document until you flatten the file.

Merge Layers

1   **In the open picnic_composite.psd document, select the cloth_texture layer.**

2   **Click the Link Layers icon on Layer 2.**

Linking layers allows you to connect two or more layers, and makes it easier to make modifications to the layers. You can merge linked layers and move them as if they were a single component. Any changes, such as scaling, opacity changes, locking, or hiding, affects all linked layers at the same time.

FIGURE 3.21

3   **From the Layers palette Options menu, choose Merge Linked.**

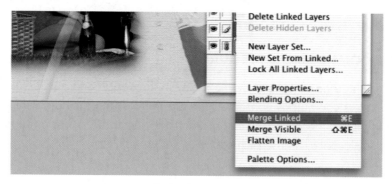

FIGURE 3.22

4   **Examine the Layers palette.**

The two layers that you linked in Step 3 are now a single layer. Notice that the name of the new merged layer was taken from the layer that was selected when you invoked the merge command. In this case, the new layer is named cloth_texture.

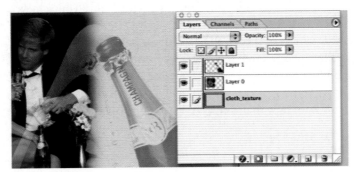

FIGURE 3.23

5   **From the Layers palette Options menu, choose Flatten Image.**

Flattening a document turns it into a single, normal Photoshop document; all layers are reduced to a single Background layer — as if you were starting all over from scratch.

FIGURE 3.24

6   **Save the file and close it when you're done.**

LESSON 5 Working with Layer Styles

In the early days of Photoshop, creating realistic shadows and other special effects was quite a chore. In many cases, creating the illusion of depth and dimension was a tedious process that required extensive use of channels and layers, as well as moving, positioning, blurring, and sharpening until you achieved the desired effect.

Today, you can achieve a wide variety of special effects without having to complete such process-intensive steps. All you need to do is use Photoshop's layer styles. They're simple to use, cause no permanent change to the image data, and can be modified or removed with a few simple mouse clicks.

In the following exercise, you learn how to use layer styles to apply special effects to objects on individual layers.

Apply Layer Styles

1   **Open bull_rider.psd from the Project_03 resource folder.**

2   **Select the type layer and examine the Layers palette.**

The document contains two layers; one contains the background image and the second contains the text found along the bottom of the poster.

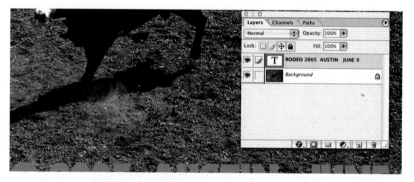

FIGURE 3.25

3   **Click the Layer Styles icon at the bottom left of the Layers palette. Choose Drop Shadow.**

FIGURE 3.26

4   **Use the dial or the value setting to set the Angle of the drop shadow to 22 degrees.**

This setting more closely matches the actual shadow of the bull and rider that's being cast by the sun.

5   **Experiment with the Distance, Spread, and Size sliders.**

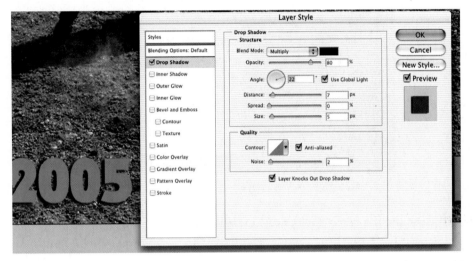

FIGURE 3.27

You can see that the possibilities presented by the Drop Shadow layer style are very extensive. Later on, when you learn about blending modes, contour, and noise settings, the creative opportunities will expand even more.

6   **Choose the Bevel and Emboss style in the list on the left side of the dialog box. Choose Chisel Hard from the Style pop-up menu.**

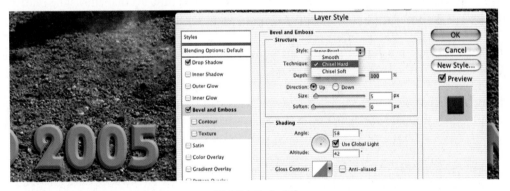

FIGURE 3.28

7   **Click OK to apply the effects. Examine the Layers palette.**

The Layers palette lets you know you applied layer styles to the type layer. To make changes to either of the two styles, you would simply double-click the style name in the palette and immediately access the related dialog box.

FIGURE 3.29

8   **Save and close the file when you're done experimenting.**

LESSON 6 Shape Layers

The shape tools can be used to create three different kinds of shapes. When you create a shape in an image document, a special shape layer is automatically created to contain the shape.

The first kind of shape is a mask shape — more specifically called a clipping mask. A ***clipping mask*** is a shape that acts like a cookie cutter, or a hole in a black (or white) piece of cardboard that allows the underlying image to show through its cut-out shape. You can apply styles to shape layers just as you can with any other layer.

The second kind of shape is a ***path shape*** — the same as the paths you can create with the Pen tool (which you'll learn about later in the book).

The third kind of shape you can create is a ***fill shape***. This shape takes the form of the tool you select and is then filled with pixels. You control shapes from the Shapes palette, which is shown in the Figure 3.30.

FIGURE 3.30

In the following exercise, you create a shape layer, add a type layer, apply effects, and link the two layers to create a graphic element that can be used anywhere on the image.

Create a Shape Layer

1 **Open wimbledon_tennis.psd from the Project_03 folder.**

The file already contains a single layer. You're going to add another layer in the next step.

FIGURE 3.31

2 **Zoom into the text on the handle of the racquet. Choose the Eyedropper tool from the Toolbox and click on the text. Zoom back to the original view.**

The foreground color is set to the same color as the logo. You'll learn a lot more about using colors and painting tools in the next project. For now, it's only important that you have a solid complementary color to use in the next steps of this exercise.

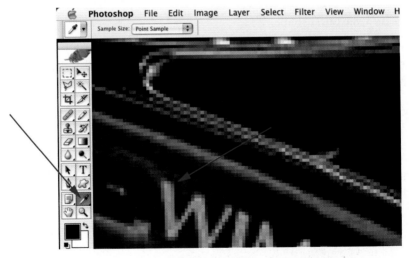

FIGURE 3.32

3 | **Choose the Custom Shape tool. It might be hiding under the Rectangle tool in the Toolbox.**

Choosing the Custom Shape tool activates the Custom Shapes pop-up palette, which appears at the top of the screen. You control the various tools' behaviors and attributes from here.

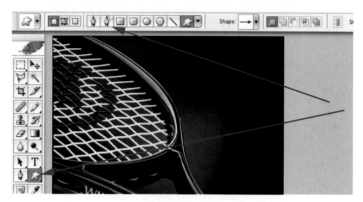

FIGURE 3.33

4 | **Use the pop-up Shape menu to choose a starburst shape.**

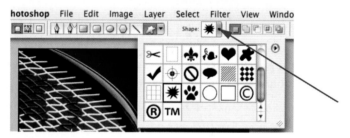

FIGURE 3.34

5 | **Drag to create a starburst shape.**

The shape is automatically filled with the foreground color — the color you selected from the handle of the racquet — as you draw it. In addition, and more importantly, a new shape layer appears in the Layers palette.

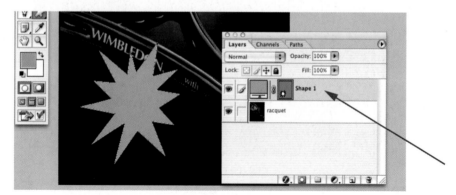

FIGURE 3.35

6   Press the "D" key to reset the default colors to black and white, and then click the Swap icon in the Toolbox.

FIGURE 3.36

7   Choose the Type tool from the Toolbox. Click the upper right of the poster. Enter "$199".

This action creates yet another layer; this time, it's a type layer. We used ATC Maple Ultra as the typeface. You can use another typeface, but the result won't look the same as the example we provide.

8   Use the Move tool to move the type onto the starburst.

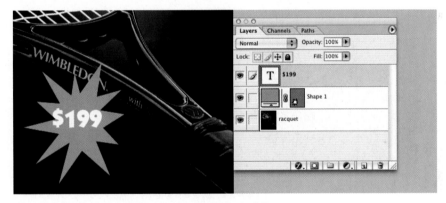

FIGURE 3.37

9   Apply a Drop Shadow effect to the type layer. Use the settings of your choice.

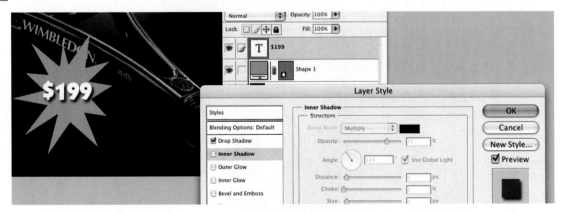

FIGURE 3.38

10 Apply a Bevel and Emboss effect to the shape layer. Experiment with the settings until you're satisfied with the results.

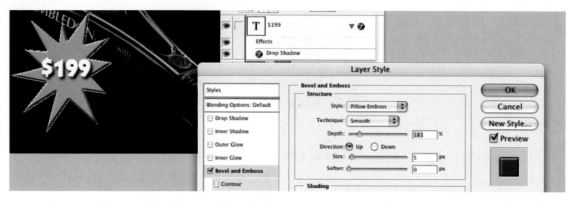

FIGURE 3.39

11 Select the type layer. Click the shape's Link Layers icon to link the two layers.

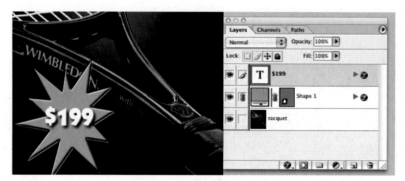

FIGURE 3.40

12 Move the linked layers around the screen.

FIGURE 3.41

13 Save the file and close it when you're done.

To Extend Your Knowledge...

BUGS

In the graphic arts industry, elements such as the starburst you just created, as well as banners, sale announcements, and discount announcements, are called *bugs*. Using layers and effects, as seen in the preceding exercise, is an excellent way to create bugs for use in multiple files. You can create a document — or series of documents — that contain various bugs and drag them into other documents as needed to create display ads, posters, sales announcements, and more.

LESSON 7 Using Layer Masks

Layer masks allow you to hide or reveal portions of the layer (or layer set) to which they're attached. Layer masks are particularly useful when you're creating composite images. You can add a layer mask to any layer or layer set.

Layer masks function in grayscale; if you paint on the mask with solid black, those areas of the layer are hidden; if you paint with white on the mask, those areas of the layer show through. If you paint on a mask with gray values, the percentage of gray determines how much of the layer objects show through. When you work on a layer mask, the foreground and background color swatches are converted to their grayscale equivalents.

You can apply special effects to a mask without affecting the actual layer. Once you're satisfied with the result, you can permanently apply the mask. You can also discard a mask without changing the layer.

Add a Layer Mask

1 Open misty_morning.psd from the Project_03 resource folder and save it in your WIP_03 folder.

2 Set the foreground color to black and the background color to white.

3 Look at the Layers palette.

There are currently two layers in the document. The topmost layer contains an image of a fisherman on a lake; the bottom layer is a simple light brown texture.

FIGURE 3.42

4   **Select the fisherman layer and click the Add Layer Mask icon at the bottom of the Layers palette.**

A layer is added to the fisherman layer. The layers are automatically linked. The palette now displays the mask as a second thumbnail immediately to the right of the layer thumbnail.

Click this icon to add a Layer Mask.

The Layer Mask appears as a thumbnail in the Layers palette.

FIGURE 3.43

5   **Choose the Brush tool.**

6   **From the Window menu, choose Brushes. Pick the Soft Round 100 brush from the list.**

You might have to scroll down to see the brush.

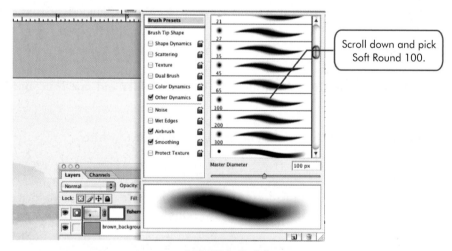

Scroll down and pick Soft Round 100.

FIGURE 3.44

7   **Use the brush to paint a circle around the fisherman.**

As you paint the mask, the underlying texture begins to show through.

FIGURE 3.45

8   **Reset the default colors and paint over a portion of the mask you created in Step 7.**

FIGURE 3.46

9   **Continue painting the mask with white until it's completely gone.**

10　Create a rectangular marquee across the top of the image.

FIGURE 3.47

11　Choose Edit>Fill. Pick 50% Gray from the pop-up menu. Click OK to apply the fill.

The area you filled with 50% gray allows 50% of the underlying texture to show through. This is an excellent method of creating highly readable text areas in an otherwise busy image.

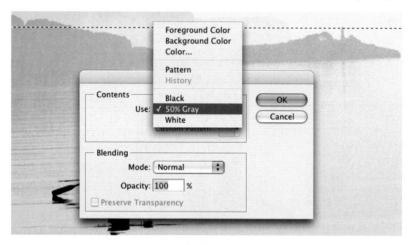

FIGURE 3.48

12　Click the trash can icon. Click Apply in the warning dialog box that appears.

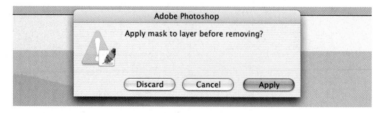

FIGURE 3.49

| **13** | **Hide the texture layer by clicking its visibility icon.** |

The rectangle you created for the mask is now a 50%-transparent area on the layer itself.

FIGURE 3.50

| **14** | **Save and close the file.** |

By default, a layer mask is linked to the layer — but you can unlink it by clicking the link icon next to mask. Once the layer and mask are unlinked, you can move the mask independently of the layer.

SUMMARY

In Project 3, you began to work with layers — one of Photoshop's most important and useful functions. Layers act as discrete, individual documents that are stacked on top of one another in a document in what is known as the stacking order. The stacking order, as well as a wide variety of other layer attributes, is controlled from the Layers palette.

Using icons on the Layers palette, you can link, hide, lock, and rename layers. You can also create layer sets, which are essentially folders that are used to organize related layers. You will work with layer sets as you complete the upcoming Skill Drills.

Being able to properly use and manage layers are critical skills you will develop as you become increasingly familiar with Photoshop. Later in the book, you will learn several techniques relative to layers, including how to use layers during color correction and image adjustment.

Layers are indispensable when you create or modify complex images. Layers allow you to apply almost unlimited modifications, special effects, and creative techniques to an image without permanently committing the changes to the original file.

KEY TERMS

Adjustment layer	Fonts	Montage
Blending modes	Layer	Opaque
Bugs	Layer mask	Shape layer
Clipping mask	Layers palette	Stacking order
Composite image	Layer set	Transparency
Fill shape	Linking layer	Type layer
Flattening	Merging	Vector object

CHECKING CONCEPTS AND TERMS

SCREEN ID

Name the following items on the Shape tool Options bar.

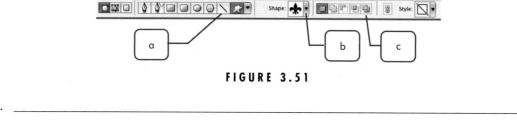

FIGURE 3.51

a. _____

b. _____

c. _____

MULTIPLE CHOICE

Circle the letter of the correct answer for each of the following questions.

1. One of the most important uses for layers is to create a _____ image.

    a. layered

    b. masked

    c. color-corrected

    d. composite

2. Layers contain the information relative to red, green, and blue color values.

    a. True

    b. False

3. Which of the following is not a layer category?

    a. Mask

    b. Correction

    c. Channel

    d. Type

    e. Shape

    f. Normal

4. The _____ layer must be converted into a regular layer before certain techniques can be applied to it.
   a. Layer 0
   b. Layer 1
   c. Type
   d. Background
   e. Shape

5. The _____ value of a layer determines how much of the underlying layers show through.
   a. transparency
   b. opacity
   c. fill
   d. shape

6. Layer effects do not actually change the contents of the layer to which they're applied.
   a. True
   b. False
   c. Depends on the type of effect you're applying.

7. Every time you add a layer _____.
   a. the file size increases slightly
   b. the file size doubles
   c. the file size remains the same
   d. the file size decreases slightly

8. Layer _____ are objects used to show or hide portions of the layer to which they're attached.
   a. channels
   b. effects
   c. masks
   d. QuickMasks

9. When you flatten an image, the only remaining layer is _____.
   a. Layer 0
   b. Layer 1
   c. a shape layer
   d. the Background layer

10. A single layer can contain both a shape and a raster object.
    a. True
    b. False

DISCUSSION QUESTIONS

1. Describe three different situations where it would be virtually impossible to develop an effective image without using layers.

2. What is the difference between layers and channels? Describe two situations where each would be more appropriate to the development of an image.

3. Describe the steps you would take to develop a drawing using shape, type, and background layers to develop a bug, and the steps you would need to take to move the bug into another document.

SKILL DRILL

Skill Drills reinforce project skills. Each skill reinforced is the same, or nearly the same, as a skill presented in the lessons. Detailed instructions are provided in a step-by-step format. You should work through the exercises in the order provided.

1. Add a Shape Layer

1. Open jillian.psd from the Project_03 resource folder. Save it into the WIP_03 folder as "jillian_working.psd".

2. Choose the Crop tool. Create a selection that discards some of the extra white space around the edges of the image.

   The exact size of the selection doesn't need to match the example, but try to get it relatively close to the aspect ratio shown in the example.

FIGURE 3.52

3. Press Return/Enter to commit the cropping command.

4. Choose the Shape tool and draw a small heart. Name the new shape layer "heart".

   It doesn't matter where on the image you create the shape; you're going to move it around later.

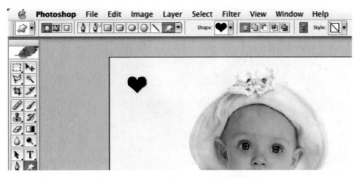

FIGURE 3.53

5. Choose Edit>Transform Path>Rotate 90 CCW.

   This turns the heart so it's pointing to the right.

FIGURE 3.54

6. Save your changes and keep the file open for the next Skill Drill.

2. Create Layer Sets

1. In the open file, use the Type tool to create a type layer that contains the word "Hats".

   You can use any font you like — but a big bold font is probably more attractive for this application.

   To change the size of the type, you can drag the text cursor over the type you want to change and then press the Shift-> (greater than) keys to make the word larger, or press the Shift-< (less than) keys to make the word smaller until it's the same height as the heart shape.

FIGURE 3.55

2. Link the Hats and heart layers.

3. From the Layers palette Options menu, choose New Set from Linked.

FIGURE 3.56

4. Name the new set "button1". Click the small triangle next to the set name in the Layers palette to display its content.

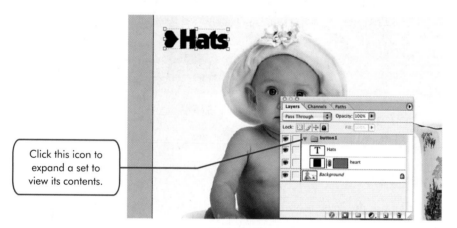

Click this icon to expand a set to view its contents.

FIGURE 3.57

5. Choose Layer>Duplicate Layer Set and name the new set "button2".

This process creates a second layer set that contains duplicates of the two layers contained in the existing set. The new set is created directly on top of the existing set.

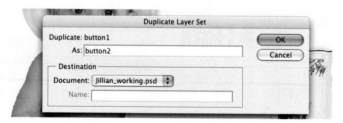

FIGURE 3.58

6. Repeat the process until you have four layer sets positioned on top of one another.

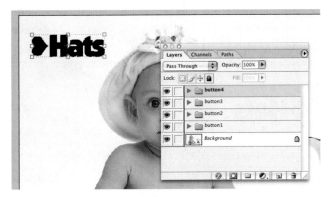

FIGURE 3.59

7. Save your changes and keep the file open for the next Skill Drill.

3. Position and Align Layers

1. In the open file, use the Move tool to drag the button4 set below the other three sets. Hold down the Shift key to constrain the movement along the vertical axis.

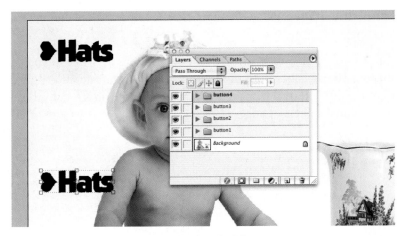

FIGURE 3.60

2. Link the four sets.

    Layer sets behave the same as individual layers; you can rename them, move them, delete them, and — as is the case here — link them. You should always consider creating sets whenever one of your images contains individual groups of related layers. This exercise presents a good example of the technique, and you will find many more once you start developing complex images.

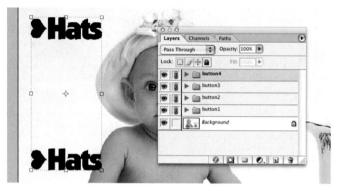

FIGURE 3.61

3. Choose Layer>Distribute Linked>Vertical Centers.

    Alignment refers to the position of a group of elements relative to one another. Objects can be aligned and distributed in the same way. Alignment is another way to control the positions of linked layers (or layers sets).

    This is only one of several alignment and distribution options available to you. In this example, you distributed the four layer sets based on their vertical centers. You can also align layers according to their tops or bottoms. If you were distributing items across the image instead of up and down, you could use the horizontal centers or edges of each element.

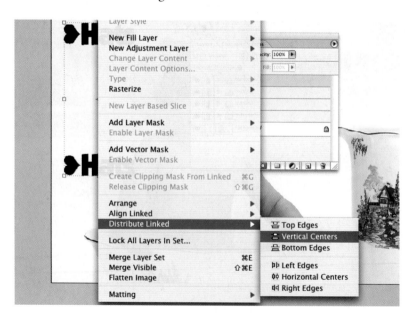

FIGURE 3.62

4. Change the text for button2 through button4 (button2=Tops, button3=Booties, and button4=Accessories).

FIGURE 3.63

5. Resize the four linked buttons so they're a little smaller.

   Design is largely a visual process, so the exact size of the reduced layers isn't as important as how you think it looks. When you are satisfied with the result, press the Return/Enter key to commit the transformation.

FIGURE 3.64

6. Move the linked sets to the upper-right side of the image.

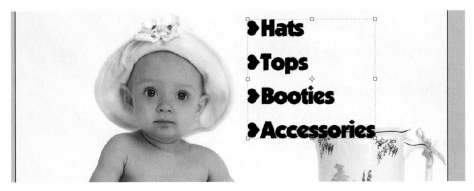

FIGURE 3.65

7. Save the file and close it.

CHALLENGE

Challenge exercises expand on, or are somewhat related to, skills presented in the lessons. Each exercise provides a brief introduction, followed by instructions presented in a numbered-step format that are not as detailed as those in the Skill Drill exercises. You should work through the exercises in the order provided.

1. Prepare a Poster Document

In the following series of Challenges, you create a new document for a poster project. Then, you import a number of images to their own layers, and then use layer masking to combine them into a single large composite image.

1. Create a new 16 inch wide by 11.5 inch high 150-ppi RGB Photoshop image named "playbill.psd". Use a transparent background.

2. Save the image into your WIP_03 folder.

3. Choose Open and navigate to the Jurors folder within the Project_03 resource folder.

4. Open all the images.

5. Choose Window>Arrange>Tile.

6. Drag all the juror images into the playbill.psd file.

7. Close the individual juror files.

8. Save the playbill.psd file, and leave it open for the next exercise.

2. Position the Main Images

1. In the open document, press the "F" key to fill the monitor with the image.

2. Use the Move tool to drag the images around.

3. Identify the image containing the entire cast.

4. Rename that layer "cast_photo".

5. Drag the cast_photo layer into the center of the workspace.

6. Save the image and leave it open for the next exercise.

3. Rough-in the Composites

1. In the open document, move the cast_photo layer to the bottom of the stack, directly above Layer 1.

2. Arrange the individual cast member layers around the cast_photo layer.

FIGURE 3.66

3.   Save the image, and leave it open.

4. Create Layer Masks

1.   In the open document, pick one of the jurors and add a layer mask.

2.   Use a soft round brush to paint around the juror to meld him or her into the background image.

3.   Continue compositing each juror into the background (cast_photo) layer using masks on each layer.

4.   When complete, fill Layer 1 with black.

5.   Open jurors_final.jpg from the Project_03 resource folder. Compare your image with our version.

FIGURE 3.67

6.   Adjust your image as necessary, save, and then close it when you're done.

Create a Montage

Your town officials hired you to create a poster for the city's 200th anniversary. They would like you to create a montage of top attractions and historical sites, similar to the playbill you created in the Challenge exercises.

1. Identify 12–15 images you would like to use in the poster project.

2. Use images you already have, or borrow a digital camera and take some pictures.

3. Identify a focal image to act as the centerpiece.

4. Composite the balance of the images around, under, above, and to the sides of the centerpiece. Don't limit your design to exactly the one we created in the Challenges; use your creativity.

5. Create the necessary layer masks to merge the images into a single composite.

6. Save the file onto a CD.

7. Output the poster on a large-format color printer. If you don't have access to a large-format color printer, call a few copy shops and get prices for "tabloid" output. This is 11 by 17 inches, the perfect size for your masterpiece.

Painting and Using Color

OBJECTIVES

In this project, you learn how to

- Work with the Brushes palette

- Use the Brush tool

- Convert images to different color modes

- Change colors

- Work with the Pencil tool

- Use the Eraser tools

- Create blends between different colors

WHY WOULD I DO THIS?

Photoshop's painting tools can be used to accomplish two types of tasks. First, painting tools are used to repair, modify, and/or improve an existing image. Repairing a damaged image, removing an unsightly element in a picture, and fixing the red eyes in a family portrait illustrate some situations where the Photoshop painting tools can be used to enhance a photograph. Painting tools are also used to create new images from scratch. Photoshop provides many ways to accomplish both of these types of tasks.

A wealth of painting tools is available in the Brushes palette, including pencils and airbrushes, watercolors and charcoals. You can customize any brush with a variety of controls. Brushes can vary in size, shape, angle, spacing, and pattern. Some of the brushes appear to have hard, distinct edges; other brushes have soft, fading edges that blend smoothly into the colors of the underlying image. You can choose the appropriate style of brush to suit the particular project under development.

V I S U A L   S U M M A R Y

Photoshop offers a wide variety of painting tools and techniques. With so many different variations on the available methods, your choices are virtually limitless. Learning which tools/methods allow you to achieve a particular result — and knowing when to use those tools — is the challenge to the new Photoshop user.

Each painting tool has an Options bar that offers control over how the tool interacts with the image. Most settings are unique to a specific tool, but the tools have some settings in common. Among the settings is the brush itself, the blending mode in use, the opacity of the "paint" being applied, and the flow of paint coming from the brush. We'll cover several other behaviors as we move forward in this project.

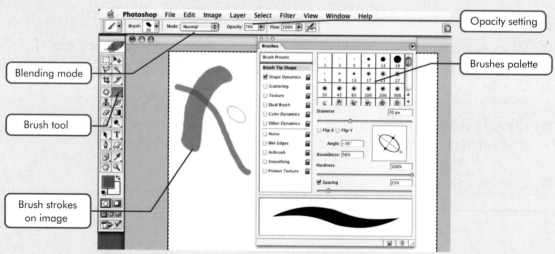

FIGURE 4.1

Some of the program's painting options allow you to apply colored and toned pixels as if they were watercolors, oils, or charcoals — the so-called natural mediums. *Natural mediums* are those that have parallels in the physical world. Other techniques, particularly those that provide healing, patching, or cloning capabilities, are limited to digital images. The *Healing brush* and *Clone tool* are used to repair and/or improve portions of an image. Repairing and otherwise modifying an original image is called retouching.

As we already mentioned, the behavior of the regular painting tools can be modified with the blending modes. *Blending modes* affect how paint interacts with pixels that lie underneath the area where you're currently painting. Blending modes can be used to darken or lighten underlying pixels, mix colors, and blend tones. They allow you to apply effects that would otherwise be difficult or impossible to achieve. Blending modes can also be applied to layers. After you complete this project, you can apply your new knowledge about blending modes to what you already know about layers.

In addition, all painting tools have an Opacity slider on the Options bar. The *Opacity slider* allows you to adjust the transparency of the color, pattern, or effect being applied to the image. When opacity is less than 100%, repeated applications of color are required to make the paint more opaque. For example, if the Brush tool is set to 25% opacity, the first stroke combines 25% of the foreground color and 75% of the image. If the area is stroked again with the same color (after releasing and then again depressing the mouse button), a bit more of the image is obscured by paint. If the brush is applied enough times, the image is entirely obscured. When the Airbrush option is chosen, the user can set the *flow rate* (how fast the paint flows from the brush) as well as the opacity.

LESSON 1   Working with the Brushes Palette

There is literally no limit to the different kinds of Photoshop brushes you can use to develop a design: brush size and behavior are fully controllable, you can create new brushes, store brushes in custom palettes, delete brushes, duplicate brushes, and more.

Clicking the Brush Tip Shape button in the Brushes palette opens a dialog box that contains many options. There is a list of style check boxes, icons representing the currently loaded tip shapes, and several controls to further modify any of the tip shapes. Let's take a closer look at some of the options in the Brush Tip Shape dialog box:

- Diameter indicates the width of the brush at its longest dimension, measured in pixels.

- The Hardness setting designates the hardness or softness of the edges of the brush. Even if the Hardness setting is at 100% (the default for Photoshop's hard-edged brushes), the edges are still softened slightly to create an anti-aliased brush stroke. Conversely, even when a brush is softened to 0% Hardness, the center of the brush is still solid.

- Anti-aliasing refers to the subtle blending of an object's (or brush stroke's) edges with the underlying pixels. Without anti-aliasing, edges are hard and jagged; with anti-aliasing turned on, the edge of a brush stroke is softer and smoother. You can see the effect in the following image; the circle on the left is anti-aliased, while the one on the right is not.

FIGURE 4.2

- The Spacing setting represents how often a brush stroke repeats. The percentage listed is a percentage of the width of a brush. For example, a round 20-pixel brush with a 200% Spacing would draw a series of dots 20 pixels in diameter, with 40 pixels between the start of the first dot and the start of the second dot. Most of Photoshop's default (hard) brushes have a spacing of 25%, which appears as solid line — similar to the continual flow from a conventional airbrush; others may vary, depending on their attributes. Unchecking the Spacing check box causes the spacing to vary according to the speed of the mouse; the faster the line is drawn, the more space between the dots.

- Changing the Roundness value creates an elliptical brush, which can then be set at any angle. Both the angle and roundness may be set by keying in the degree of rotation and percent of roundness, or by manipulating the graphic in the center of the dialog box.

Other things you should know about brushes:

- You can save or load sets of custom-created brushes, as well as append one set of brushes to another, by clicking the black triangle in the upper-right corner of the Brushes palette. This activates a drop-down menu. You can also use this menu to reset the Brushes palette to the default (original installation) settings.

- Photoshop allows you to define irregularly shaped brushes; select any area of the image using the selection tools, and then choose the Edit>Define Brush command.

- Brush shape, color, and other dynamic attributes allow you to fade brush strokes from foreground to background, from foreground to transparent, or to fade the weight of the line. Using these three settings, you can achieve almost unlimited effects while you paint.

- Support for graphics tablets, such as those by Wacom, allow users to control the paint stroke via pen pressure, pen tilt, and stylus wheel. Settings for these controls can be made in the Control submenu for each applicable brush style. The Fade control is found here as well; it allows the user to set the number of steps over which the stroke fades.

Select and Use a Brush

1 Create a 5-inch by 5-inch 200-ppi RGB image named "paint_practice". Choose White for the Background Contents.

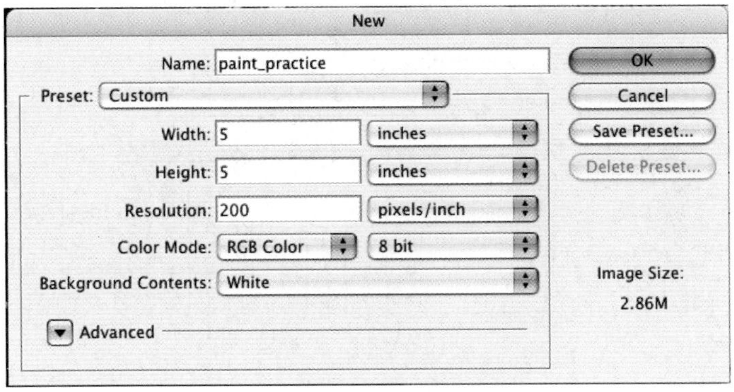

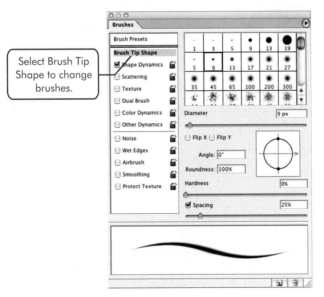

FIGURE 4.3

2 Choose the Brush tool in the Toolbox.

Make sure you select the regular Brush tool. If you're not sure, refer to the Toolbox illustration in Project 1.

3 Activate the Brushes palette. Choose Brush Tip Shape from the list on the left of the palette.

The Brushes palette is often docked in the Palette Well, the area at the upper right of the workspace, where you can store your most frequently used palettes.

FIGURE 4.4

4 On the tool Options bar, set Opacity to 100% and Blending Mode to Normal.

5   Select the Round 9-pt brush from the Brushes palette. Draw a squiggly line.

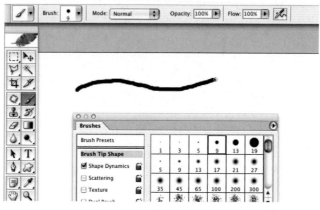

FIGURE 4.5

6   Select another brush from the Brushes palette. Use it to paint another shape on the page.

In this example, we chose a 46-pixel Scatter brush.

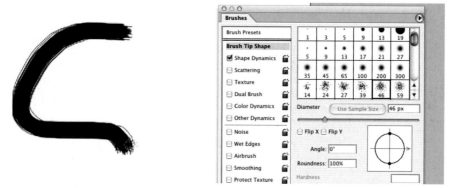

FIGURE 4.6

7   Continue to experiment with different brushes.

8   Save and close the document.

The name you entered (paint_practice) when you created the new document in Step 1 is automatically used for the name of the file.

LESSON 2   Working with Color Modes

Photoshop supports several different color modes. A ***color mode*** (also known as ***color space*** or ***color model***) is a mathematical representation of a set of colors that can be produced using a particular process or device. The range of colors that can be reproduced using a specific process is known as the ***gamut***. The ***visible spectrum*** consists of all colors normally perceived by the human eye.

Change the Color Mode of an Image

1 Open lineworker.tif from the Project_04 resource folder.

2 Choose Image>Mode. Examine the drop-down menu.

There is a checkmark next to RGB Color, telling you this is an RGB image. Notice that Duotone and Bitmap modes are grayed out, indicating that they aren't available for selection.

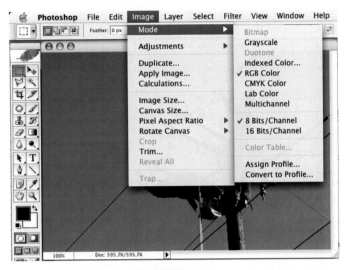

FIGURE 4.7

3 Save the file into the WIP_04 folder, accepting the existing values when prompted.

4 Choose Duplicate from the Image menu to create a copy of the image.

5 Name the copy "lineworker_cmyk.tif", and save it into the same WIP_04 folder.

From this point forward, save the remaining duplicates in the WIP_04 folder.

FIGURE 4.8

To Extend Your Knowledge...

UNDERSTANDING COLOR MODES

One of the most effective ways to gain someone's attention is through the tasteful use of color. The exact method of selecting colors depends on how you're going to distribute your artwork. If you're going to print your images, you usually select either CMYK color or grayscale. Grayscale images contain only black, white, and shades of gray. If the final printed output will be reproduced in color, then you should work with CMYK, a method used to create the illusion of full color using only four colored inks, namely cyan, magenta, yellow, and black. For images that are destined for the Web or distributed in some other electronic manner, the correct color mode to use is RGB, which stands for red, green, and blue.

An **additive color mode** contains colors that are created by adding together different wavelengths of light. A good example of an additive color device is a computer monitor. All of the colors the monitor shows are created by light emitted from three guns — red, green, and blue — at varying intensities. RGB is an additive color mode.

Subtractive color modes encompass colors that are created when light strikes an object or image and certain wavelengths are absorbed (subtracted). The light that is reflected from the object is perceived as a particular color. Subtractive color modes include all color in printed materials. They are comprised of dyes and pigments. CMYK is a subtractive color mode.

These modes overlap, but they do not coincide completely. For example, there are manmade pigments that do not appear in nature, and there are many colors in nature that can't be emulated on a monitor or printing press. More importantly, there are many colors that do not appear in both the large additive mode (the monitor) and the much smaller subtractive mode (the printed page).

Figure 4.9 shows RGB and CMYK color gamuts within the range occupied by commercial printing, computer monitors, and the human eye.

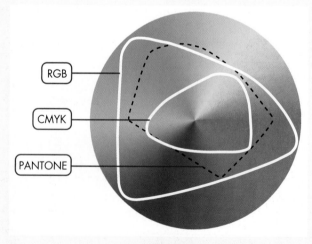

FIGURE 4.9

To Extend Your Knowledge...

UNDERSTANDING COLOR MODES (CONTINUED)

RGB Color. Colors in the RGB color mode are created by combining red, green, and blue light. This additive color mode is used to describe the colors produced by the computer monitor. Other devices that use the RGB color mode include spotlights with colored gels, and film recorders, such as those used to create slides and transparencies.

RGB images are also known as 24-bit or True Color images. Each pixel in an RGB image contains 8 bits of information for each color channel (red, green, and blue). In the RGB color mode, 100% each (256 levels) of red, green, and blue light combine to make white; 0% of each define the absence of color (black).

CMYK Color. CMYK is a subtractive color mode, which reproduces the range of possible colors using combinations of the four primary process colors (cyan, magenta, yellow, and black). This color mode is also referred to as *four-color process*, and is used in commercial printing and for most color desktop printers.

Zero percent (0%) each of cyan, magenta, yellow, and black produces white in the CMYK mode. CMY is the mathematical opposite of the RGB color mode. Theoretically speaking, as 100% each of RGB combine to make white, 100% each of CMY should combine to make black. In reality, however, printing pigments are impure. The result of mixing 100% of these colors is usually a muddy, purplish brown. Consequently, black is added to produce a true black, add depth to shadows and details to edges, and to reduce the amount of ink on the page.

An image in the CMYK color space yields a file 33% larger than an RGB file — it uses 8 bits of information per color channel, similar to an RGB file, but it has 4 channels information (C, M, Y, and K), totaling 32 bits of information as compared to 24 bits for RGB.

Indexed Color. An *indexed color image* is another 8-bit-per-pixel format. Similar to an 8-bit grayscale image, each pixel is represented by a value from 0 to 255. Instead of a shade of gray, however, the value refers to a position on a color look-up table. Each position on the table contains a specific color, with 0 (zero) as black, and 255 as white. Indexing is often used to reduce the range of colors stored in an image to only those actually used — storing, for instance, 4 or 5 colors instead of 256 or 16,000,000. When a particular color is not found, the Indexed Color option uses the color closest to it in the Index palette.

Grayscale and Bitmap Images. Grayscale images contain only shades of black and white. A grayscale image uses far less disk space than RGB images. In fact, each of the most commonly used color modes requires a different amount of space. Grayscale images show a variety of shades of gray (also referred to as *tonal values*). A *bitmapped image* (also called a *bitmap*) contains only black and white pixels. To convert a color image into a bitmap, it must first be converted into a grayscale image.

6   **Choose Mode>CMYK Color from the Image menu.**

This converts the image from RGB to CMYK. You probably see a shift in the color on the screen. Notice, too, that the Title bar of the Image window displays the new color mode next to the image title.

7   **Save the file and keep it open.**

Discard Color Information

In this exercise, you create grayscale and bitmap images. The process of converting a color image to grayscale and bitmap discards the color information. Be careful: once you convert a color image to grayscale or bitmap, you can't retrieve the color.

1   **Continue working in the open file. Choose Duplicate from the Image menu to make a copy of the file. Name the copy "lineworker_grayscale.tif".**

2   **Choose Grayscale from the Image>Mode menu. Click OK when the warning dialog box asks if you want to discard all color information.**

The image is converted from CMYK to Grayscale. Click the Mode menu. All of the options in the Mode menu for a grayscale images are now available for selection.

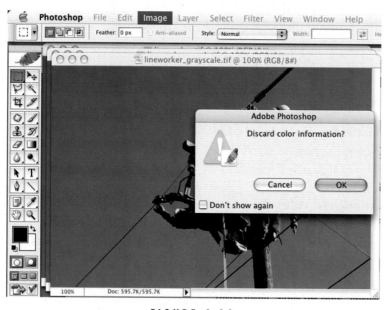

FIGURE 4.10

3   **Save the image.**

4   Duplicate the image again. This time, choose Bitmap from the Mode menu. Use the default settings for the bitmap conversion.

FIGURE 4.11

5   Save the image as "lineworker_bmap.tif".

Zoom in and look at what the program did to reproduce the image using only black and white pixels.

FIGURE 4.12

6   Choose Window>Arrange>Tile to view all four images at the same time.

The difference between the four images should be apparent: the best color can be seen in the original RGB image; the CMYK version appears flatter; the grayscale image is a clean version, perfect for use in a one-color publication or a laser-printed document; the bitmap image, using only black and white pixels, still presents a recognizable version of the original.

FIGURE 4.13

7   Close all the images.

To Extend Your Knowledge...

In most cases, even though an image will eventually be converted to the CMYK or Grayscale color mode, we strongly recommend that you work in RGB until the conversion is finalized. That way, you can save the image in the correct mode when the time is right, yet preserve the original color values. This is important because in most cases, you'll want to keep the RGB originals so that if you have to make any changes, you can go back to the pre-converted color mode.

8 | **Look in the folder (from the desktop) and compare the relative sizes of the files.**

The largest of the color modes is the CMYK version, weighing more than 900 KB. The original image is 312 KB, while the grayscale image is only 172 KB. The bitmap image, which doesn't contain much tonal information, weighs in at 108 KB. Depending on your system, the size of the files might vary a bit, but you'll still be able to see the difference in the relative sizes of files using different color modes.

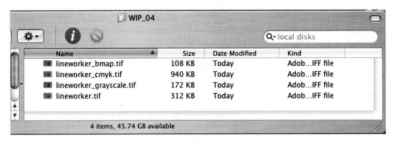

Name	Size	Date Modified	Kind
lineworker_bmap.tif	108 KB	Today	Adob...IFF file
lineworker_cmyk.tif	940 KB	Today	Adob...IFF file
lineworker_grayscale.tif	172 KB	Today	Adob...IFF file
lineworker.tif	312 KB	Today	Adob...IFF file

4 items, 45.74 GB available

FIGURE 4.14

LESSON 3 | Painting with Color

Photoshop's painting tools allow you produce a remarkable variety of artwork. You can use them to add new objects, add colors and shapes to your images, erase portions of an object (or a mask), retouch/remove portions of an image that shouldn't be there (such as offending signs or logos, or distracting items such as street signs and electric wires), and paint portions of one image onto the surface of another.

The best way to learn about all the myriad effects you can create with painting tools is to experiment. In the following exercise, you do just that — you get a feel for applying digital "paint" onto your images.

Set the Foreground and Background Colors

1 | **Create a new document with a Width of 500 pixels, Height of 500 pixels, and Resolution of 240 pixels/inch (ppi). Apply the RGB Color Mode and choose White for the Background Contents.**

New

Name: Untitled-1	OK
Preset: Custom	Cancel
Width: 500 pixels	Save Preset...
Height: 500 pixels	Delete Preset...
Resolution: 240 pixels/inch	
Color Mode: RGB Color 8 bit	
Background Contents: White	Image Size:
	732.4K

Advanced

FIGURE 4.15

2   **Make sure the Brushes palette is visible on your screen.**

3   **Click the Default Color icon at the bottom of the Toolbox.**

This sets the foreground color to black and the background color to white. You can reset the default colors at any time by pressing the "D" key.

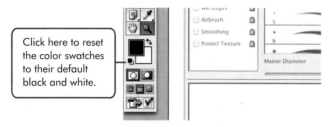

Click here to reset the color swatches to their default black and white.

FIGURE 4.16

4   **Choose the Brush tool in the Toolbox. Choose Brush Presets from the Brushes palette. Scroll down to the brush that resembles a single blade of grass.**

5   **Paint back and forth with this brush.**

Your strokes should resemble dune or desert grass — different shades of gray appear in each blade. Imagine how it would look if this were green grass instead of the gray blades you are creating.

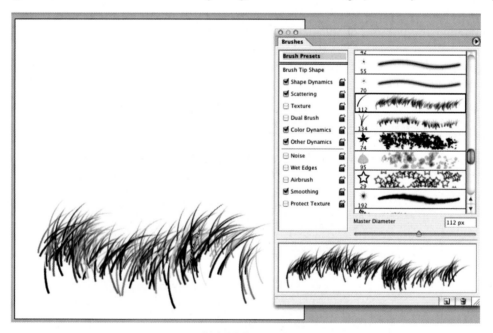

FIGURE 4.17

6 **Click the Foreground Color swatch.**

The Color Picker dialog box appears.

7 **Move the arrow on the vertical color slider into the green range.**

The main Color Picker dialog box displays a range of green colors.

8 **Choose a green foreground color from the main Color Picker and click OK.**

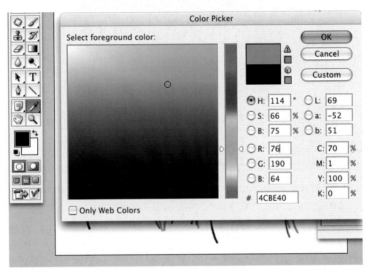

FIGURE 4.18

9 **Repeat the process, but this time, choose a different green for the background color swatch.**

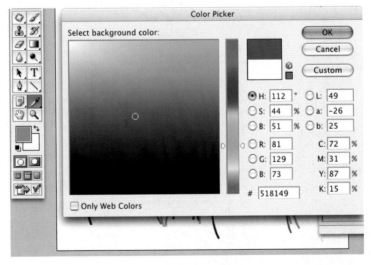

FIGURE 4.19

10   **Paint with the brush again.**

Rather than being rendered in shades of gray, the blades of grass are created in shades that vary between the foreground and background greens.

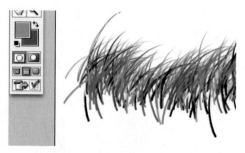

FIGURE 4.20

11   **Save the file as "color_practice.tif" and keep it open for the next exercise.**

Modify Brush Size and Orientation

We mentioned earlier that the variations you can create with the Brushes palette are practically limitless. In the next exercise, you see how changing the shape, size, and orientation of a brush offers countless creative opportunities.

1   **Continue working in the open file. Choose Brush Tip Shape from the list on the Brushes palette.**

Using the Brush Tip Shape options, you can simultaneously resize a brush and change its orientation. The active foreground and background colors for the brush being used don't change, so the changes can be made while you're painting without causing any unsightly color changes.

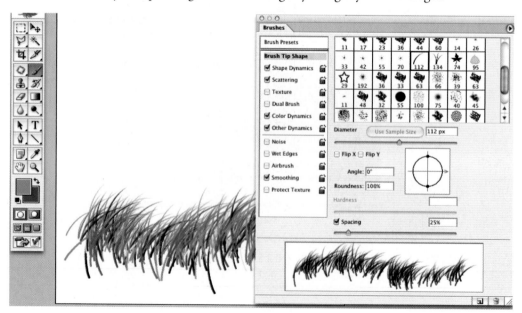

FIGURE 4.21

2 Move the Diameter slider to the right or left to increase or decrease the size of the brush.

The preview window in the lower part of the dialog box changes interactively to reflect the changes you make to the brush. This real-time feedback can be very helpful when you're working on a critical project that requires very accurate brush sizes and shapes to achieve a specific result.

A brush can be sized anywhere from 1 to 999 pixels; the actual size you need depends on what you're trying to accomplish and the image you're working on. Remember that the preview window is only about 50 pixels high, and can't provide an accurate representation of an item larger than that. This is a minor problem because you will seldom work with brushes larger than 50 pixels; when you do, seeing the preview isn't as important as when you're doing very detailed work.

3 Change the roundness of the brush by moving the small dot displayed on the brush tip icon.

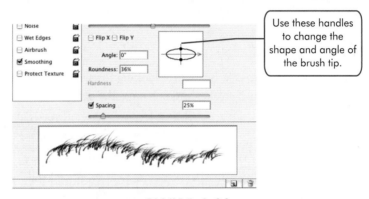

> Use these handles to change the shape and angle of the brush tip.

FIGURE 4.22

4 Move the arrow on the right side of the icon to change the orientation of the blades.

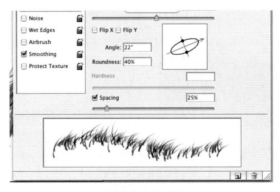

FIGURE 4.23

5   **Paint again with the brush to see the new effect.**

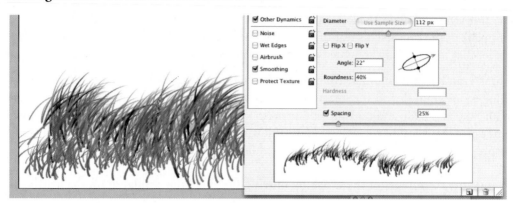

FIGURE 4.24

6   **Flip the X and Y axes of the brush.**

This turns the brush around and over. When you're looking for a random effect, flipping these values increases the randomness of the brush strokes and enhances the design.

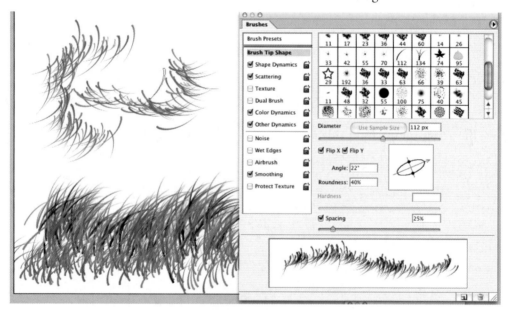

FIGURE 4.25

7   **Continue to experiment with different brushes.**

Try changing the foreground and background colors while you're experimenting. Many brushes use both colors at the same time.

8   **When you're done, save and close the file.**

From the Brushes palette Options menu, located below the pop-up icon on the upper-right side of the palette, you can save custom brushes, load additional sets of brushes, restore brush defaults, and many other features.

As part of your practice, load various brush palettes found at the bottom of the Options menu. When you're done, you can reset the brushes to their original conditions. When you load a brush palette, you have the option of replacing the current brushes or appending the new brushes to the existing set. Appending an existing set extends the choices you can make from the Brushes palette.

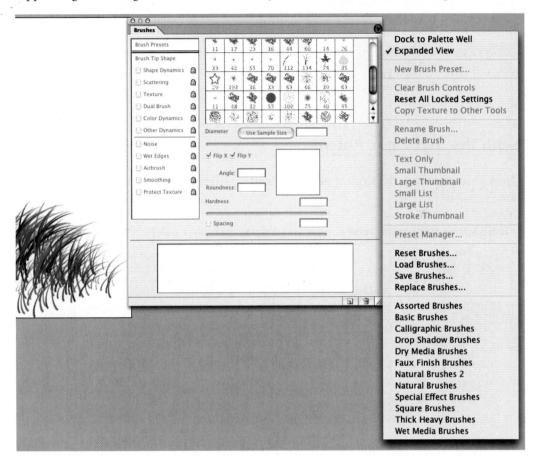

FIGURE 4.26

To Extend Your Knowledge...

COLOR DYNAMICS

When you used the blade brush in the preceding exercise, you should have noticed how the color of each blade of grass randomly shifted between the foreground and background colors you selected. Cycling between the foreground and background colors is known as **color dynamics**. You can select this option from the Brushes palette before you begin to paint. If this option is turned off, a brush paints using only the foreground color. Remember to turn on the option when you want to create a more random and natural effect.

LESSON 4 ┃ Using the Swatches Palette

In the previous exercise, you used the standard Color Picker to select colors for the blades of grass. Another method of setting the foreground and background colors is to use the Swatches palette, which offers a more intuitive way to pick colors. In fact, using the Swatches palette is very similar to picking from a box of crayons.

The Swatches palette is usually docked with the Color and Styles palettes. For now, it's best to leave these three palettes docked. From this group of palettes, you can apply the colors that are already defined in the palette, access a collection of swatches that came with the application, define new colors, create your own custom palettes, and more.

Work with the Swatches Palette

1 Open grass.psd from the Project_04 folder and save it into your WIP_04 folder. Assign the same name to the file.

2 If it isn't already open on your screen, display the Swatches palette (Window>Swatches).

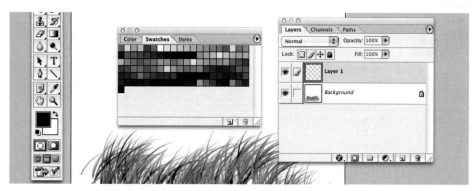

FIGURE 4.27

3 Choose Small List from the Swatches palette pop-up Options menu.

We find this view is more useful than the simple thumbnail palette because it allows you to see color chips, as well as the names of the colors.

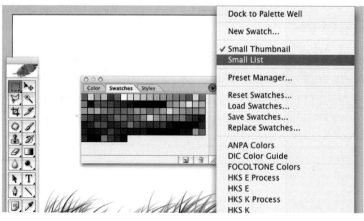

FIGURE 4.28

4 Resize the palette so you can see more of the color chips.

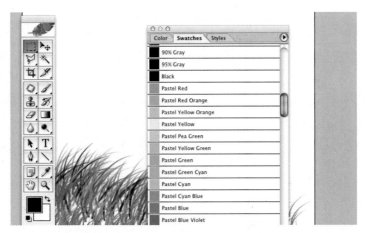

FIGURE 4.29

5 Scroll down until you see Medium Cool Brown. Click that color.

The foreground color is instantly set to the color you click in the palette.

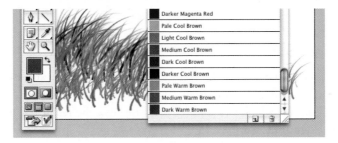

FIGURE 4.30

6 Hold down the Command/Control key and choose Dark Cool Brown.

The background color is set to the second color you choose from the palette. This process is very simple and allows you to select exact colors, rather than the random method of clicking in the Color Picker window.

FIGURE 4.31

7 Choose one of the larger sampled brushes.

8   Choose the Airbrush and Color Dynamics options. Set the Opacity value to 50%.

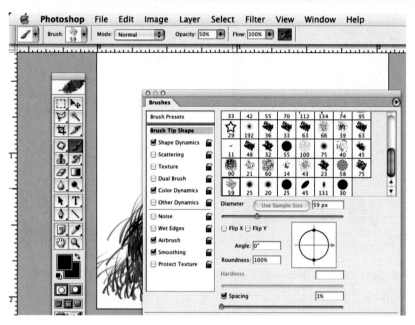

FIGURE 4.32

9   Use vertical strokes to paint some earth at the bottom of the image.

As you paint over an existing stroke, the color darkens. This is the result of the Opacity setting; each time you go over an area, more "paint" is applied and darkens the region. If you paint the same place enough times, the buildup of color reaches 100%. For now, the result is a more natural mixing of the foreground and background colors.

10   Rename the Background layer "Grass", and the current layer "Dirt".

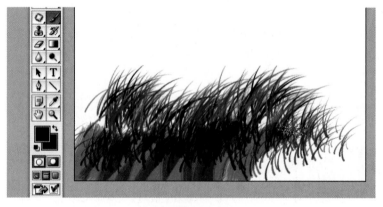

FIGURE 4.33

11   Save the file and keep it open for the next exercise.

LESSON 5 Creating Gradients

Blends, also called *gradients*, are smooth transitions between two or more colors. Photoshop makes it simple to create blends. They are often used to fill selections (such as the sky), and can be useful whether you're creating new artwork or repairing existing images.

In the following exercise, you work with several different types of blends to enhance the artwork you began earlier.

Work with Gradients

1 In the open grass.psd file, create a new layer at the top of the stack and name it "Sky".

2 Use the Swatches palette to set the foreground color to Pastel Cyan and the background color to one of the Blue Violets.

FIGURE 4.34

3 Choose the Gradient tool from the Toolbox.

As soon as you choose the tool, the Options bar reflects the change. From the Options bar, you can choose different types of blends, control the opacity and behavior of the tool, and change the blending mode.

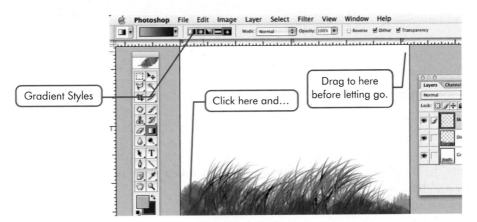

FIGURE 4.35

4   **Click the first of the five gradient-fill icons (Linear) on the Options bar.**

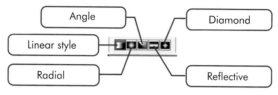

FIGURE 4.36

5   **Click in the lower-left corner of the image and drag to the upper-right corner.**

When you release the mouse button, the blend appears. Where you start and end the dragging process determines the location of the light blue and dark blue regions of the sky. Right now, you can't see the grass or the dirt, but that's OK; it's better if you focus exclusively on what happens when you use different blends, and how the location of the first and last clicks affect the end result.

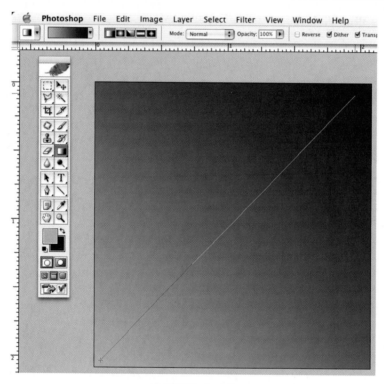

FIGURE 4.37

6   **Drag the tool from the center of the sky to the top center.**

The blend changes. The direction you drag the tool and where you release the mouse button affect the starting and end range of the blend.

7   **Choose the Radial style. Click in the center of the image and drag to the upper-left corner to create a radial blend.**

The Radial Gradient tool is the second of the five style icons. Where you start and end the dragging process determines how the gradient appears on the page. Experiment with all five of the blend styles. You will reset the blend at the end of this exercise.

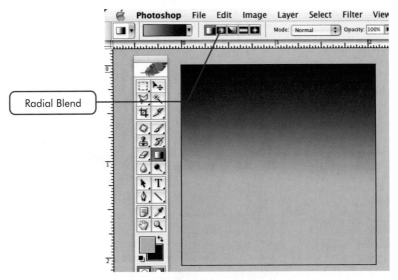

FIGURE 4.38

8   **Reset the blend to a linear gradient that starts in the lower left and ends in the upper right of the image.**

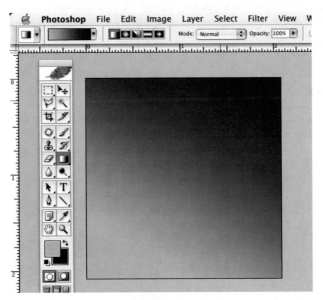

FIGURE 4.39

9   **Save your changes and keep the file open for the next exercise.**

This type of blend goes through a transition from one solid color to another. In some cases, you'll need a blend to transition from one color (the foreground) to transparent. You apply this technique in the following exercise.

Create a Transparent Blend

1 **Continue working in the open file. Create a new layer named "Sun".**

The new layer should be on top of the stack. If it's not, drag the layer to the top.

2 **Use the Swatches palette to set the foreground color to Pure Yellow.**

At this point, the blend is moving from Pure Yellow to the dark blue you used as part of the sky gradient. We're going to change that in a moment.

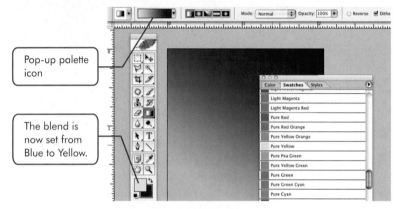

FIGURE 4.40

3 **Use the pop-up palette to set the gradient style from foreground-background to foreground-transparent.**

This blend behavior is the second icon in the top row. You'll see a number of different preset blends in this menu.

FIGURE 4.41

4 **Create the sun using a small radial blend in the middle-lower-left of the image.**

Since you're now blending from Pure Yellow to transparent, the appearance of the sun in the lower left of the blue sky appears quite natural.

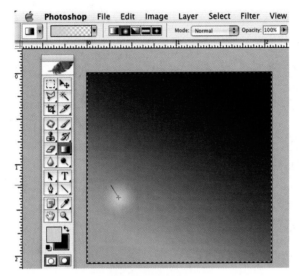

FIGURE 4.42

5 **Save your changes and keep the image open for the next exercise.**

As is the case with virtually every aspect of Photoshop, creating gradients isn't something that can be easily classified into a table containing every option; virtually endless design choices are available when you use the gradient tools in combination with colors and styles.

LESSON 6 Removing Color with the Eraser Tools

The Eraser tool can be used in the same way as any of the painting tools (the Brush, Airbrush, or Pencil tools), or it can be used as a simple square block. You can select the tool's behavior from the drop-down list on the Eraser tool Options bar. Except when the Block option is specified, you can assign a level of opacity to the Eraser.

Instead of painting with the foreground color, which is the case with the other painting tools, the Eraser paints in one of three ways:

- If you are working on a background layer — a layer that contains no transparency — the Eraser paints with the background color.

- If you are working on a layer that allows transparency, the Eraser removes all image data, making the area transparent.

- If the Erase to History box is checked, the tool actually restores image data from the state you designate in the History palette. It is important to remember that the changes made by the Eraser are, for the most part, not editable; many tasks that appear to be candidates for erasure should probably be handled with layer masks instead.

Paint with the Eraser

1 Continue working in the open document. Move the Grass layer to the top of the stack.

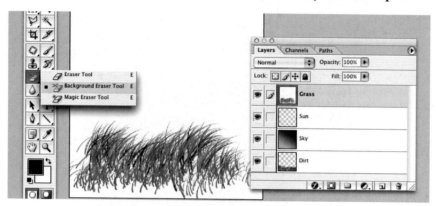

FIGURE 4.43

2 Choose the Background Eraser tool.

The Background Eraser tool is one of the options found under the Eraser tool icon in the Toolbox.

3 Set the Diameter of the brush to 50 pixels, and set the Hardness to 50.

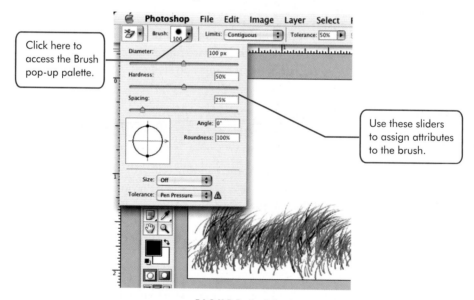

FIGURE 4.44

4 Show the other three layers (click their visibility icons), but keep the Grass layer selected.

5 | **Paint with the Background Eraser tool on the white background.**

As the background is removed, the blue gradient begins to show through. Note that the edges of the area you're painting are rather soft. This is the result of the Hardness setting.

FIGURE 4.45

6 | **Choose the Magic Eraser tool.**

This is another of the Eraser tool options in the Toolbox.

FIGURE 4.46

7 | **Click the Magic Eraser tool on the white background.**

Almost all of the white is removed, but some white remains between the blades. You could click around with the Magic Eraser tool to remove the rest of the white, but there's a much easier way to finish the task.

8 Change the Blending Mode of the layer to Darken.

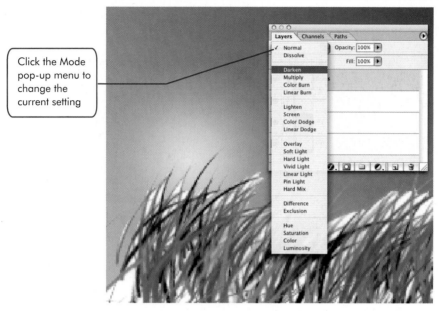

> Click the Mode pop-up menu to change the current setting

FIGURE 4.47

9 Examine the result.

This change in blending mode results in a perfect blending of the blades into the underlying layer. Now, only pixels that are darker than the underlying layers appear; the white background of the blades is eliminated from the mix.

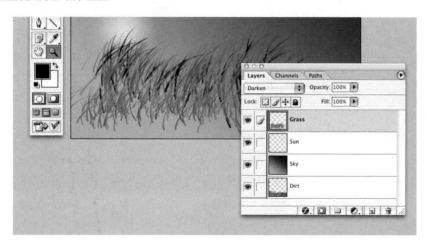

FIGURE 4.48

10   **Position the Dirt layer on top of the Sky layer.**

Experiment with the position of the various layers until the scene begins to resemble a primitive paint-ing. The goal of this exercise is to gain a bit of familiarity with the various Photoshop painting tools, not to create a sophisticated painting.

FIGURE 4.49

11   **Save your changes and keep the file open for the next exercise.**

LESSON 7 Using the Pencil Tool

The Pencil tool is unique among the painting tools. It is ideally suited for use with bitmap (black-and-white) images, or for creating hard outlines using horizontal or vertical strokes. The tool allows you to place individ-ual pixels on the page using the foreground color. The Pencil tool has no anti-aliasing attribute; as such, it has somewhat limited range, and is rarely used with photographic images.

Draw with the Pencil Tool

1   **Continue working in the open document. Reset the default colors to black and white.**

2   **Zoom into the lower-right corner of the artwork.**

3   **Choose the Pencil tool from the Toolbox.**

The Pencil tool is the alternate to the Brush tool. To access it, click and hold the Brush tool until the pop-up provides access to the Pencil tool.

FIGURE 4.50

4   **Use the Pencil tool to write your name.**

The line is choppy. In computer art terms, these stair-stepped pixelated lines are called *jaggies*.

FIGURE 4.51

5   **Save your changes and close the file.**

C A R E E R S   I N   D E S I G N

THE NATIONAL PHOTOSHOP USERS GROUP

Scott Kelby, a Florida Photoshop guru, is the founder and executive director of the Photoshop Users Group — an organization dedicated to the use of the world's most popular and powerful imaging and image-editing application. If you are interested in taking your Photoshop skills to the next level, the Photoshop Users Group is one of the best resources we've come across.

If you want to be the best that you can be, knowing what other users are doing and becoming part of an user group is an invaluable step in the right direction. Among the many benefits of membership in the organization is the magazine *Photoshop User*. Each month the publication is packed full of new tips, tricks, functions, and reviews of products related to the use of Photoshop. The reviews alone are worth the price of membership, not to mention that we can guarantee that you'll learn something new with each issue.

In addition to the magazine, the organization sponsors training seminars and annual get-togethers known as Photoshop World. The event is held in several different venues, so participation is convenient no matter where you work and live.

SUMMARY

In Project 4, you learned that Photoshop can function as several different programs. First and foremost, it is an image-editing program — allowing the graphic designer to modify existing images in many ways. Photoshop is also a painting program, providing almost unlimited ways to apply color to a page. You experienced a number of these coloring methods, and there's much more to learn. As you gain proficiency with the Photoshop features, functions, and tools, and you gather experience working on different types of assignments, you'll intuitively know which tool is best suited for a specific design task.

As you worked with the Brush tool, applied various brush types and behaviors, and changed the opacity and other characteristics, you began to build your painting skills. Those skills will grow stronger as you complete the following Skill Drills and Challenges. As you continue to use the program, your ability to paint naturally and effectively will become second nature. Over time, you will be able to use your painting skills to make an image come alive.

KEY TERMS

Additive color mode

Bitmapped image

Blending mode

Clone tool

Color dynamics

Color mode (also color space, color model)

Color Picker

Eraser tools

Flow rate

Four-color process

Gamut

Gradient

Hardness

Healing tools

Indexed color image

Jaggies

Natural media

Opacity slider

Pencil tool

Retouching

Subtractive color mode

Swatches palette

Tonal value

Visible spectrum

CHECKING CONCEPTS AND TERMS

SCREEN ID

Describe the following items found on the Brushes palette.

1. _____

2. _____

3. _____

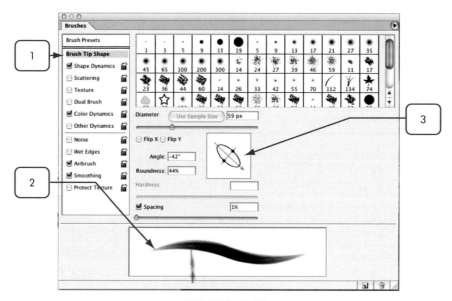

FIGURE 4.52

Name these two components of the Swatches palette.

1. _____

2. _____

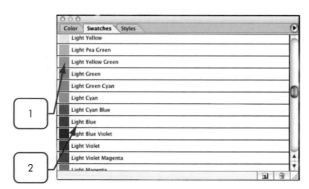

FIGURE 4.53

MULTIPLE CHOICE

Circle the letter that matches the correct answer for each of the following questions.

1. Which color mode should you use for a four-color printed brochure?
    a. CIE/LAB
    b. Grayscale
    c. Bitmap
    d. RGB
    e. None of the above.

2. CYMK is an acronym for four different colored
    _____ .
    a. pixels
    b. channels
    c. inks or colorants
    d. layers

3. The harder a brush, the more _____ its edges.
    a. defined
    b. jaggy
    c. fuzzy
    d. soft
    e. colorful

4. To change the size or orientation of a brush, which option from the Brushes palette would you choose?
    a. Color Dynamics
    b. Brush Tip Shape
    c. Blending Mode
    d. Hardness

5. Once you create a color in an image using RGB values, you can't create another color using CMYK values.
    a. True
    b. False

6. What happens if you create a selection on an image, and use a paint brush to paint on top of it?
    a. Only the area within the selection is affected by the brush.
    b. Only the area outside the selection is affected by the brush.
    c. Both areas are affected, depending on the Opacity setting for the layer.
    d. The effect depends on the blending mode and the opacity for the layer.

7. The blending mode has an effect on _____.
    a. how newly painted pixels interact with pixels that are already on the layer
    b. how the pixels on one layer interact with pixels on underlying layers
    c. how one color blends with another
    d. b and c above.
    e. a and b above.

8. Mixing cyan and magenta produces what color?
    a. Deep purple
    b. Light violet
    c. Dark brown
    d. Dark blue

9. A color not attainable using CMYK colors must be reproduced using _____.
    a. RGB color
    b. a solid colored ink
    c. a spot color channel
    d. None of the above.

10. Images destined to be printed at a commercial site must be converted into CMYK before you do anything to the image.
    a. True
    b. False

DISCUSSION QUESTIONS

1. Define the term "color space."

2. When would you use the RGB color space?

3. Why would you want to keep a copy of an original image in the RGB color space, even if you only need it for a commercial printing project?

SKILL DRILL

Skill Drills reinforce project skills. Each skill reinforced is the same, or nearly the same, as a skill presented in the project. Detailed instructions are provided in a step-by-step format. You should work through the exercises in the order provided.

1. Use the Background Eraser Tool

1. Open the file named mountain_child from the Project_04 folder.

2. Choose the Background Eraser tool from the Toolbox.

FIGURE 4.54

3. Set the brush Diameter to 60 pixels and the Hardness to 50.

4. In the pop-up palette, set Limits to Discontiguous, Tolerance to 10%, and Sampling to Once.

These settings result in a brush that picks up a color from the center "hotspot" of the brush cursor, and only erases that color — within a 10% range on either side. The Discontiguous setting causes any pixels touched by the brush to be erased, even if they're not connected to each other.

FIGURE 4.55

5. Click the blue sky and begin to paint with the brush.

FIGURE 4.56

6. Change the Limit setting to Contiguous. Paint the lower skyline and the boy's head.

7. Continue removing the sky.

FIGURE 4.57

8. Keep the file open for the next Skill Drill. Do not save your changes.

2. Use the Magic Eraser Tool

1. Continue working in the open file. Choose File>Revert to restore the sky.

2. Choose the Magic Eraser tool from the Toolbox.

3. Set the Tolerance to 10, check Anti-Alias and Contiguous, and set the Opacity to 100%.

   The Use All Layers selection is only useful if you're working in a multi-layer document. If you are, this command allows you to use different settings for different layers, or one set of attributes for all the visible layers in the document.

Use All Layers isn't helpful unless you're working in a multi-layer document.

FIGURE 4.58

4. Click anywhere in the sky.

   Many pixels are instantly erased.

FIGURE 4.59

5. Increase the Tolerance setting to 30. Click in several different places on the sky.

The increased Tolerance setting results in a wider range of selected pixels. This behavior is similar to the Tolerance setting of the Magic Wand tool.

FIGURE 4.60

6.   Close the file without saving it.

3. Use the Clone Stamp Tool

In the following exercise, you work with the Clone Stamp tool. This tool is critical for retouching and repairing images, as well as for simply duplicating portions of an image.

1.   Open the file named head_shot.psd from the Project_04 resource folder.

2.   Use the Magnifying Glass tool to zoom into the bottom of the image.

In Figure 4.61, you can clearly see that the model's thumb inadvertently appears in the picture. It would look a lot better if you removed the offending element, but simply erasing it would result in a large, ugly hole in the picture.

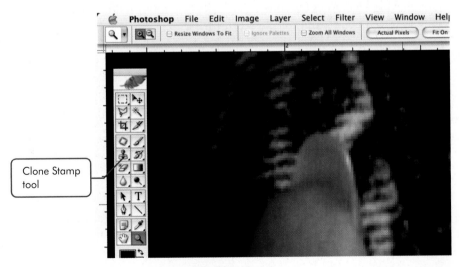

Clone Stamp tool

FIGURE 4.61

3. Choose the Clone Stamp tool from the Toolbox.

4. Set the Diameter to 40 pixels and the Hardness to 20%. Make sure that Aligned is checked.

    Rather than simply erasing the thumb, you're going to remove it without leaving any evidence. As you've learned, retouching is the process of using painting tools and techniques to repair or modify an original image.

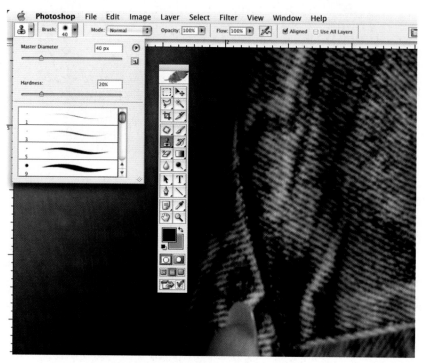

FIGURE 4.62

5. Hold down the Option/Alt key and click the cloth directly above the thumbnail.

    Option/Alt-clicking establishes the source pixels that the tool uses for the repair. This source region is then used as the content (paint) of the brush.

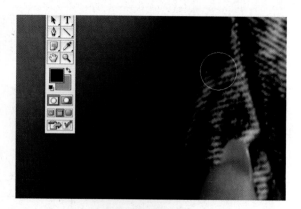

FIGURE 4.63

6. Slowly and carefully, paint over the thumb with the Clone Stamp tool.

    When you use the Clone Stamp tool, it's better to apply many short, delicate strokes rather than long strokes. Click, paint, let go; click, paint, let go. Remove only the tip of the thumb and nail.

FIGURE 4.64

7. Option/Alt-click a little higher above the thumb to sample another source.

    When retouching, it's a good idea to keep changing the source region to avoid repetitive patterns. These patterns cause visible artifacts (objects), which are often called "railroad tracks" by professional image retouchers.

8. Remove the rest of the thumb.

9. Zoom out and look at your work.

FIGURE 4.65

10. Save the file into your WIP_04 folder. Keep it open for the next exercise.

4. Use the Healing Brush

Many artists prefer to work with multiple layers when they retouch an image. This ensures they preserve original data in the event that they make a mistake and need to start over. In the following Skill Drill, you add a new layer before you work with the Healing Brush.

1. Continue working in the open file. Create a new layer by making a duplicate of the Background layer.

    The easiest way to create a copy of a layer is to Option/Alt-drag the layer you want to copy onto the New Layer icon at the bottom of the Layers palette.

FIGURE 4.66

2. Zoom into the area under the model's left eye (on your right).

    There are several small wrinkles. Typically, professional image editors remove such features on photos of their models in an attempt to perfect their appearance.

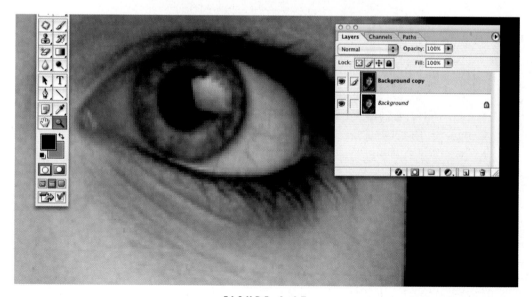

FIGURE 4.67

3. Choose the Healing Brush from the Toolbox. Set the Size to 20 and the Hardness to 50.

   The Healing Brush works in much the same way as the Clone Stamp tool. Instead of simply cloning (duplicating) pixels from one area of the image and applying them in another area, the Healing Brush picks up more subtle aspects, such as tonal values and general appearance, and mixes them into the area where you're painting. This tool is very effective when you're working with skin tones, facial characteristics, and other areas of subtle color differences.

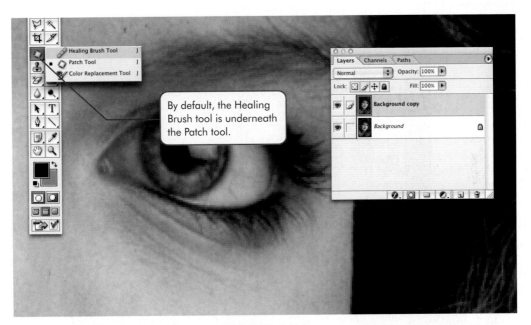

FIGURE 4.68

4. Option/Alt-click in the smooth area directly below the model's eye. Gently paint away the wrinkles with the Healing Brush.

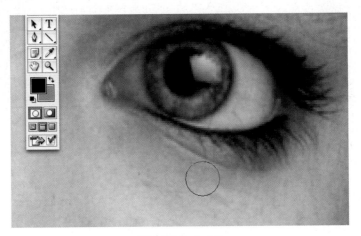

FIGURE 4.69

5. Use the Hand tool to move the image so you can see the other eye.

6. Repeat the process with the Healing Brush to repair the wrinkles on the other eye.

   You will enjoy greater success if you simply click the brush, rather than drag it across the area. This dabbing technique often results in less apparent changes. The soft brush helps achieve excellent results. Retouching is considered an art form — not simply a Photoshop skill that you read about, try once, and achieve professional results. This technique takes time and effort to master, and the rewards are substantial when you do so. Professional retouchers are very well compensated for their talents.

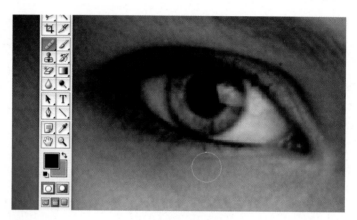

FIGURE 4.70

7. Zoom out and examine the newly retouched image.

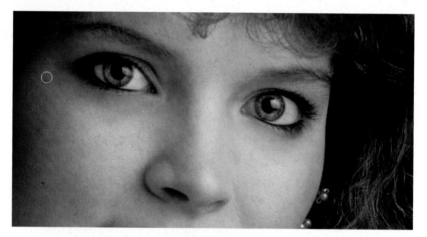

FIGURE 4.71

8. Save your changes and close the file.

CHALLENGE

Challenge exercises expand on, or are somewhat related to, skills presented in the lessons. Each exercise provides a brief introduction, followed by instructions presented in a numbered-step format that are not as detailed as those in the Skill Drill exercises. You should work through the exercises in the order provided.

1. Use the Clone Stamp Tool to Add Elements to a Photo

You took a picture of a wild turkey you saw in the woods near your house. To make the picture more interesting, you want to add a few more turkeys to the scene — turning the single turkey into a virtual flock of birds.

1. Open the file named turkey.psd from the Project_04 folder.

2. Add a new layer with a transparent background, and then select the original layer.

3. Choose the Clone Stamp tool, and then Option/Alt-click in the center of the turkey to establish the source for the tool.

4. Switch to the new layer and paint a copy of the turkey.

FIGURE 4.72

5. Use the Transform command to resize the new turkey layer and create a smaller turkey.

6. Move the small turkey toward the back of the image.

FIGURE 4.73

7. Save the image and leave it open.

2. Remove Artifacts

Artifacts are obvious flaws in an image; retouching or cloning often leaves behind such glitches. Be sure to remove them so they don't stand out as obvious errors in your work.

1. In the open file, zoom into the smaller turkey and select its layer.

2. Choose the Eraser tool from the Toolbox.

3. Choose a small, soft brush.

4. Erase the bright edges of the bird so the Background layer shows through.

5. Work all the way around the bird until all the bright edges are gone.

FIGURE 4.74

6. Save your changes and close the file.

3. Clean up a Floral Image

Oftentimes, nature is blemished; but dead leaves on the picture of a plant, brown spots on the lawn of a promotional image, and wrinkles on an otherwise perfect model aren't visible when the images are printed or posted on the Web because the blemishes have been removed. In the following exercise, you practice removing such blemishes from an almost flawless image of an orchid.

1. Open the orchid.psd file from the Project_04 resource folder.

2. Save it into your WIP_04 folder.

3. Look at the image closely. You see a number of blotches and dust particles.

4. Repair the image using the Clone Stamp tool and the Healing Brush.

5. Print and compare the repaired image to the original.

4. Paint with Blends

There is virtually an infinite number of ways that you can combine tools to create artwork in Photoshop. In this Challenge, you use layers, blends, and an existing file containing text elements to create a Web object.

1. Open the file named metalsmith.psd from the Project_04 resource folder.

2. Hide the two layers containing the type.

3. Choose the Gradient tool in the Toolbox. Click the pop-up palette icon on the Gradient tool Options bar.

4. Using the pop-up palette menu, select Metals from the bottom of the list.

5. Click Append in the dialog box.

6. Create a new layer and position it below the two existing layers.

7. Pick one of the metal blends that you just loaded.

8. Choose the Reflective Gradient style from the Options bar.

9. Create a blend from the center of the layer to the top.

10. Experiment with different locations and start/stop points.

11. Experiment with different Gradient styles.

12. Apply Layer styles to the two type layers.

    You can change the entire look of the banner logo simply by using the Gradient tool on the layer containing the blends. Try changing the blend mode of the Gradient tool (to Screen, Lighten, or any of the others) and applying the blend. You will probably get results you never expected. Change the blend style and the blend mode at the same time — you can never tell what will happen next.

13. Save the file into your WIP_04 folder and close it when you're done.

FIGURE 4.75

P O R T F O L I O   B U I L D E R

Make Color Selections

Most designers have definite preferences when it comes to color combinations; some prefer warm earth tones, while others lean toward bright and shocking colors. Your assignment is to build an image that you can use to store a few of your favorite combinations. That way, you can open the document and use it as a visual guide for color selections in the future.

1.   Create a new letter-size document and save it as "color_combos.psd".

2.   Use the Rectangular Marquee tool to create a small square "swatch" toward the upper-left corner of the document.

3.   Use the Color Swatches palette to select a favorite color, and use it to fill the selection.

4.   Use the Move tool to drag the selection to the right. Repeat Step 3 to fill the new selection with a complementary color.

5.   Continue creating pairs of colors that you feel work well together. Create at least ten sets.

6.   Save the file when you're done.

7.   To use your combinations, open the file, and then copy and paste the samples into your new document. From there, you can use the Eyedropper tool to assign them to either the foreground or background color swatches in the Toolbox.

Using Type Elements

O B J E C T I V E S

In this project, you learn how to

- Create type elements
- Control font attributes
- Manage type layers
- Work with paragraph attributes

- Warp type
- Create type masks
- Add special type effects

WHY WOULD I DO THIS?

A picture may be worth a thousand words, but its message may be open to interpretation without accompanying text. In this project, you learn how to add type elements to your images — and to effectively incorporate what many designers feel is the single most important component of their work.

For projects that contain a great deal of text, such as magazine articles, newsletters, or product brochures, you should utilize a page-layout program rather than try to complete the job in Photoshop. In some cases, a dedicated illustration application may be the correct tool to use. For the vast majority of design projects, however, Photoshop is the correct choice for incorporating text within an image. Many such projects come to mind: posters, flyers, artwork for ads, retouching assignments, and a very important graphic element that many designers work on today — the Web. The type elements you see on the Internet, or at least much of the text and copy you find in the design elements, were created in Photoshop or another image-editing program capable of adding text to pictures.

Understanding how to incorporate text into your Photoshop documents is an important skill, one that you will often use. Photoshop's type functions have become quite sophisticated; in fact, the program's type-control features are competitive with those found in the industry-leading illustration programs. Even though you will not use Photoshop to construct newsletters and brochures, type elements are required in the vast majority of graphic design projects. Proficiency in applying type elements to images will not only enhance your output, it will help you to become a well-rounded artist.

VISUAL SUMMARY

Depending on what needs to be done to a particular image, you need to know the best approach to add text to an image to ensure a successful end product. You have two basic choices. The first choice is to add text to a painting, image, or other artwork. Examples of this type of text element include Web banners, postcards, and posters. In Figure 5.1, you can see a Web banner under development; this is an example of adding type elements to an existing image to develop artwork for a specific purpose.

FIGURE 5.1

The second category of type assignment is retouching, where the type already present in an image must be changed. In Figure 5.2 below, you can see how Photoshop was used to remove the original artwork that read "K-SWISS" and replace it with the word "NIKE".

FIGURE 5.2

Bitmap versus Vector Graphics

You can create two types of graphics on your computer. The first type is called a raster (or bitmap) graphic. Bitmap graphics are comprised of individual pixels, which are called **bits**. No matter how high the resolution of a specific bitmap image, you can see the pixels when you examine the image closely.

FIGURE 5.3

Photoshop is primarily designed to create and edit bitmap images. The only exceptions are type elements and paths. You learn the basics about paths in this project, and discover advanced features in a later project that focuses on paths.

The second type of graphic element you can create is called a vector object. Vector objects aren't made of individual pixels; they are created from mathematical descriptions of paths (also called **strokes**) and the colors or tones contained within those paths (called the fill). If you examine a vector object closely, you'll see that it's comprised of lines connected by points (often referred to as **anchor points**). Each point contains information about the curves or corners defined by the points, and can be moved and/or reshaped.

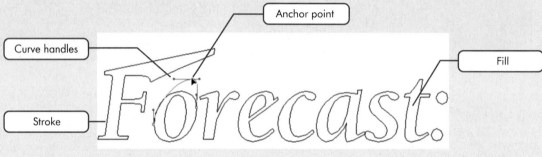

FIGURE 5.4

Before you begin the lessons in this project, you must load the ATC font families supplied in the resource files for this Essentials Series book. For information about loading fonts onto your system, please refer to the documentation that came with your system, or access the operating system Help function under "Loading Fonts."

LESSON 1   Creating Type Elements with the Type Tool

Placing type in your Photoshop documents is straightforward and quite easy to do. Controlling the appearance of type, as well as using text elements effectively and tastefully, requires practice, experience, and skill.

Let's take a moment to review the features of the Type tool Options bar shown in the following image:

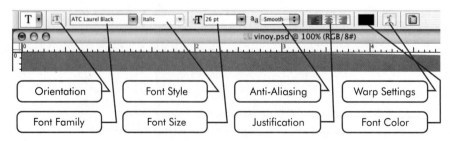

FIGURE 5.5

- *Orientation* refers to the direction of the type. Type can run from left to right or top to bottom.

- *Font family* is the name of the typeface you are using in the document. Examples include Times Roman, Arial, Helvetica, Courier, and Wingdings.

- Type *Style* refers to the differences between regular, italic, bold, and bold italic types. Some fonts have additional "weights," such as heavy and extra bold. Type weight determines the thickness of the strokes that comprise the characters.

- *Size* of the type is measured in points, which is an old typographer's term. A *point* is roughly 1/72 of an inch.

- *Anti-aliasing* is a technique used to soften the hard edges of type (and other objects) by creating a grayscale ramp along the edge. The higher the anti-aliasing setting, the softer and more natural the type appears; the lower the setting, the more you see the jagged edges (jaggies). This visual trick makes bitmapped type appear to have a softer edge and helps eliminate pixelization. The effects of anti-aliasing are most apparent in the rounded letterforms.

- *Justification* settings determine how the type fits within the space allotted. Left-justified type has a ragged right-hand border. Right-justified type aligns with the right side of the area, and the left side is ragged. Centered type is centered on the page with ragged left and right borders. Full Justification forces type to fit evenly on both the right and left sides of a text region.

- *Warp settings* allow you to distort, stretch, and otherwise modify text elements so they follow a shape, create a circle, appear to be on the face of a banner or cloth, and more.

Point Text versus Text Boxes

Photoshop provides two methods for setting text. Simply clicking anywhere in the image and typing creates what is known as *point text*. Point text works well for headlines and titles; but as line breaks must be added manually for multi-line copy, point text becomes cumbersome when more than a few words are placed on the page.

A *text box* is created when you click the Type tool on the page and drag to create a box. You can then place the cursor inside the text box and enter text. You can resize a text box with the handles on the sides and corners of the box. Simply hold the cursor over the handle of a text box, wait until the cursor changes to an arrow, and then resize as necessary. Depending on what you intend to do with the type, text boxes can be more flexible than point text. Once you've created the text box, it can be resized, rotated, and repositioned anywhere on the page.

Explore the Type Options Palette

1 Open the file named **vinoy.psd** from your Project_05 folder.

2 Save a copy of the file into your WIP_05 folder. Assign the same file name.

3 Choose the Type tool in the Toolbox.

4 Examine the features of the Type tool Options bar at the top of the window. Hover the cursor over each of the features until the tool tip pops up.

5 Keep the file open for the next exercise.

Place Type on an Image

1 In the open vinoy.psd file, choose ATC Laurel from the Font menu. Choose Book from the Style pop-up menu.

FIGURE 5.6

2 Set the Size to 30 pt., and set Anti-Aliasing to None.

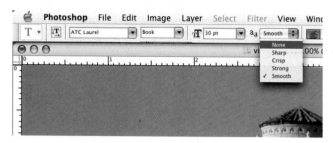

FIGURE 5.7

3 Click in the blue sky to the left of the bell tower.

When you click the Type tool on the page, a vertical bar appears. This bar is called the ***insertion point***, which tells you where the text will appear when you begin typing characters.

4 Type the word "History" and press Return/Enter to commit the text to the page.

As you type, the text appears at the insertion point. You should also note that as soon as you create the type, a new layer appears in the Layers palette.

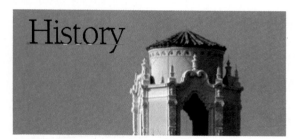

FIGURE 5.8

5 Save the file and keep it open for the next exercise.

Set Anti-Aliasing Values

1 **In the open vinoy.psd file, zoom in close enough to see the edges of the text.**

This text has obvious stair-stepping, which is due to the anti-aliasing setting you chose in the previous exercise. Photoshop normally softens the edges of type elements, and offers several automatic settings designed for that purpose. Remember that anti-aliasing softens the edges of type (and other elements) by stepping down from the color of the type to the color of the background (or to transparent).

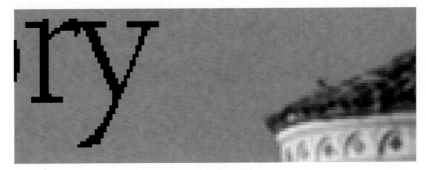

FIGURE 5.9

2 **Highlight the text; zoom in if necessary.**

To select text, activate the Type tool and simply drag over the characters that you want to select. An alternative is to click the Type tool in the text to set an insertion point, and then choose Edit>Select All (or press Command/Control-A) to select the entire range of type. You can also double-click the word or triple-click to select an entire paragraph.

FIGURE 5.10

3 **With the type selected, change the Anti-Aliasing setting to Crisp.**

Examine the text and note the improvement. The edges of the type appear much smoother and more natural. Experiment with different settings and note the changes. Examine the type close-up, as well as at 100% magnification.

FIGURE 5.11

4 **Save the file and keep it open for the next exercise.**

To Extend Your Knowledge...

SPELL CHECK UTILITY

Photoshop provides a spell check utility under the Edit menu. This utility works in a similar manner to other spell checkers and is complete with multi-lingual capabilities. Spell checking is no substitute for good proofreading, however, as certain words can be used out of context, even though they are spelled correctly. Remember: never proof your own copy; always enlist the aid of a willing, knowledgeable assistant.

LESSON 2 | Controlling Type Attributes

You can control many type attributes from the Type tool Options bar, but another method provides even greater control over the appearance of text elements — it is called the Character palette.

By default, the Character palette is docked with the Paragraph palette. Take a moment to examine the various settings and functions identified in the following illustration. Some of the functions are the same as those found in the Type tool Options bar. Others are unique features found only in the Character palette.

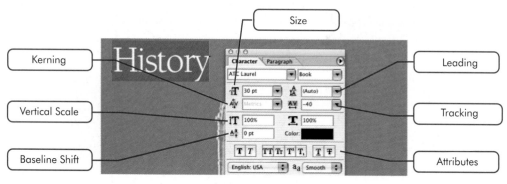

FIGURE 5.12

Here's a brief description of the settings that are highlighted in Figure 5.12:

- *Kerning* refers to the space between two individual letters. Kerning is an important attribute when you must align your type precisely. Certain letter pairs — To, Wa, and Ta, for example — tend to appear too far apart in most font families. Kerning allows you to reduce the space between two characters to make them more visually attractive.

- *Tracking* follows the same principle as kerning, but it works on an entire line of text or a paragraph. Larger tracking values add space to a line of text; smaller values reduce the space in the line of text.

- *Vertical Scale* and *Horizontal Scale* distort the type along the respective axis. Vertical scaling stretches type up and down, while Horizontal Scaling makes type wider or narrower. Both methods distort the type characters, so use caution when modifying these settings.

- **Baseline Shift** moves type above or below the baseline. A font's **baseline** is determined by the bottom of the letter "M." Parts of some characters naturally fall below the baseline, such as the tails of the letters "y" and "g." Letters that extend below the baseline are said to exhibit **descenders**.

- The **Attributes** settings offer character formatting options, including **Bold**, *Italics*, ALL CAPS, SMALL CAPS, Superscript ($E=Mc^2$), Subscript (H_2O), <u>Underline</u>, and ~~Strikethrough~~.

In the following exercise, you use the Character palette to change the appearance of existing type elements, as well as add new type elements to the image.

Resize and Position Type

1   **In the open vinoy.psd file, select the word "History".**

2   **Choose Window>Character.**

The Character palette opens. Take a few moments to explore the Character palette.

3   **Choose the Type tool in the Toolbox. Click an open area and enter the words "Florida Style". Place the words as shown in Figure 5.13.**

FIGURE 5.13

The type is in the same font and style that you used earlier.

4   **Choose Select>All to select the text you just typed.**

You can also press Command/Control-A to select all of the text elements.

5   **Click the All Caps icon in the Attributes section of the Character palette.**

All the characters in the line are converted to capital letters.

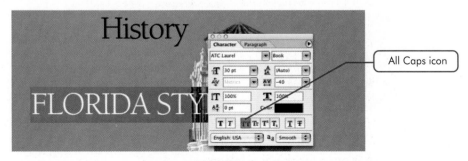

FIGURE 5.14

6   **In the Character palette, change the typeface (font) to 8-pt ATC Elm Normal.**

The Character palette provides a great deal of control from one easy-to-access location. We recommend that you keep the Character palette open while you work with text elements. Even though many of the same controls are available from the Type tool Options bar, numerous useful functions are only available from the Character palette. Some users find the Character palette easier to use than the Options bar.

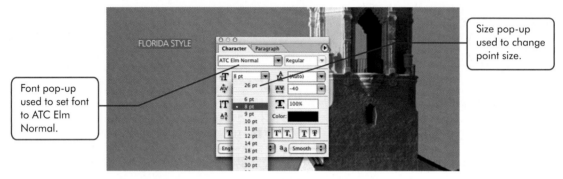

FIGURE 5.15

7   **Choose the Move tool in the Toolbox. Place the Florida Style text element underneath the word History.**

You can grab the text element and move it wherever you prefer. You can also use the handles to distort and resize the type.

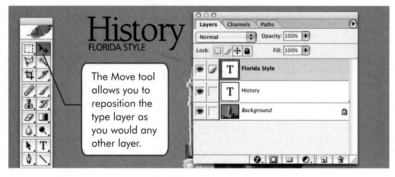

FIGURE 5.16

8   **Press Command/Control-Return/Enter to complete the move, or click the checkmark icon.**

FIGURE 5.17

9   **Save the file and keep it open for the next lesson.**

To Extend Your Knowledge...

FAUX FONTS

If bold or italic fonts are available in your chosen font family, always use them in preference to Faux Bold or Faux Italic. The actual bold and italic styles of a font family reproduce much better than faux fonts.

LESSON 3 Managing Type Layers

As we discussed earlier, every time you click the Type tool on the page, a new type layer is created. Type layers behave the same as any other layer. Let's use the open vinoy.psd to illustrate type layers.

At this point, the document contains three layers. The first layer, called the Background layer, was created when you first opened the file. Two additional layers were created when you used the Type tool to place the text elements onto your image — one layer for the word "History", and one layer for the words "Florida Style". The two type layers contained in vinoy.psd are part of a single element; together, they form a single graphic element. To ensure that the visual integrity of the graphic remains constant, you must link the two layers.

In the following exercise, you use some of the knowledge you gained in the Layers project (Project 3) to manage these type layers.

Link Related Type Layers

1   **In the open vinoy.psd file, double-click the Background layer and rename it "bell_tower".**

Renaming the Background layer changes it into a normal layer. As you already know, default Background layers are protected; to apply certain effects to the layer, it must be changed to a normal layer.

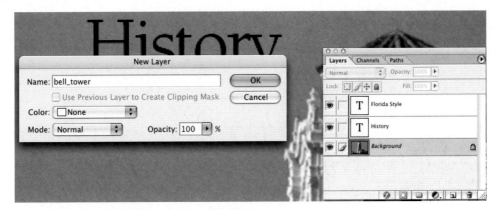

FIGURE 5.18

2 | Select the History layer and click the Florida Style layer's Link icon to link the layers.

The Link icon is located to the left of the layer name.

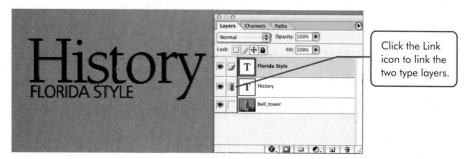

Click the Link icon to link the two type layers.

FIGURE 5.19

3 | Move the two layers to the right of tower.

Now that the two layers are linked, they act as a single layer. This allows for precise positioning. No matter where you move the linked layers, the appearance of the element remains unchanged.

FIGURE 5.20

4 | Click the visibility icon next to the bell_tower layer.

Hiding the layer containing the image of the bell tower at the Vinoy hotel allows you to see that both linked type layers are transparent, except for the actual text characters. Remember that the checkerboard background tells you the layer is transparent.

FIGURE 5.21

5 | Redisplay the Bell_tower layer, and then save the file; keep it open for the next exercise.

Merge Type Layers

It is oftentimes easier to simply merge two layers rather than link them. There is, however, a downside when you do so — once merged, the layers can no longer be edited. In this short exercise, you merge the two linked layers to see how the type elements change from a vector object to a bitmap object.

1   **In the open vinoy.psd file, select the History layer and select the text.**

You can see that although the two type layers are linked, you can still select the individual words.

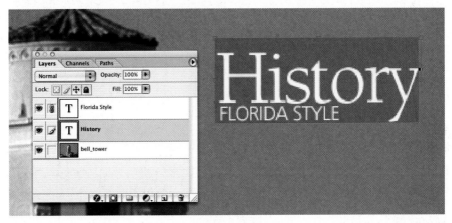

FIGURE 5.22

2   **From the Layers palette Options menu, choose Merge Linked.**

FIGURE 5.23

3   **Try to edit the text.**

You can no longer edit the text. Merging the linked layers *rasterized* the text — turned it into a bitmap — which cannot be edited. Rather than select the type elements, Photoshop automatically creates yet another type layer.

FIGURE 5.24

4   **Choose File>Revert to restore the file. Keep the file open for the next exercise.**

FIGURE 5.25

To Extend Your Knowledge...

FLATTENING TYPE LAYERS

When you create type in Photoshop, the result is a vector object. It can be edited however you choose — as long as you keep the file in native .psd format. If you create a document that's meant to be used in another file (such as a page-layout program or as a Web application), you should save a copy of the document and keep the original .psd file intact. That way, if you need to make changes to the text later, it is intact and editable. If you flatten the document (merge the layers), the type becomes rasterized and you lose the ability to make changes with the type tools.

If you flatten a document containing type, make sure it's still readable; the process rasterizes type elements, and can result in blurry or unreadable text. This is particularly true with serif typefaces set at small point sizes.

LESSON 4   Working with Paragraphs

So far, you've created text that resides on a single line. You created point text by clicking once with the Type tool and entering text. While this type of text object is fine for headlines and one-line graphic elements, there will be times when your text simply won't fit on a single line. To include multi-line copy, you must know how to manage paragraphs. A ***paragraph*** is a collection of words and sentences that begins when you start typing and ends when you press the Return/Enter key. Many of your Photoshop documents will contain multiple paragraphs of text.

Paragraphs have special characteristics and features. For example, you can:

- Control where a word breaks at the end of the line
- Eliminate hyphens altogether
- Indent a paragraph by moving the first line away from the margin
- Add extra space before or after a paragraph
- Control the amount of space between lines within the paragraph
- Cause punctuation symbols (periods, question marks, commas) to reside outside the normal margins of the paragraph

To incorporate paragraphs of text in an image, you must create box text. ***Box text*** is contained within a region (a text box) that you define by dragging the Type tool on the page.

In the following exercise, you create box text and apply various paragraph attributes to the copy — which you import from another document and paste into the region. A text file is included in the Resource folder for this exercise.

Copy Text from Another Application

| 1 | **From the Finder (Macintosh) or Explorer (Windows), navigate to the RF_Photoshop_L1 folder.** |

| 2 | **Open the Project_05 folder. Double-click the file named "history.txt".** |

Depending on how your system is configured, the file opens in MS Word, WordPad, Notepad, or another text editor. It makes no difference which program your system uses to open the history.txt file. You only need to open the file so you can copy the text to the clipboard.

| 3 | **Click anywhere in the text. Choose Edit>Select All to select the text.** |

| 4 | **Choose Edit>Copy to copy the selected text to the clipboard.** |

| 5 | **Close the file and quit the application.** |

Create a Text Box

Now that the text has been copied to the clipboard, it's time to create a text box to receive the content.

1   **In the open vinoy.psd file, press Command/Control-R to turn on the rulers (if they're not already showing).**

2   **Grab the ruler on the left side of the image and drag it to the 4-inch mark.**

A non-printing vertical guide is placed on the image.

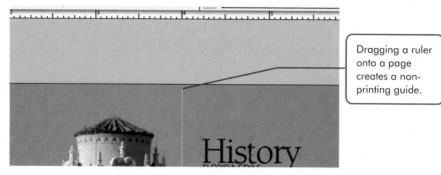

> Dragging a ruler onto a page creates a non-printing guide.

FIGURE 5.26

3   **Place a second vertical guide at 5-1/2 inches.**

FIGURE 5.27

4   **From the top ruler, drag a horizontal guide to the top of the tower.**

FIGURE 5.28

5   Drag another horizontal guide to the 3/4-inch mark.

6   Drag the linked type layers into the upper-left corner of the rectangle formed by the guides.

Guides are magnetic; objects snap to the guides when they get close enough. You can control this feature from the Preferences dialog box.

FIGURE 5.29

7   Choose the Type tool in the Toolbox. Draw a rectangle in the guides below the History object.

When you use the Type tool to draw a rectangle, it becomes a text box, ready to contain the type you enter. The text box constrains the type to a specific horizontal width (also called a *measure*), and causes the type to wrap within the space you designate.

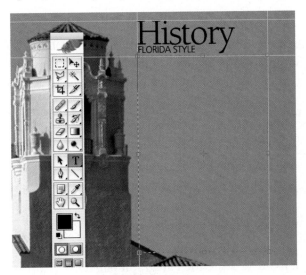

FIGURE 5.30

8   Use the Type tool Options bar to change the typeface to 10-pt ATC Jacaranda Regular.

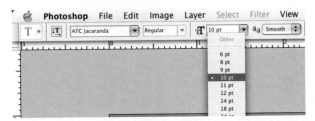

FIGURE 5.31

9   Choose Edit>Paste (or press Command/Control-V) to paste the text from the clipboard into the text box you created in Step 7.

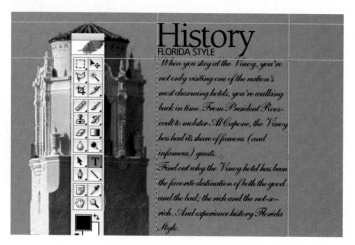

FIGURE 5.32

10   Save the file and keep it open for the next exercise.

Copyfit Text

The process of fitting text into a predefined space is called *copyfitting*. In the following exercise, you change the typeface and use several techniques to make the content of the text box visually appealing, as well as easier to read.

1   In the open vinoy.psd image, rename the new layer "body_copy".

Body copy is the common term for paragraphs of text that carry the primary "body" of the story, article, or advertisement. We strongly recommend that you name your layers with descriptive names.

2   Select all the body copy. Change it to 9-pt ATC Pine Normal.

This font is easier to read than the original. Be objective concerning the readability of type. Avoid typefaces that are too small or too ornate.

3   Click the Paragraph tab to activate the Paragraph palette.

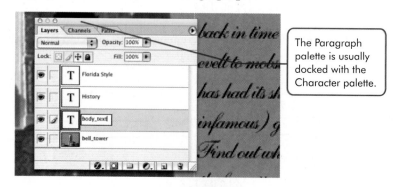

The Paragraph palette is usually docked with the Character palette.

FIGURE 5.33

4   **With the text selected, apply several of the Justification options. Finish with Justify Last Left.**

Click through all of the Justification options to see the results. Notice that when you apply Full Justification, the space between the words in the paragraphs expands. Try to avoid large, unsightly gaps. In many cases, left-justified paragraphs result in a better-looking block of copy.

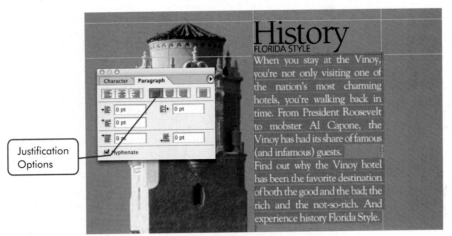

FIGURE 5.34

5   **Enter "9" in the Space After field.**

The Space After control increases the amount of space between each paragraph. In this case, you are adding space to the end of each paragraph, which avoids the first paragraph from being bumped down.

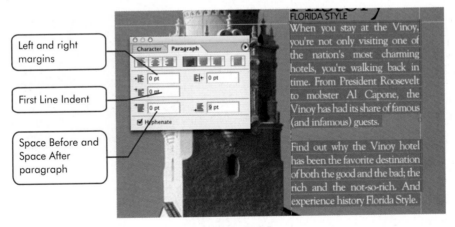

FIGURE 5.35

6   **Use the Move tool or Down Arrow key to move the body copy down a few pixels.**

Adding space between the lead-in graphic and the body copy creates a cleaner look for the entire area. Rely on your visual sense to ensure the appeal of your artwork. More than anyone else, you understand the artistic vision for your work.

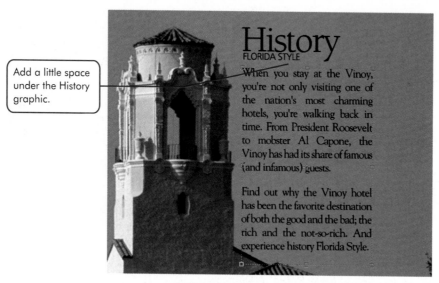

Add a little space under the History graphic.

FIGURE 5.36

7   **Click the Link icon to link the body_copy layer to the History layer.**

All three layers are linked, and will move as a single object.

FIGURE 5.37

8   **Save the file and keep it open for the next exercise.**

To Extend Your Knowledge...

ORGANIZE YOUR LAYERS

Organizing your layers is very important — especially as your images become increasingly complex. The critical need for organization is illustrated in a typical Web project, which contains buttons, backgrounds, navigation bars, images, and other elements that can easily number in the hundreds.

LESSON 5   Distorting Type

In addition to using the Layers, Character, and Paragraph palettes to modify text elements, you can modify the appearance of text from the Warp Text dialog box, which contains 15 warp options. In addition to the standard warps, you can further alter the warps to achieve a variety of interesting effects. Even after text has been warped, it can be edited and layer styles can still be applied. You can use the sliders in the Warp Text dialog box to apply an almost unlimited number of effects — so many in fact, that we can present only a small percentage of them in the confines of this lesson. We recommend that you take some time to experiment with this feature and become accustomed to the concept of warping text.

In the following exercise, you explore Photoshop's ability to distort text elements using the Warp functions, and learn how to wrap type around a shape. In doing so, you create a company logo. The first step is to create the type and ensure the letter spacing and general appearance of the text is visually appealing.

Fine-Tune Text Elements

1   **In the open vinoy.psd file, enter the word "VINOY" to the upper left of the tower. Format the text as 40-pt ATC Oak Bold.**

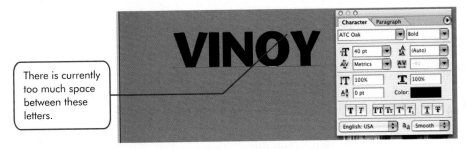

There is currently too much space between these letters.

FIGURE 5.38

2   **Place an insertion point between the "O" and the "Y".**

There's too much space between these two letters. You need to apply a kerning value to remove some of that space. Remember that kerning is the space between pairs of letters. In many fonts, the default kerning settings — called the *metrics* — are not perfect.

3   **Use the Kerning pop-up menu to change the value to –50.**

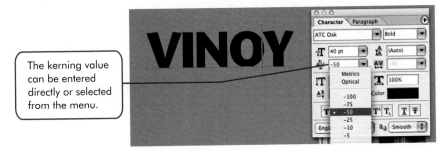

The kerning value can be entered directly or selected from the menu.

FIGURE 5.39

Notice that this value does not resolve the kerning problem.

4   Use the Kerning pop-up menu on the Character palette to change the value to –100.

5   Select the letter "O" and set the Horizontal Scaling value to 90.

This value is measured in percentages of the original horizontal width of the character. Reducing it to 90% of its default width makes this "O" appear lighter.

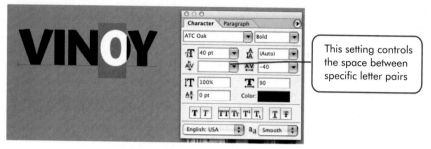

FIGURE 5.40

6   Save the file and keep it open for the next exercise.

Warp Text

The fine-tuned word would look better as a pure graphic element. You can use the Warp function to bend and shape the word.

1   In the open file, select the word "Vinoy" with the Type tool.

2   Choose Layer>Type>Warp Type to access the Warp Type dialog box.

3   Choose Arc from the Style pop-up menu.

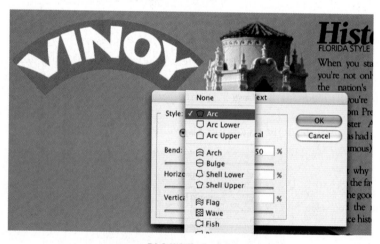

FIGURE 5.41

4   Experiment with changes in the values for Horizontal and Vertical Distortion.

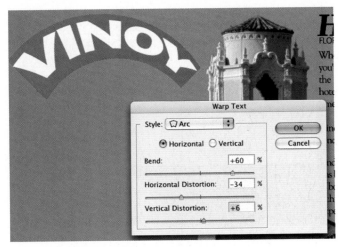

FIGURE 5.42

5   Set the Bend to 50% and Horizontal and Vertical Distortion to 0%. Click OK to apply the change.

6   Use the corner handles to scale down the type to the size of the lower-right curved window. If you're on a Windows system, hold down the Alt key to make the handles appear.

Move the object as necessary to position it correctly.

FIGURE 5.43

7   Adjust the size as necessary.

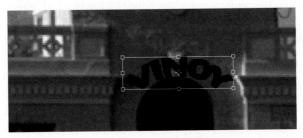

FIGURE 5.44

8   Select the type and increase the Bend value until it fits the curve.

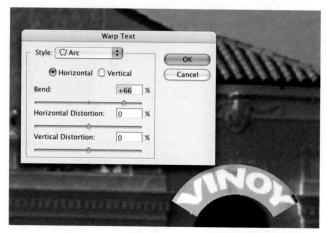

FIGURE 5.45

9   Commit the text, and adjust the layer's opacity so the object fades into the building. Zoom out to see the result.

These changes create a more realistic appearance.

FIGURE 5.46

10   Save the file and keep it open for the next exercise.

LESSON 6   Creating Type Masks

To create colored type elements, you can choose a color for the foreground, and any type you create from that point forward assumes that color. You can also change the color of type that's already in the image by selecting it and then choosing a different foreground color.

Beyond simply changing text from one color to another, your options are somewhat limited. Type — or more accurately editable type — is a special kind of object. As type, it retains spacing information, point size, font family, and other type-specific information. Photoshop does not allow you to color type with a gradient or apply filters (more about filters in the next project). In order to apply blends or filters to type, it must first be rasterized — turned from a vector object into a bitmap representation. Once you rasterize type, you can't change the point size, font, style, or spacing.

There is another alternative, however, when you want to add special effects to type. You can apply a type mask. A *type mask* is simply a selection of the exact same shape and size as the type from which it's created. It is layered over the original text element, and can be filled with a gradient or a filter can be applied; the original type element remains intact. For all intents and purposes, the type mask appears to be the type element in the image.

Color Type

1	In the open vinoy.psd file, select the word "History".

2	Open the Color Swatches palette (if it's not already visible).

3	Select a color from the palette. Commit the text.

To see the color of the type, select another tool to deselect the text.

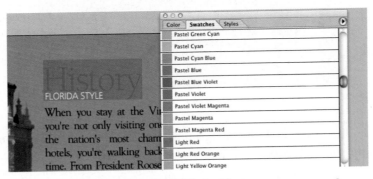

FIGURE 5.47

4	Save your changes and keep the file open for the next exercise.

Create a Type Mask

1	In the open vinoy.psd file, Command/Control-click the History layer.

This technique automatically creates a mask using the shape of the type. The selection is active, as you can tell from the marching ants that are moving around the characters.

FIGURE 5.48

2	Create a new layer directly above the History layer.

You can't fill the mask while it's on the type layer; it must be on a layer of its own.

3 Choose the Eyedropper tool in the Toolbox. Set the Sample Size to 5 by 5 Average.

FIGURE 5.49

4 Click the sunny left side of the tower to set the foreground color to light pink.

5 Option/Alt-click the shady front of the tower to set the background color to dark pinkish brown.

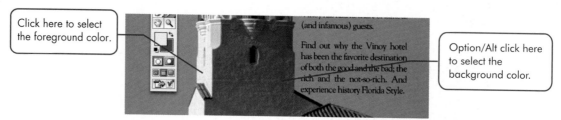

FIGURE 5.50

6 Choose the Gradient tool. Pick the Foreground to Background blend option from the pop-up menu. Select the fourth blend option.

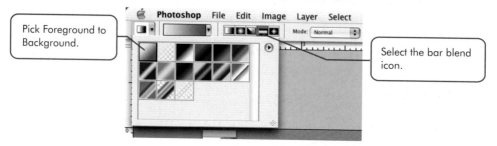

FIGURE 5.51

7 Press Command/Control-H to hide the edges of the mask.

Hiding the selection edges makes it easier to see the effect of the gradient.

8 Drag the Gradient tool from the lower left to the upper right of the word "History".

This simulates the same lighting as seen on the tower — bright on the left and darker on the right.

FIGURE 5.52

9 Save the file and keep it open for the next exercise.

Apply Layer Effects to Type Layers

Even though type layers have certain special characteristics, they're still layers, which means they can contain layer effects. In the following exercise, you apply a drop shadow effect to the layer containing the History text.

| **1** | **In the open file, select the History layer.** |

| **2** | **Click the Layer Effects icon along the bottom of the Layers palette. Choose Drop Shadow from the list of options.** |

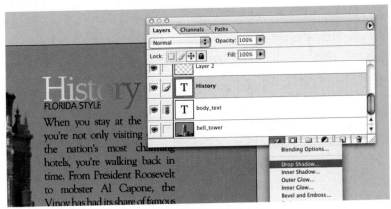

FIGURE 5.53

| **3** | **Change the Angle of the shadow to 180 degrees.** |

The sun is shining on the left side of the tower, so the angle of the shadow must be from the left side of the scene.

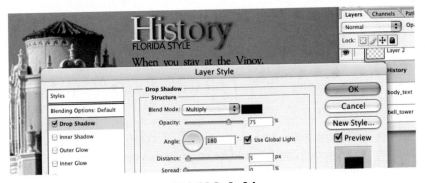

FIGURE 5.54

| **4** | **Save your changes and close the file.** |

To Extend Your Knowledge...

LEARNING ABOUT TYPOGRAPHY

This book is dedicated to Photoshop, and focuses on those skills and techniques necessary to become proficient in using the many features of the program. In this project, we touch on the subject of **typography**, which is the art of using typefaces tastefully and effectively. It is an important subject, but one that we can only briefly introduce here.

To learn more about typography, and discover how to select and utilize the correct typeface for each job, we suggest that you look into the *Type Companion for the Digital Artist*, one of a series of books available from Pearson/Prentice Hall. These books focus on design, art, photography, Web design, copywriting, typography, and other subjects that are important to the burgeoning designer or artist.

RESTRICTED MODES

Type layers aren't available in several color modes, including Indexed, Bitmap, and Multichannel. If you're working in one of these and use the Type tool, you'll create a type mask, not a type layer.

SUMMARY

In Project 5, you learned how to place text elements into images. You discovered that even though Photoshop offers powerful font and text tools, it is not designed to be a page-layout program. You learned that Photoshop is, however, quite capable of incorporating bitmap and raster graphics elements, resulting in powerful design combinations that can be used for posters, Web graphics, and other artwork that benefits from supporting text.

You learned the difference between raster and vector graphics, and explored the strengths of both types of images. You learned how to use the Character and Paragraph palettes, and discovered the differences between character formatting and controlling the format of an entire paragraph. You learned how to create point type and text boxes, and know when to apply each. You learned how to control the look and feel of your type, and how to manage type layers.

You also learned how to create type masks and apply special effects to type layers. You will learn more about type as you move forward; but for now, you should be comfortable modifying type in a wide variety of ways, including warping text, filling it with graphics, and converting it into a normal selection.

KEY TERMS

Anchor point	Justification	Stroke
Baseline	Kerning	Style
Baseline Shift	Measure	Text box
Bitmap graphic	Orientation	Tracking
Body copy	Paragraph	Type
Box text	Pixelated	Type layer
Copyfit	Point	Type mask
Descenders	Point text	Warp Setting
Font family	Raster graphic	Weight
Insertion point	Rasterized	

CHECKING CONCEPTS AND TERMS

MULTIPLE CHOICE

1. Kerning is a term that defines _____.
  a. the space before a paragraph
  b. the space after a paragraph
  c. letter-spacing for a paragraph or line of text
  d. spacing between specific pairs of letters

2. You can use the Gradient tool to add a blend to editable type.
  a. True
  b. False

3. To create a type mask, you would _____.
  a. select the type and choose Select>Add to Selection
  b. create the type with the selection tools
  c. Option/Alt-click a type layer
  d. All of the above.

4. Parts of characters that fall below the baseline are called _____.
  a. ascenders
  b. descenders
  c. tails
  d. None of the above.

5. Dragging with the Type tool _____.
  a. creates a type mask
  b. creates point text
  c. creates a text box
  d. activates the Paragraph palette

6. Which of the following is not a type style?
  a. Tracking
  b. Italics
  c. Bold
  d. Underline
  e. Strikethrough

7. Tracking applies to the space between letters.
  a. True
  b. False

8. To use a font, _____.
  a. it must be installed on your system
  b. it must be compatible with Photoshop
  c. it must be registered with the font company
  d. All of the above.

9. A typeface refers to all the characters in a font family.

    a. True

    b. False

10. Using the wrong font can negatively affect a design.

    a. True

    b. False

DISCUSSION QUESTIONS

1. Describe the difference between raster graphics and vector graphics.

2. How would you fill type with a gradient?

3. What types of projects would benefit from Photoshop's type tools?

SKILL DRILL

Skill Drills reinforce project skills. Each skill reinforced is the same, or nearly the same, as a skill presented in the project. Detailed instructions are provided in a step-by-step format. Work through these exercises in the order provided.

1. Set the Color for Type Objects

There are two ways to apply color to type. First, you can select the color you want before you create the text object. If the type is already on the image and you want to change the color, you select the text and then pick a color from the Swatches palette or Color Picker to apply it to the object.

In this drill, you use the first option — select the color from the image before you create the type layer.

1. Open the file named bike.psd from your RF_Photoshop_L1>Project_05 folder.

2. Save the file into your WIP_05 folder using the same name.

3. Use the Eyedropper tool to select the red color from the stripe on the bike.

    This selects the red color as the foreground, and, as a result, sets the color for the type you're going to create.

Use the Eyedropper with a 5×5 sampling size to pick the red stripe from the bike.

FIGURE 5.55

4. Save the file and keep it open for the next exercise.

2. Establish Font Attributes

You can set all the type attributes before you create the text, or you can select existing type and change the attributes from the Character palette, the Paragraph palette, or the Type tool Options bar. In this exercise, you set the type Style and Justification option before you create the type.

1. In the open file, choose the Type tool in the Toolbox.

2. Use the Type tool Options bar to set the typeface to 24-pt ATC Oak Bold Italic.

FIGURE 5.56

3. In the Options bar, set the Anti-aliasing to Strong, and the Justification to Centered.

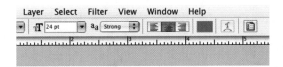

FIGURE 5.57

4. Keep the file open for the next exercise.

3. Create a Type Layer

Every time you click the Type tool on the page, a new type layer is automatically created. The name of the layer is the same as the text you enter. This is acceptable for short text elements such as headlines; but in other cases, it's better to assign a descriptive name to the layer. This allows you and others who are working on the image to know exactly what is contained on the layer.

1. In the open file, click the Type tool in the center of the image above the bike.

2. Type "Not for the Weak of Heart".

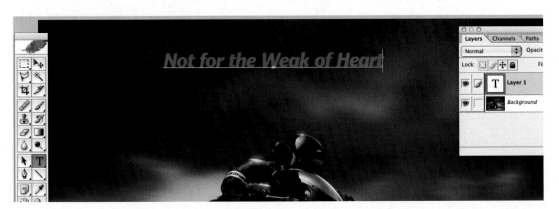

FIGURE 5.58

3. Rename the type layer "Headline".

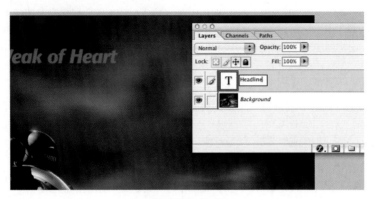

FIGURE 5.59

4. Select all the type and resize it manually to about 50 points by pressing Shift-Command/Control-> (greater-than symbol).

   Using keyboard commands to resize type is far more productive and much easier than selecting the size from any of the menus or palettes.

FIGURE 5.60

5. Use the Move tool to position the type in the top center of the image.

FIGURE 5.61

6. Save the file and keep it open for the next exercise.

4. Apply Layer Effects

You can apply layer effects to type layers; but other techniques, such as filters or gradients, cannot be applied. In this exercise, you apply a layer effect to the image.

1. In the open file, select the Headline layer.

2. Choose Layer>Layer Style>Blending Options to activate the Layer Style dialog box.

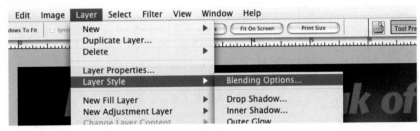

FIGURE 5.62

3. Check the Bevel and Emboss option.

    This sets the basic style for the type layer. Remember, you can apply layer styles to editable type, but you cannot apply gradients or filters. To use a gradient or filter with type, you must create a type mask.

4. Set the Bevel Style to Inner Bevel and the Technique to Chisel Hard.

    This is only the beginning of what can be accomplished with layer effects. These built-in and customizable styles are at their best when you're working with type elements.

5. Slowly move the Depth slider to the right and back again.

    Notice the subtle (yet striking) effect. When you are satisfied with the appearance of the image, release the slider. We used a Depth value of 151 to achieve the result in Figure 5.63.

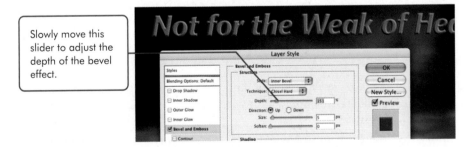

Slowly move this slider to adjust the depth of the bevel effect.

FIGURE 5.63

6. Experiment with the Size and Softness of the Bevel.

This effect simulates chiseled stone or glass. Adjusting the opacity of the type layer further enhances the illusion.

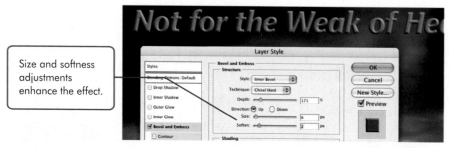

FIGURE 5.64

7. Adjust the Shading angle to match the natural light.

This setting is more visual than numeric; you must get a feel for working with any effect that produces the illusion of lighting. In this case, the light is striking the biker from more than one angle. (The bike and rider were shot in a studio, and the background was dropped in later.)

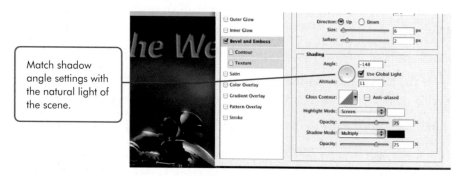

FIGURE 5.65

8. Save the file and keep it open for the next exercise.

5. Create a Type Mask

Next, you create a type mask, add a layer to hold it, and then fill it with the same foreground color that you picked for the text in the first Skill Drill exercise.

1. In the open file, command/Control-click the Headline layer to create the type mask.

FIGURE 5.66

2. Add a layer to hold the selection.

3. Press Option/Alt-Backspace to fill the selection. Press the "D" key to deselect the text.

    Since the red you used for the type is still the foreground color, the selection fills with red.

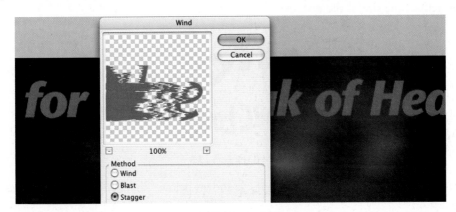

FIGURE 5.67

4. Choose Filter>Stylize>Wind.

    You will learn more about filters in Project 6.

5. Click the Stagger radio button and then click OK.

    Stagger is the strongest of the wind filters; it takes a few seconds to complete the filter process.

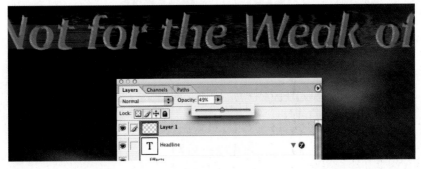

FIGURE 5.68

6. Reduce the Opacity of Layer 1 to around 50%.

    This reduces the wind effect so you can see the chiseled glass appearance of the letters.

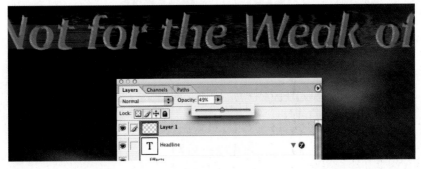

FIGURE 5.69

7. Save the file and close it when you're done.

CHALLENGE

Challenge exercises expand on, or are somewhat related to, skills presented in the lessons. Each exercise provides a brief introduction, followed by instructions presented in a numbered-step format that are not as detailed as those in the Skill Drill exercises. You should work through the exercises in the order provided.

1. Test the Warp Settings

1. Create a new RGB document, 800 pixels wide, 400 pixels high, with a Resolution of 200 dpi.

2. Choose the Type tool in the Toolbox. Set the Font to 30-pt ATC Oak Bold.

3. Enter the word "ARC".

4. Open the Warp Text dialog box. Warp the text using the default Arc setting.

5. Choose the Move tool. Option/Alt-drag the word "ARC" to make a duplicate; add the word "Lower".

6. Apply the Arc Lower warp setting, select all, and press the Shift-Command/Control-< (less-than) keys to reduce the size of the text.

FIGURE 5.70

7. Experiment with each of the Warp settings as shown below. Change the type as necessary.

FIGURE 5.71

8. Save the file in your WIP_05 folder as "warping.psd" and close it when you're done.

2. Create a Personal Signature Graphic

In this exercise, you create a personal graphic that can be used to "sign" your name to your work.

1. Create a new RGB document with 400-pixel Width, 200-pixel Height, at 200-dpi Resolution.

2. Type your name.

3. Choose any typeface you prefer.

    It doesn't have to be an ATC typeface; any typeface you like — as long as it is installed on your system — can be used in this exercise.

4. Warp the type with any style you prefer.

5. Apply a layer style.

    Feel free to experiment with the myriad layer style effects.

6. When you're done experimenting, flatten the image. Choose Flatten from the Layers palette Options menu.

7. Save the file as "personal.psd" and close it when you're done.

3. Create an Advertisement for a Local Point of Interest

1. Take a picture of an interesting location in your town.
    Either download it from your camera or scan it.

2. Add type as a headline.

3. Apply a style to the headline.

4. Create a type mask and fill it with a gradient.
    The gradient should include colors from the image itself.

5. Enter copy that describes the location.

6. Save the file as "location.psd", and leave it open for the next exercise.

4. Use Your Personal Signature

In this exercise, you add your personal signature to the image you created in the previous Challenge.

1. In the open image, choose File>Place and drop your personal signature into the image.

2. Choose Edit>Free Transform to resize and position the signature graphic in one of the corners of the image.

3. Reduce the opacity of the signature layer to tone it down.

4. Save your work and close the file.

PORTFOLIO BUILDER

USE FONTS IN DESIGN

Understanding how fonts affect a design is a critical factor in an artist's development. The goal of this Portfolio Builder is to begin your education on using fonts as a unique and specific design element.

1. Go to your local library and check out one or more books on fonts.

2. Learn the difference between a serif and a sans-serif font.

3. Identify the categories of the fonts installed on your system.

4. Redo one or more of the exercises in this project using alternative fonts.

5. Analyze the effect on the overall look and feel of the piece/s.

Using Filters

OBJECTIVES

In this project, you learn how to

- Work with the Filter Gallery

- Use the Extract filter

- Combine filters with selections

- Use filters and layer masks

- Combine displacement maps and textures

- Create custom textures

- Use the Liquify filter

WHY WOULD I DO THIS?

Filters are specialized tools that allow you to apply a seemingly endless number of special effects to your images – whether they're photographs, line-art drawings, or paintings. A large number of filters are already built into Photoshop when you first install it, and wide arrays of third-party filters are available for nominal fees.

Filters are small programs that "plug into" the core Photoshop application and add features that weren't originally present. In fact, the underlying technology that powers filters is called ***plug-in technology***.

Filters fall into specific categories that you'll learn about in detail in this project. Filters can be applied to entire images or to portions of an image (when you use them in conjunction with selections, channels, or masks). Simply put, filters allow you to accomplish many design-oriented tasks that cannot be completed any other way. A Photoshop designer must know how to take full advantage of filters; without this critical skill, your creative capabilities are limited. After you complete the lessons in this project, you will have a working understanding of the full battery of Photoshop filters, and know how and when to apply them to your artwork.

VISUAL SUMMARY

As you work through this project, you'll discover that filters can be used in one of two ways. First, they can be used to enhance images, create artwork, and simulate traditional mediums, such as watercolors, oils, pastels, and pencils. They can be used to add realistic lighting to your images. When used in combination with the Photoshop painting tools, you can use filters to develop dramatic and compelling artwork.

The image of a northern pike shown in Figure 6.1 is an enhanced version of the original photograph; painting techniques and targeted use of filters were applied to the photograph. (Photo courtesy of photographer and image-maker, Wynn Wollof, Tampa, Florida.) What was originally an excellent picture of equipment and a freshly caught fish evolved into what could be mistaken as an original watercolor.

FIGURE 6.1

Filters can also be used to **_extract_** portions of an image to create what are commonly called silhouettes (also called silos). A **_silhouette_** is an object, person, or image component that is separated from its background. Silhouettes are often created with the intention of creating composite images or to replace one background with another.

In Figure 6.2, you can see model Connie Hayes. On the left is the original image; on the right is the silhouette.

Posing model is separated from background, creating a silhouette.

FIGURE 6.2

The second way filters are employed by the professional artist, designer, or image specialist is more utilitarian and arguably not as much fun as the artistic application of the tools. In the real world, however, the utilitarian use of filters to repair damage, improve sharpness and apparent focus, soften harsh details, and perform production-related processes far outweighs artistic application.

In Figure 6.3, the original image of the Agave cactus on the left was sharpened using a tool known as a High-Pass filter, with the result shown on the right. This represents an advanced technique, but you have access to many easy-to-use filters for repairing flaws in damaged originals. One example is the Dust & Scratches filter that softens areas of large color and effectively removes dust marks on an image that originated on the photograph's negative.

FIGURE 6.3

Figure 6.4 is a perfect example of an image that would be difficult to create without the use of filters. On the left side of the piece is a line-art representation of the bridge image you saw earlier in the book; it seamlessly blends into a watercolor version on the right side. This effect was accomplished with filters and layer masks. You apply the same technique later in this project.

FIGURE 6.4

The Filter Menu

All filters are accessible from a single source, which is the Filter menu. More than 80 filters are available from this menu. Fortunately, the latest version of Photoshop offers a Filter Gallery, which you explore in the first lesson. This gallery allows you to browse through the available filters, similar to how you browsed the Image Gallery in Project 1.

With so many filters, it is impossible to present each and every one of them in the confines of this project. We recommend that you learn the basics of the filters we present here, and then take whatever time you need to explore the features and functions of the remaining filters in the Filter menu.

The Filter menu is divided into several categories. Take a moment to explore the categories and the related filters.

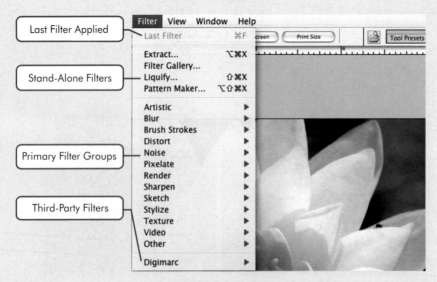

FIGURE 6.5

- The first category of filters is known as ***stand-alone*** filters. Stand-alone filters aren't part of the general (primary) filter groups.

- The second category contains the ***primary*** filter groups. They're organized in folders based on their general functionality, such as artistic filters.

- Last in line are the filters available from third-party companies. You can buy these filters and add them to Photoshop. They appear at the bottom of the menu once they're installed. One third-party filter, named Digimarc, is available when you install Photoshop. Digimarc is a company that provides certified watermarks. A ***watermark*** is an invisible identification object that's placed into an image to protect the photographer or artist's ownership rights.

FIGURE 6.6

LESSON 1   Using the Filter Gallery

The Filter Gallery, as we already mentioned, is indispensable — especially while you're learning about filters and aren't sure how a filter will affect your image. The ***Filter Gallery*** is a dialog box that shows generic previews of how each filter affects a single image of a sailboat. It also provides a preview window on the left side of the dialog box that allows you to see how the filter will affect your own image.

Before we continue with the Gallery hands-on activity, you should know that not all filters in the Filter menu are available in the Gallery. Many important filters — particularly those used to fix and repair images, and to create textures and other important functions — can only be accessed from the Filter menu. Still, the Gallery is a useful tool, and learning how to use it is well worth the time and effort.

In the following exercise, you use the Filter Gallery while you work on a high-resolution picture of a water lily in full bloom.

Work with the Filter Gallery Interface

1   **Open the image named waterlily.psd from the Project_06 resource folder. Save a copy in your WIP_06 folder.**

This is a good, clear image that contains enough resolution to show off some of what can be accomplished with Photoshop's filter technology.

2   **Choose Filter>Filter Gallery.**

3 **Click the small arrow icon at the top right.**

The Thumbnail Gallery opens. It presents some, but not all, of the filters available on your system.

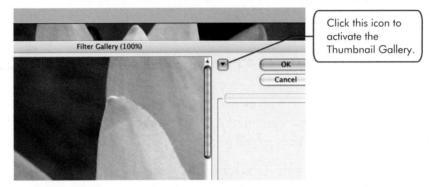

Click this icon to activate the Thumbnail Gallery.

FIGURE 6.7

4 **Examine the Thumbnail Gallery and select any of the filters.**

Depending on what you've been doing with Photoshop, there may or may not be a filter selected when you first activate the Filter Gallery. Regardless, this is the basic Gallery window. In this case, the Watercolor filter was selected and its effect shows in the preview window on the left side of the interface.

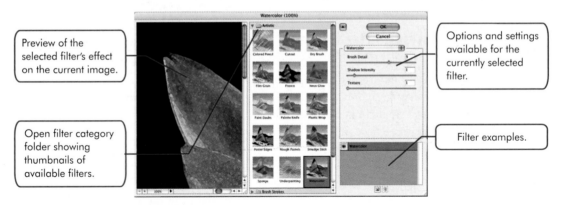

Preview of the selected filter's effect on the current image.

Open filter category folder showing thumbnails of available filters.

Options and settings available for the currently selected filter.

Filter examples.

FIGURE 6.8

5 **Click the small arrow to the left of the Artistic folder.**

This closes the folder and shows you the rest of the categories available in the Gallery.

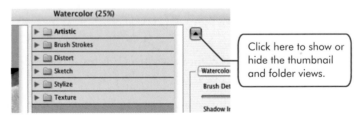

Click here to show or hide the thumbnail and folder views.

FIGURE 6.9

6   **Click the Show Thumbnails icon to enlarge the Preview window.**

Once you've selected the filter you want to use, you can take advantage of the increased preview size to fine-tune the filter's settings. Use the adjustments on the right side of the window. You can also use the regular operating system resize handles in the lower right of the Gallery dialog box to resize the entire Gallery window.

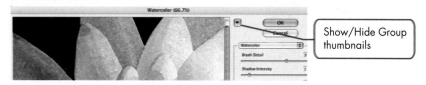

FIGURE 6.10

7   **Use the plus (+) and minus (-) signs in the lower left of the window to change the size of the Preview window.**

When you're using filters, it's important to zoom in and out of an image to see how the process affects the small details, while you keep the bigger picture in mind.

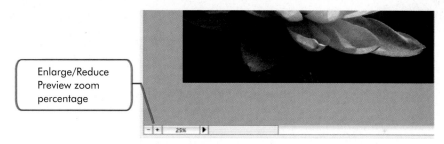

FIGURE 6.11

8   **Keep the file open for the next exercise.**

Apply a Filter from the Gallery Interface

In this exercise, you see the various components of the Gallery interface when you apply an artistic filter to the image of the water flower.

1   **In the Filter Gallery window, open the thumbnails and close the Artistic group folder (if necessary).**

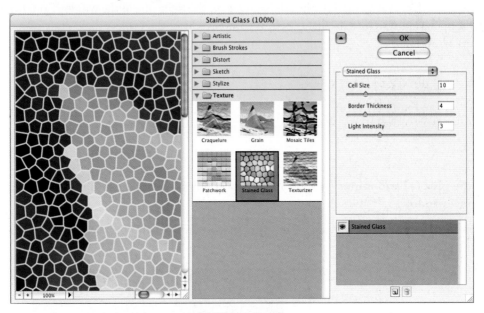

2   **Open the Texture group. Select Stained Glass.**

The Stained Glass dialog box opens.

FIGURE 6.12

3   **Close the Thumbnail section to enlarge the Preview window.**

This gives you a better view of the effect of the filter.

4   **Adjust the sliders to change the effect of the filter.**

In this example, we reduced the size of the individual pieces of glass (Cell Size), changed the width of the lead lines (Border Thickness), and increased the intensity of the light (Light Intensity).

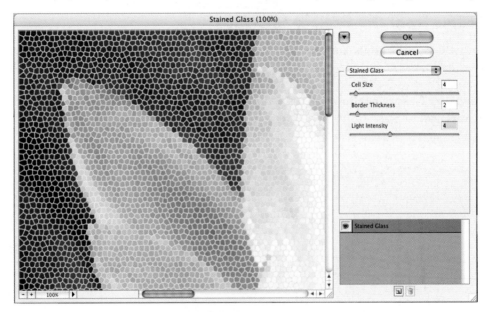

FIGURE 6.13

5   Adjust the size of the Preview window to see the large-scale effect of the changes you made.

FIGURE 6.14

6   Keep the file open for the next exercise.

Use the Filter Gallery to Combine Filters

The Filter Gallery is an excellent tool for experimenting with different types of filters to see what will happen before you actually apply the filter to an image. In this case, you're working with a file that weighs more than 7 MB. Although a good size for instructional purposes, this file is small in comparison to the files you'll work with in real-world situations. There, applying a filter to an image that weighs 35 MB or more can take significant processing time. Using the Filter Gallery allows you to see the result of the filter in much less time.

You can also use the Filter Gallery to view the result of combining two or more filters. In the following exercise, you learn how to use this important feature.

1   In the open file, click the visibility icon next to the Stained Glass filter's name.

This hides the effect of the Stained Glass filter.

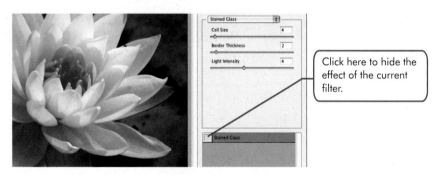

Click here to hide the effect of the current filter.

FIGURE 6.15

2 **Click the New Filter icon.**

This adds a new filter to the list. Note that the new filter is also hidden. When you add a new filter to the list, it takes on exactly the same attributes as the last filter you added, including its name.

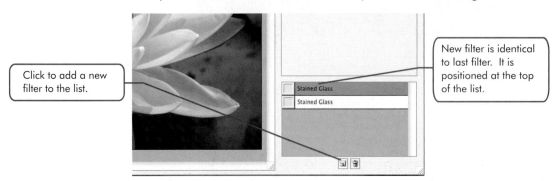

Click to add a new filter to the list.

New filter is identical to last filter. It is positioned at the top of the list.

FIGURE 6.16

3 **Select Poster Edges from the Filters pop-up menu.**

When you select the new filter, nothing happens because the visibility icon is still turned off.

FIGURE 6.17

4   Add another new filter to the list. This time, make it a Watercolor filter.

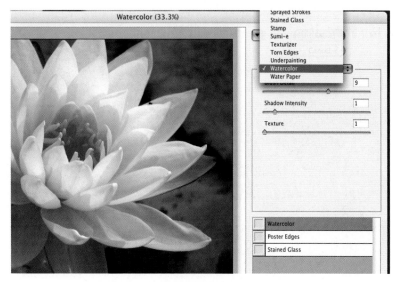

FIGURE 6.18

5   And one more filter — the Texturizer.

At this point, you have four filters in the list, and all of their effects are hidden because you turned off their visibility icons.

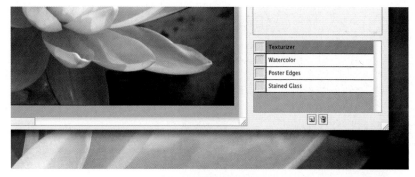

FIGURE 6.19

6   Make the Texturizer filter visible and experiment with the settings.

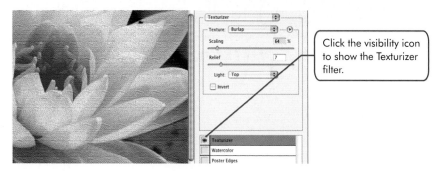

FIGURE 6.20

7   **Hide the Texturizer filter and show the Watercolor filter.**

Once again, take some time to experiment with the Watercolor filter. Many artists use the Watercolor filter, usually in combination with painting techniques and other filters.

FIGURE 6.21

8   **Hide the Watercolor filter and show both the Poster Edges and Texturizer filters.**

The Preview window displays the effect that both filters have on the image when applied at the same time.

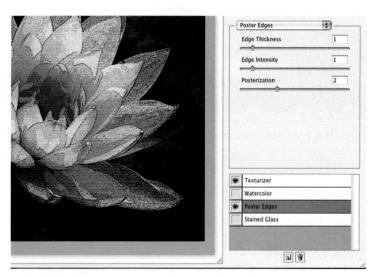

FIGURE 6.22

9 │ **Drag the Poster Edges filter to the top of the list (above the Texturizer filter).**

The relative stacking position of each filter changes the way it interacts with the other filters in the list. The (visible) filter at the top of the list is applied first; the next one in the list moving down is then processed, and so forth. Experiment with different filters and filter combinations on your own, using this or other images.

FIGURE 6.23

10 │ **Click OK to apply the selected filters. Save the file and close it when you're done.**

To Extend Your Knowledge...

APPLYING THE LAST FILTER

To re-apply the last filter you used, press Command/Control-F. Whatever settings were used the last time are automatically applied. If you want to apply the filter again, but with different settings, add the Option/Alt key to the Command/Control-F combination. The filter's dialog box appears, and you can adjust the values as necessary.

LESSON 2 Using the Extract Filter

The Extract filter is one of the stand-alone filters. It provides a selection method that makes it easy to extract a portion of an image so you can apply pens, brushes, and other painting techniques to it. The Liquify and Pattern Maker filters are the other members of the stand-alone filter group.

The reason these filters are separated from the primary filters group is because they are essentially miniature programs. They take over the Photoshop interface when you use them. They offer so many options and settings that putting them into a standard filter interface would limit their functionality.

In the following exercise, you use the Extract filter to create a silhouette of a bike rider, and then apply the Blur filter to simulate depth of field. ***Depth of field*** refers to a photographic technique that allows you to blur a background or keep it in perfect focus. It helps make the subject stand out in an otherwise busy picture when you soften the background, making it less distracting to the viewer.

Use the Extract Filter

1 **Open the file named amsterdam_biker.psd from the Project_06 folder. Save it in your WIP_06 folder.**

2 **Ensure that the Layers palette is visible.**

If not, choose Window>Layers to open the palette.

3 **Drag the Background layer onto the New Layer icon.**

This copies the Background layer. You will apply the Extract filter to the Background copy layer.

FIGURE 6.24

4 **Choose Filter>Extract.**

A number of different tools are available within the Extract filter. For now, the only two you need to use are the Edge Highlighter tool and the Fill Bucket. The Edge Highlighter is used to paint the outside edges of the item (or area) you want to extract. Once you create the outline, use the Fill Bucket to fill it. When you click OK to invoke the filter, the areas surrounded by the Edge Highlighter and filled with the Fill Bucket are protected from deletion. Anything not surrounded by the Edge Highlighter and filled with the Fill Bucket will be deleted to transparent when you apply the Extract filter.

Edge Highlighter tool

Fill Bucket

Cleanup tool. Makes edges transparent. Hold down the Option/Alt key to restore extracted backgrounds.

Edge Cleanup tool. Used to enhance edges of selection.

Brush and Tool Options

FIGURE 6.25

5 Change the Brush Size to 10 pixels and turn on Smart Highlighting.

Smart Highlighting is helpful when the edge of the subject is well defined, as in this case. You can drag the cursor a little faster when Smart Highlighting is turned on. The highlight follows the subject's edge quite well.

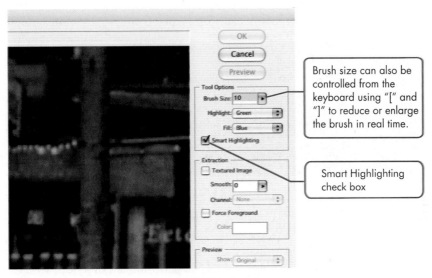

Brush size can also be controlled from the keyboard using "[" and "]" to reduce or enlarge the brush in real time.

Smart Highlighting check box

FIGURE 6.26

6 Use the Smart Highlighting tool to paint a border around the biker.

FIGURE 6.27

7   **Add a border along the two open areas underneath the subject's coat flaps.**

Always look for areas that should be cleared upon extraction; the two openings underneath the biker's arms could easily be missed. You can always extract them later, but it pays to get the selection right the first time. On very high-resolution images, the filter requires significant processing resources and time to take effect, particularly when you're making a complicated extraction. This is a relatively simple example of using the Extract filter; many real-world assignments are far more complicated.

Make sure there are no gaps.

FIGURE 6.28

8   **Use the Fill Bucket to fill the painted borders.**

Painting the border is the first of two parts; the second part is to fill the intended extraction with the Fill Bucket to protect it from being cleared when you perform the extraction. To fill a region, you must make sure that it's closed; there can't be any openings or gaps in the borders, or the fill will "leak out" and fill the entire image.

9   **Click the Preview button.**

Preview shows you what will happen when you apply the filter. It provides an opportunity to clean up the selection area and enhance the edges of the extracted subject before you commit the filter.

FIGURE 6.29

10   **If necessary, use the Cleanup tools to clean the edges and make them more distinct.**

11   Click OK. Hide the Background layer to see the entire extraction.

FIGURE 6.30

12   Rename the Background layer "Layer 0" and save the file.

FIGURE 6.31

13   Keep the file open for the next exercise.

Add the Blur Filter

1   In the open file, select Layer 0.

2   Choose Filter>Blur>Gaussian Blur.

Notice the several blur filters, all of which blur or soften an image or the area within a selection. Gaussian Blur is a controllable and visually appealing blur. Professional designers and artists use this filter on a very regular basis.

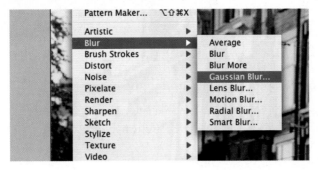

FIGURE 6.32

3   Click the plus (+) and minus (–) signs to enlarge and reduce the image within the Preview window.

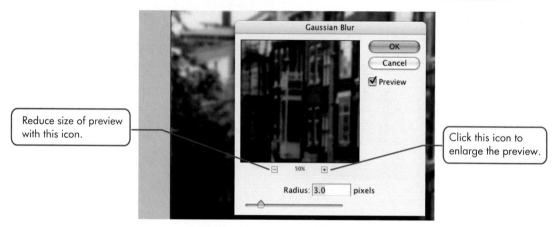

FIGURE 6.33

4   Use the slider to increase the Radius value to between 7 and 8 pixels. Click OK.

Changing the radius of the Gaussian blur filter enlarges the number of pixels it uses in its blur calculations; the result of increasing the radius adds a greater amount of blurring, while reducing it proportionately reduces the effect.

FIGURE 6.34

5   Select the Crop tool. Draw a rectangle around the biker.

Cropping is a process where a portion of an image is retained, and the rest cut off and discarded. Using the Crop tool, you can draw a rectangle, press Return/Enter, and effectively change the size and shape of an image.

FIGURE 6.35

6   **Press the Return/Enter key.**

The image is cropped. It presents a completely different aspect of the scene than the original. If you want, open the original and compare the two.

FIGURE 6.36

7   **Save the file and close it when you're done.**

This is a simple example of simulating a specific photographic method using only filters and selection techniques. In the next lesson, you combine repair techniques (from the painting project) with filters and a bit of artistic license to create artwork that could never come directly from a camera.

To Extend Your Knowledge...

ARTISTIC FILTERS

Artistic filters are grouped together under a dedicated Filter submenu, but one could argue that a number of filters found within other categories can also be used to achieve artistic effects.

An artistic filter is one that — through the manipulation of pixels and colors — simulates an otherwise traditional method of creating artwork. Artistic filters include several that you've already seen, such as the Watercolor filter.

LESSON 3   Combining Filters and Masks

Whenever you apply creative filters, it's important that you first repair or remove all obvious or glaring flaws in the picture. Otherwise, when you apply your filters and create your artwork, those flaws will not only be clearly visible, they will be very difficult to fix.

Filters and masks go together like coffee and cream, or a horse and carriage. Masks protect portions of an image, and can provide a soft transition from one area to another, where a filtered area blends almost imperceptibly into a non-filtered area.

A piece of artwork you saw earlier in the project showed a bridge that was a watercolor on the right and a line-art illustration on the left. With minimal effort, the artist was able to simulate that work-in-progress by creating a mask on the left and applying a watercolor filter on the right. Once the watercolor was done, the artist masked that portion, and used several filters to remove the color and reduce the left side of the image to black and white lines. Without the intelligent application of masking and filter combinations, this artwork could not have been produced.

In the following set of exercises, you combine masks and filters. Before you actually do so, however, you repair a bit of damage. You should always make sure you perform any repairs before you apply your filters; otherwise, you'll enhance the damage, and end up creating unnecessary work for yourself.

Prepare an Image for Masking and Modification

1.   **Open the image named white_vanda.psd from the Project_06 folder. Save it in your WIP_06 folder.**

   Saving a copy of the image in your WIP_06 folder ensures that the original document remains intact, in case you want to repeat a specific lesson or exercise.

2.   **Choose the Clone Stamp tool in the Toolbox.**

3   Use a small soft brush to remove the large fungus spots on the petals of the flowers.

FIGURE 6.37

4   Continue repairing the image. The big, obvious spots aren't the only flaws in the picture.

As this image develops into a work of art (or at least an example of artistic filters), you'll see that fixing blemishes such as these fungus spots would be very difficult once you combine masks, filters, and layers to create the final artwork.

FIGURE 6.38

5   When you're satisfied with the appearance of the flowers, save the image and keep it open for the next exercise.

Mask the Image

In this exercise, you create two different layer masks, and use them to selectively apply a few filters to the image.

1　In the open image, rename the Background layer to "flowers".

Remember, the default Background layer doesn't behave the same as a regular layer. This step ensures you can do whatever you want to the image.

2　Click the New Layer icon to add a new layer.

The new Layer 1 is added to the top of the layer list.

FIGURE 6.39

3　Click the Add Layer Mask icon.

4　Choose the Gradient tool.

5　Select the Linear Gradient and set the Style to Foreground to Transparent using the pop-up palette. Set the Foreground Color to Black, if necessary.

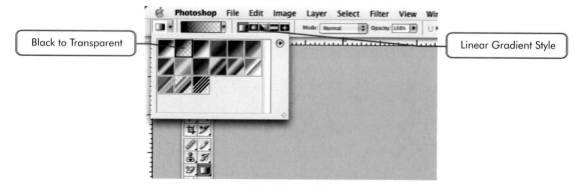

FIGURE 6.40

6 **Drag the Gradient tool from the lower right to the center of the image.**

Look in the Layers palette at the Layer Mask icon. You should see the lower-right side of the thumbnail is black and seems to fade to white.

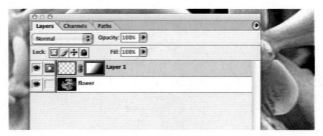

FIGURE 6.41

7 **Add another layer and accompanying layer mask.**

8 **Create another gradient coming down from the upper left to the center of the image.**

You have two different layer masks at this point, and the thumbnails of the layer masks should look like mirror images. Another way to do this is to simply reverse one mask to create a mirrored image; creating the effect by hand, as you're doing here, results in a more natural-looking finished image.

One mask comes in from the upper left, and another from the lower right.

FIGURE 6.42

9 **Save your changes and keep the file open for the next exercise.**

Combine Filters and Masks

1 **In the open white_vanda.psd image, Command/Control-click the Layer 1 mask to load it as a selection.**

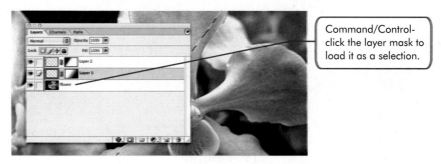

Command/Control-click the layer mask to load it as a selection.

FIGURE 6.43

2 Select the flower layer.

3 Choose Image>Adjustments>Desaturate.

This process removes the color tones from the unmasked areas, while the protected lower-right side of the image retains its original shades. You can press Command/Control-U to accomplish the same effect.

FIGURE 6.44

4 Choose Filter>Brush Strokes>Accented Edges.

We reduced the Edge Width to 1, increased the Edge Brightness, and reduced the Smoothness value to 2. Feel free to experiment with different values; but before you're done, return them to the values shown in the following image (Figure 6.45).

FIGURE 6.45

5   **Apply the Stylize>Find Edges filter.**

The Find Edges filter doesn't allow you to change any values. This one-size-fits-all filter produces a pen-and-ink type of effect.

FIGURE 6.46

6   **Choose Image>Adjustments>Levels. Slide the right slider to the left to reduce the gray tones in the image.**

This accentuates the black lines and removes some of the detail in the image.

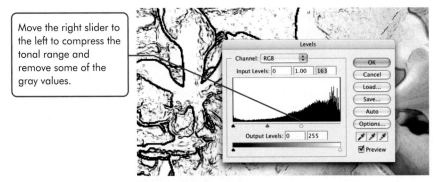

Move the right slider to the left to compress the tonal range and remove some of the gray values.

FIGURE 6.47

7   **Choose Filters>Blur>Blur.**

This softens the lines a little bit.

8   **Select Layer 2. Command/Control-click the layer mask to load the layer as a selection.**

9   **Select the flower layer.**

10   **Choose Filter>Pixelate>Facet.**

11 **Press Command/Control-F twice to apply the filter two more times.**

The Command/Control-F process re-applies the last filter you used. This is particularly useful when you're applying an artistic or painterly filter that benefits from multiple applications. The Facet filter reduces tonal gradations each time you apply it, essentially flattening details and reducing color gradations within the mask.

12 **Hide the selection areas and examine the image.**

FIGURE 6.48

13 **Delete the two layers containing the masks.**

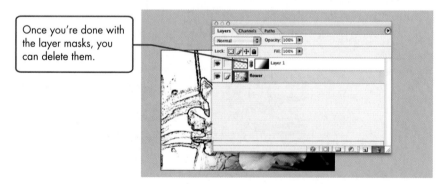

Once you're done with the layer masks, you can delete them.

FIGURE 6.49

Once you've used the two layer masks to create the selections, you can delete them to reduce the size and complexity of the final image.

14 **Save your changes and close the file.**

There's nothing special about simply applying a standard Watercolor filter to an image; instead, use your creativity and imagination when you apply filters. Using a combination of masks, selections, and filters presents literally infinite possibilities to create unique artwork from otherwise every-day photographs. Remember, though, that the use of filters can be taken too far. When it comes to filters, a little bit goes a long way.

To Extend Your Knowledge...

RESETTING THE DEFAULT IMAGE

When you're working in the Filter Gallery or a filter dialog box, you can reset the filter or the image by holding down the Option/Alt key. When you do, the Cancel button temporarily turns into a Reset button.

Holding down the Command/Control key, on the other hand, turns the Cancel button into the Default button, which resets the preview and deletes all the current filters from the list on the lower right of the dialog box.

LESSON 4   Using Filters to Create Custom Textures

Besides the obvious application of filters to modify and enhance regular images, they can also be used to create images from scratch. A good example of this is the creation of customized textures. In Lesson 2, you used the regular Texturizer filter, which allows you to apply textures to existing images. In addition to the Texturizer, a few other filters are classified under the Texture submenu, which you can see in Figure 6.50.

FIGURE 6.50

What do you do when you need a texture that isn't found within the category? You make your own. In the following exercise, you learn one way (there are many more) to generate custom textures.

Create a Custom Texture

1   Create a new RGB document with a 4-inch Width, 5-inch Height, 300-ppi Resolution, and a White Background.

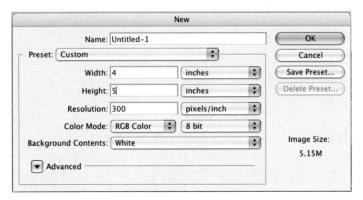

FIGURE 6.51

This relatively high-resolution image is suitable for mid- to high-quality color printing (although you would convert it to CMYK before it went to the printer).

2   Reset the foreground and background colors to their default black and white.

3   Choose Filter>Render>Clouds.

FIGURE 6.52

4   Apply Render>Difference>Clouds.

FIGURE 6.53

The result is a dark, mottled field. Next, you turn it into stone.

5   **Choose Filter>Stylize>Emboss.**

Embossing is a useful filter, one that essentially takes details and raises them, adding shadows to enhance the illusion of depth. Embossing can result in very realistic textures, which you see in a moment.

6   **Set the Angle to 135 degrees (the default), the Height to 4 pixels, and the Amount to 250%.**

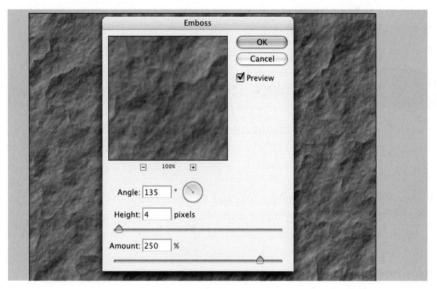

FIGURE 6.54

7   **Choose Image>Adjustments>Hue/Saturation, and colorize the texture.**

A blue-gray color helps simulate the illusion of slate, but feel free to make it any color you prefer.

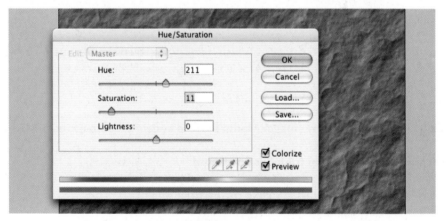

FIGURE 6.55

8   **Save the file in your WIP_06 folder as "slate.psd".**

9   **Close the file when you're done.**

This exercise gives you an idea of what can be done with the texture filters. In the next exercise, you create realistic-looking linen — another texture that can be utilized in a wide variety of design assignments.

To Extend Your Knowledge...

WORKING ON LAYERS

Filters are powerful tools; they are also potentially damaging. It's good practice to drag the layer you're working on to the New Layer icon in the Layers palette before you apply filters. That way, you preserve the original in perfect condition.

LESSON 5   Using Filters and Displacement Maps

You can use filters in combination with a ***displacement map***, which is a texture or shape used as a backdrop to add depth and dimension to an image. Displacement maps are particularly useful when used in conjunction with filters.

In the following exercises, you create an image map and a cloth texture. In order to use an image as a displacement map, it must be in grayscale; color modes don't work. In the first steps of the exercise, you create the grayscale image, and then you use that displacement map to add shape to a piece of cloth.

Create A Displacement Map

1   Create a new document and apply the same resolution and dimensions as you did in Step 1 of the previous exercise, but select Grayscale as the Color Mode.

2   Choose Filter>Render>Difference Clouds.

This creates the basic tones for the displacement map.

3   Save the file in your WIP_06 folder as "cloth_map.psd". Keep the file open for the next exercise.

Create A Cloth Texture

1   In the open document, select Image>Mode>RGB to convert the image into RGB color mode.

2   Save the file in your WIP_06 folder as "cloth.psd".

3   Choose Edit>Select All, and then delete the existing image.

4   From the Filter menu, choose Noise>Add Noise.

The Add Noise dialog box appears.

5   Set the Amount to 300, Distribution to Gaussian, and check the Monochromatic option. Click OK to apply these settings.

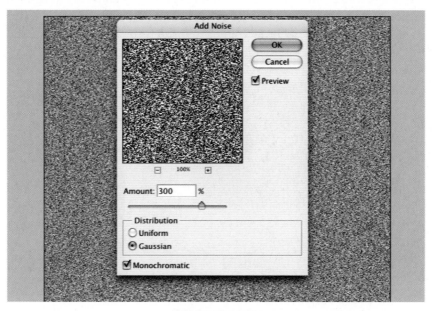

FIGURE 6.56

6   Rename the Background layer to "horizontal", and then drag it to the New Layer icon in the Layers palette to create a copy.

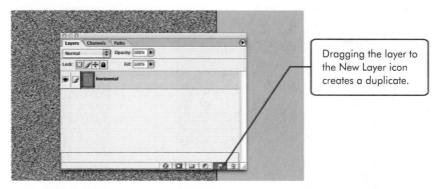

Dragging the layer to the New Layer icon creates a duplicate.

FIGURE 6.57

7   Rename the horizontal copy layer to "vertical".

8   Select the horizontal layer.

9   **Choose Filter>Blur>Motion Blur. Set the Angle to 0 and the Distance to 50 pixels.**

This results in a blur that simulates threads running in one direction – left to right. The larger the distance, the more cohesive the lines resulting from the effect. The angle controls the direction; if you had set it to 45 degrees, the lines would run from the upper-left corner to the lower right.

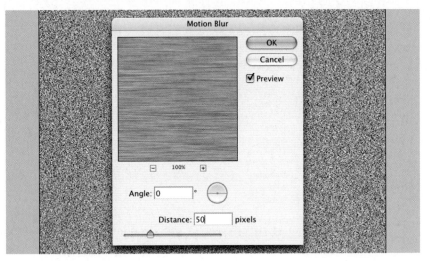

FIGURE 6.58

10   **Select the vertical layer and apply another Motion Blur with a 90-degree Angle and a Distance of 50 pixels.**

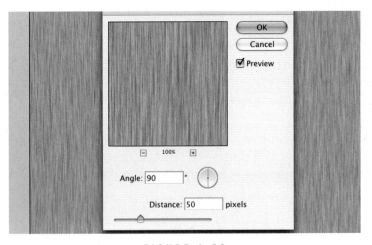

FIGURE 6.59

11 Change the Blending Mode of the vertical (top) layer to Multiply.

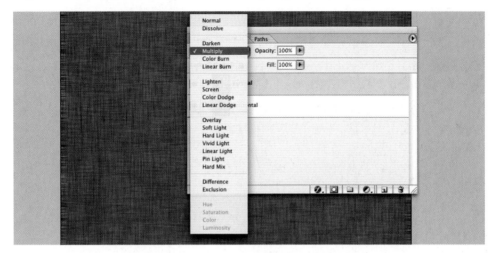

FIGURE 6.60

12 Save your changes and keep the file open for the next exercise.

The combination of the two blended layers results in a fairly convincing texture. Next, you add some shape to the cloth, since cloth is rarely as flat as it appears here.

Apply the Displacement Map to the Cloth

1 In the open file, flatten the image.

Flattening an image combines all visible layer components into a single layer, which is a normal default Background layer. It's as if you did all that work without using a single extra layer. Remember, every layer you have in an image adds to the size and memory requirements, so whenever you're done working on a complex image, flatten it to reduce the file size.

2 Choose Image>Adjustments>Hue/Saturation to color the cloth a light brownish-yellow.

This lightens the cloth, as well as changes the color to a more realistic tone. Feel free to make the color of the linen whatever shade you prefer.

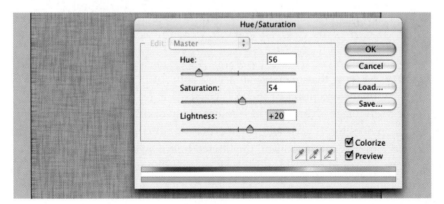

FIGURE 6.61

3 **Choose Filters>Distort>Displace.**

Displacing pixels moves them in specific directions, and can be used to apply a shape file, such as the one you created in the previous exercise.

4 **Set the Horizontal and Vertical Scale values to 20%, the Displacement Map option to Stretch to Fit, and Undefined Areas to Repeat Edge Pixels.**

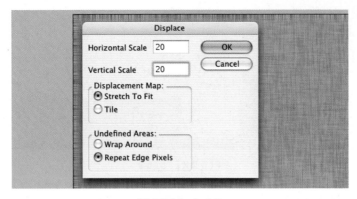

FIGURE 6.62

As soon as you click OK, the Open dialog box appears.

5 **Navigate to the cloth_map.psd image you created earlier in the lesson. Open the file.**

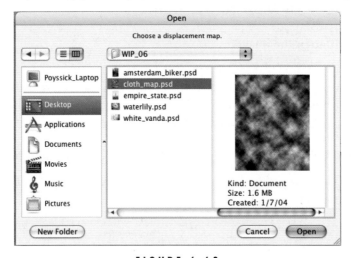

FIGURE 6.63

Dimensionality is a term that refers to an artist's ability to create the illusion of depth where none actually exists. With the exception of the 3-D glasses you get at the movie theater, the only way you can add depth to an image is through the intelligent use of distortion, shadows, and lighting. Using a displacement map does just that. It takes light areas and imparts that brightness to the image being filtered; dark areas simulate lower spots on the filtered image by adding shadow detail. In the case of this cloth assignment, you're making the cloth look rumpled by using the random shadows generated by rendering the clouds.

6 **Save the file and close it.**

To Extend Your Knowledge...

USING THE HISTORY PALETTE

When working with filters, activate the History palette (Window>History). It provides an unlimited "undo" function by recording everything you do while you work on your images. You can click anywhere in the list of commands and techniques you applied to your image to move back in time to that position. Then, you can begin again and overwrite the original history.

You can also use the History palette to take a "snapshot" of the current state of your work. This allows you to jump back to that point in time if necessary.

LESSON 6 Using the Liquify Filter

The *Liquify filter* is a fascinating and powerful digital-editing tool that allows you to push pixels around as if they were wet paint. Although the opportunity or need to use the tool doesn't occur every day, the Liquify filter allows you to apply effects to graphic images that couldn't possibly be done to physical photographs.

In the following exercise, you learn how the various liquify tools work. Remember, this is a stand-alone filter that has its own interface and tool set.

Work with the Liquify Filter

1   Open the file named **checkerboard.psd** from the Project_06 folder.

2   Save it in your WIP_06 folder.

3   Choose Liquify from the Filter menu.

   The stand-alone Liquify filter opens on your screen. Notice the tools lined up along the left edge of the interface. They are the liquify tools.

4 **Choose the top tool in the list of liquify tools.**

This is the Forward Warp tool.

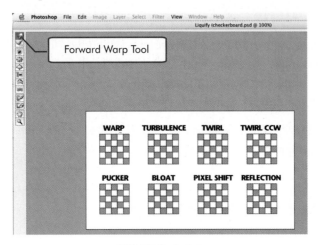

FIGURE 6.64

5 **On the upper-right side of the interface window, set the Brush Size to 60 pixels.**

You can use the "[" key to reduce the size of the brush and the "]" key to increase it. For now, use the interface method to set the brush size.

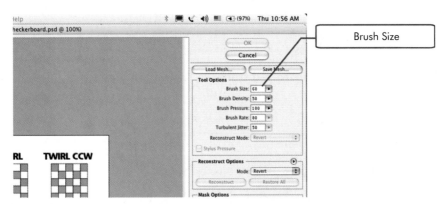

FIGURE 6.65

6 **Use the Forward Warp tool to push the corners of the first grid pattern outward.**

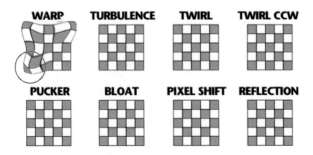

FIGURE 6.66

7 Select the Turbulence tool from the list of liquify tools.

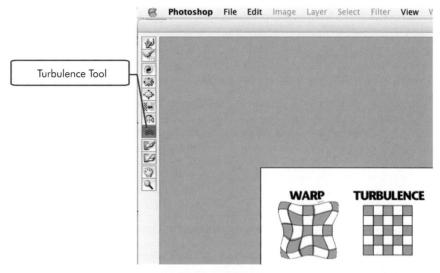

Turbulence Tool

FIGURE 6.67

8 Place the Turbulence tool cursor over the appropriate checkerboard and move it slightly.

No dragging is necessary with this tool. It "turbulates" the pixels while you hold down the mouse button.

FIGURE 6.68

9 Select the Twirl Clockwise tool from the list of tools. Click and hold the tool on the Twirl checkerboard box.

Similar to the Turbulence tool, no clicking is necessary to create the twirling effect.

10 Hold down the Option/Alt key while you hold the Twirl tool on the Twirl CCW checkerboard box.

Adding the Option/Alt key reverses the direction of the twirl; the same tool is used for both clockwise and counterclockwise effects.

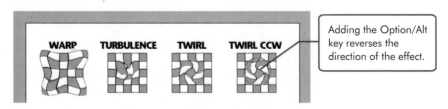

Adding the Option/Alt key reverses the direction of the effect.

FIGURE 6.69

11 One at a time, explore the rest of the liquify tools.

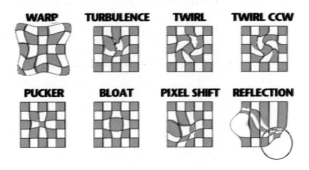

FIGURE 6.70

12 Use the Reconstruction tool to paint over the distorted graphics.

The Reconstruction tool restores the original image and removes the effects of the other liquify tools. You can use a combination of distortion and restoration to create some bizarre visuals.

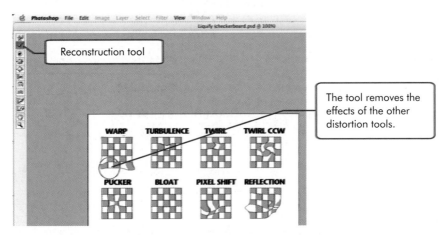

FIGURE 6.71

13 Select the Freeze Mask tool and paint a mask over the text above the checkerboards.

A *Freeze Mask* is a mask that protects portions of the image from the effects of the liquify tools. If you've already distorted the text, use the Reconstruction tool to restore the text to its original condition before you apply the Freeze Mask.

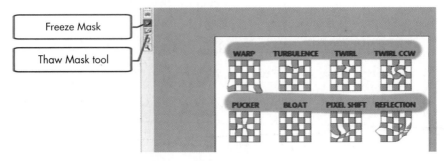

FIGURE 6.72

14 **Use the Turbulence tool to distort the text and checkerboards.**

Passing the brush over the text elements has absolutely no effect because you froze the region with the Freeze Mask tool. You can use the Thaw Mask tool to erase the freeze mask.

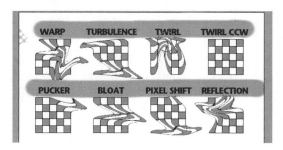

FIGURE 6.73

15 **In the View Options box on the right side of the interface, click the Show Mesh button.**

The mesh/grid shows you a visual representation of the original "metrics," or geometry, of the image. The mesh is useful when you're trying to keep distortion relative to the objects in the original image.

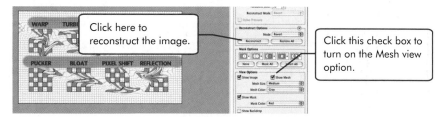

FIGURE 6.74

16 **Reconstruct the file. Continue your experimentation with the various tools and options.**

17 **When you're done, close the file without saving your changes.**

You can use this file to experiment with an effect before you commit it to one of your own images.

THE PHOTOSHOP HELP SYSTEM

No single book could ever provide you with the entire scope of what can be done with Photoshop. In fact, there are so many aspects of the program that even the most dedicated and experienced artists — people who work with the program every day — discover something new almost every time they complete a project or create an image. Fortunately, Photoshop is quite evolved. Built into the thousands (perhaps millions) of lines of programming code is an equally mature Help system. There are several different ways to use it.

The Search option allows you to type in a term or phrase; you will then see a series of steps that show you how to apply that specific technique. Since the Help function is part of the program, it's easy to perform the process while the appropriate Help screen is visible on top of the workspace.

The second way to use the Help system is through the built-in alphabetical index. Starting with "Absolute Colorimetric rendering intent" and ending with "Average Key Images" (an image that contains an average balance of gray tones), the index provides examples of virtually everything the program can do.

Finally, you can use the Contents feature, which is similar to a table of contents. This option provides a series of exercises that show off all the features built into the world's most popular imaging application.

Following is an example taken directly from the Help system, discussing the general use of the Dust & Scratches filter.

To use the Dust & Scratches filter:

1. Choose Filter > Noise > Dust & Scratches.
2. If necessary, adjust the preview zoom ratio until the area containing noise is visible.
3. Drag the Threshold slider left to 0 to turn off the value, so that all pixels in the selection or image can be examined.

   The Threshold determines how different the pixels' values should be before they are eliminated.

   Note: The Threshold slider gives greater control for values between 0 and 128—the most common range for images—than for values between 128 and 255.

4. Drag the Radius slider left or right, or enter a value in the text box from 1 to 16 pixels. The radius determines how far the filter searches for differences among pixels.

   Adjusting the radius makes the image blurry. Stop at the smallest value that eliminates the defects.

5. Increase the threshold gradually by entering a value or by dragging the slider to the highest value possible that eliminates defects.

SUMMARY

In Project 6, you explored the fantastic world of Photoshop filters. As you learned in the Visual Summary, there are so many filters available that if you dedicated five minutes to each filter, and applied them all to a single image, it would take more than six and one-half hours to complete the process — and that's without fully exploring any of the tool's features and functions.

You learned that filters are divided into several broad categories and a number of subcategories. There are stand-alone filters (such as the Extract, Liquify, and Pattern Maker filters), primary filter groups, and third-party filters available as commercial products.

As you become more experienced with the Photoshop filters, you will find that the majority cannot be used on every file type, color mode, or image format. Through trial-and-error, you will discover which tool is best for each type of task.

KEY TERMS

Artistic filters	Filter Gallery	Sharpen
Blur	Freeze mask	Silhouette
Cropping	Gaussian Blur	Smart Highlighting
Depth of field	History palette	Stand-alone filter
Dimensionality	Liquify filter	Texture
Displacement map	Pattern Maker filter	Watercolor filter
Extract filter	Plug-in technology	Watermark
Filter	Primary filters	

CHECKING CONCEPTS AND TERMS

MULTIPLE CHOICE

Circle the letter that matches the correct answer for each of the following questions.

1. Which of the following is not a stand-alone filter?

a. Extract filter

b. Gaussian Blur filter

c. Pattern Maker filter

d. Liquify filter

e. They're all stand-alone filters.

2. Blur filters are often used to _____.

a. remove detail

b. add color

c. repair damage

d. All of the above.

3. Pressing Command/Control-F _____.

   a. activates the last filter used

   b. activates the Filter menu

   c. removes the last filter effect

   d. None of the above.

4. You should never apply a filter to a Background layer.

   a. True

   b. False

5. You can't apply all filters to the Background layer.

   a. True

   b. False

6. The History palette _____.

   a. allows you to go back to a specific place in the image development

   b. keeps track of previous versions of an image

   c. can be used to take a "snapshot" of an image

   d. uses large amounts of memory when you work on large images

   e. All of the above.

   f. None of the above.

7. You should always _____.

   a. fix damaged areas of an image before applying artistic filters

   b. apply filters to an image and then fix damaged areas

   c. make a decision based on the specific image you're working on

   d. All of the above because it depends on what you're trying to do.

8. You can add new filters to Photoshop.

   a. True

   b. False

9. The more filters you have installed, the more memory you need.

   a. True

   b. False

10. Once you apply any of the liquify filters, you cannot reverse the effect.

   a. True

   b. False

DISCUSSION QUESTIONS

1. What is plug-in technology?

2. Why should you keep an image in RGB color mode while working with filters?

3. Why is it a good idea to copy the active layer before applying filters?

4. Explain the use of the History palette and why it is particularly useful when using filters to enhance the creative process.

SKILL DRILL

Skill Drills reinforce project skills. Each skill reinforced is the same, or nearly the same, as a skill presented in the lessons. Detailed instructions are provided in a step-by-step format. You should complete the exercises in the order provided.

1. Use the Filter Gallery

1. Start Photoshop and open any image.

2. Choose Filters>Filter Gallery. The Filter Gallery opens.

3. Make a list of filters that aren't in the gallery.

4. Write a brief explanation of why certain filters aren't available in the gallery.

2. Create a Custom Filter Gallery

1. Start Photoshop, if it is not already running.

2. Using the list you developed in the first Skill Drill, create a personal gallery of filters for yourself.

3. Use barn.psd or waterlily.psd as the basis for your personal gallery.

3. Use the Extract Filter

1. Start Photoshop, if it is not already running.

2. Open the desert_rose.psd image from the Project_06 folder.

3. Choose Filters>Extract.

4. Use the Extract tools to carefully create a selection border around the plant.

5. Be sure to include any "holes" in the graphic that allow the background objects to show through.

6. Complete the extraction.

7. Save the image as "extracted_dr.psd" and close the file.

4. Create Textures

1. Start Photoshop, if it is not already running.

2. Open the waterlily image you used earlier in the project.

3. Use the Extract filter to isolate the image of the flower from the background clutter.

4. Create three additional layers.

5. Position the layers below the flower layer.

6. Create different custom textures on each of the layers.

7. One at a time, activate the custom textures to serve as backgrounds for the flower.

8. Save and print three different copies of the flower with the custom textures by hiding and showing the appropriate texture layers for each version.

CHALLENGE

Challenge exercises expand on, or are somewhat related to, skills presented in the lessons. Each exercise provides a brief introduction, followed by instructions presented in a numbered-step format that are not as detailed as those in the Skill Drill exercises. You can work through one or more exercises in any order.

1. Combine the Liquify Filter, Layers, and Gradients

This challenge requires you to use the painting tools, gradients, layers, and the Liquify filter. It tests your understanding of combining techniques and methods. In the exercise, you create a bottle, apply a gradient, and use the Liquify filter to shape the glass. Then, you make a genie come out of the top of the bottle.

1. Open the file named big_man.psd from the Project_06 folder.

2. Rename the Background layer to "Layer 0". Add a new layer with a White Background.

3. Turn on your rulers.

4. Draw a tall rectangular selection about 2 inches tall and 1/2 inch wide.

5. Fill it with a banded vertical blend (gradient) from blue to yellow.

6. Choose the Liquify filter from the Filter menu. Choose the Bloat tool. Set the Brush Size to 600 pixels. This is the largest setting you can apply. This size works well for the following task.

7. Use the Bloat tool to enlarge the base of the bottle.

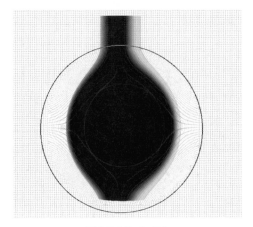

FIGURE 6.75

8. Use other liquify tools to shape the mouth and base of the bottle.

9. Open beach_walk.tif from your Project_06 folder.

10. Drag the bottle and genie layers from the big_man.psd file into the beach scene.

11. Use the Magic Eraser tool to remove the backgrounds from the bottle and genie layers.

12. Reduce the size of the bottle, lay it on its right side, and place it on the sand with a drop shadow layer effect.

FIGURE 6.76

13. Activate the Liquify filter. Turn on the other two layers. Apply the Backdrop option to show only the Background layer.

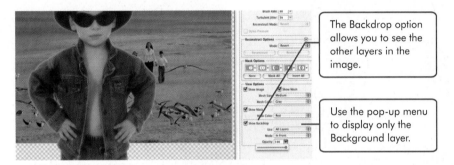

The Backdrop option allows you to see the other layers in the image.

Use the pop-up menu to display only the Background layer.

FIGURE 6.77

14. Use the liquify tools to squeeze the genie's legs so they appear to be coming out of the bottle.

15. Click OK to apply the filter and position the elements.

FIGURE 6.78

16. Save the file in your WIP_06 folder. Close the file when you're done.

2. Filters on Multiple Layers

This exercise shows what can be done when you combine filters and layers, which allows you to combine filters and unfiltered portions of an image.

1.   Open barn.psd from the Project_06 folder.

2.   Rename the Background layer to "Layer 0". Make two copies of the renamed layer.

3.   Hide the top and bottom layers. Create a silhouette on the middle layer that contains the barn and eliminates most of the bushes and trees.

4.   Make the bottom layer visible and active. Apply the filter of your choice.

5.   Draw a feathered selection around the barn on the top layer. Apply another filter to the top layer.

6.   Move the middle layer to the top. Apply a Screen blending mode to the layer.

7.   Use a soft-edged eraser to combine the barn silo with the two filter layers.

FIGURE 6.79

8   Save and close the file when you're satisfied with the image.

3. Repair an Image with Filters

As we mentioned earlier, the effective use of filters can go a long way toward restoring damaged images. In this exercise, you take an old black-and-white image of a high school basketball game and remove dust and scratches.

1.   Open old_game_photo.psd from the Project_06 folder.

2.   Save it in your WIP_06 folder.

3.   Choose the Filters>Noise>Dust & Scratches filter.

4.   Adjust the Preview to ensure proper results.

5. Try two or more Radius and Threshold settings until the image is cleaned up to your satisfaction.

6. Use the Clone Stamp tool to remove any remaining large scratches or flaws.

7. Choose Filter>Sharpen>Unsharp Mask. Experiment with several settings until the image is sharper and cleaner.

8. Save the file as "repaired_game.psd" and close it.

4. Combine Grayscale and Color in the Same Image

Making a single element in a black-and-white image full color is a technique that's widely used and very effective. To accomplish this difficult task, you use layers and filters.

1. Open desert_rose.psd from the Project_06 folder.

2. Save the file in your WIP_06 folder.

3. Duplicate the existing layer.

4. Desaturate the top layer and use a combination of filters to convert it into line art.

5. Select a soft-edged brush and erase the top layer wherever there are flowers on the plant.

6. Toggle the visibility of the top layer to make sure you remove all the flowers.

7. Flatten the image when you're done. Save the file as "colored_flowers.psd".

8. Close the file.

COLORIZING IMAGES

The technique of colorizing black-and-white images has been around for many years. During a traditional colorization project, an artist painstakingly used brushes and special dies to hand-paint colors into a black-and-white original. With Photoshop, the process has been dramatically simplified. Look in high-quality magazines; it won't be long before you find several examples of the colorization process.

In this Portfolio Builder, you explore some of the basic methods of colorizing black-and-white images, which result in unique appearances.

1. Pick one of the images from the Resource folders. If you want, you can use one that's already black and white, or you can convert a color image into grayscale.

2. Once converted, change the image back into RGB. This establishes a grayscale base for the colorization process. The conversion to grayscale discards what color information was originally in the piece.

3. Use the Brush tool to apply appropriate colors for the specific regions of the image you wish to colorize.

4. Experiment with transparency and blending modes for the brush you're using to determine which combination achieves the effect you are hoping to achieve.

5. Consider working on a layer above the base image while you experiment.

6. Flatten the image when you're done to reduce the complexity and size of the document.

Photoshop and the Web

O B J E C T I V E S

In this project, you learn how to

- Prepare images for the Web
- Create backgrounds for Web pages
- Create graphic assets
- Add text to a Web page

- Slice images
- Save Web pages as HTML
- Edit simple HTML code
- Create image maps

WHY WOULD I DO THIS?

Knowing how to use Photoshop to create, repair, and otherwise modify images is certainly very important; the intended goal of a particular image, however, is ultimately the most significant consideration in design development. Unless you are in a very specialized field, the images you create in Photoshop are going to be used for one of two things: print media or the Web.

Photoshop is a wonderful design environment for developing creative concepts — as well as for creating Web page components such as buttons, backgrounds, pictures, and other graphical assets. An *asset* is a single component used to create a Web page or site.

Understanding how to properly prepare images for use on the Web is essential. If you don't prepare images properly, they could take too long to download, their appearance could display significantly different than you intended, or they might not appear at all.

In this project, you learn how to design Web pages, create assets, and discover which file formats you should use to ensure the best results.

V I S U A L   S U M M A R Y

The incredible expansion of the Internet from a text-only network of mainframe computers to its current ubiquitous position in everyday life is largely due to the evolution of specialized programs called browsers. A *browser* interprets HTML code and displays both text and graphics on your screen. HTML is short for Hypertext Markup Language, and is at the core of most Web pages.

What's noteworthy to you as a designer using Photoshop is that a large majority of all Web pages are constructed not from text, but from images and supporting text. Any of the images you see on the Web can be either created from scratch using Photoshop, or, if they originated in another source such as a digital camera or scanner, can be prepared for use on the Web (or for print projects) using Photoshop or its companion application, ImageReady.

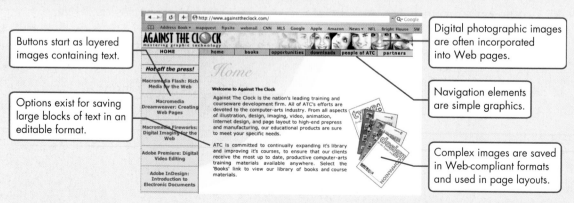

FIGURE 7.1

Whether your career is that of a dedicated Web site designer, or you work on a broad range of design assignments, the ability to create and manage elements for Web sites is a critical skill. The more you know about putting your images onto the Web, the easier and more effective your marketing efforts will become — and marketing your own talents is at least as important as successfully developing branding, messaging, and other marketing materials for your clients.

LESSON 1   Preparing Images for the Web

When you're creating images for use on the Web, there is one overriding consideration you must always bear in mind — the size of the final image. File size determines how long it will to take an image to download to the viewer's browser over a standard (slow) telephone modem. This file size, and the resultant impact that file size has on download time, is referred to as the file's *weight*. You must keep the weight of your final images at a manageable size. Even in today's world of high-speed cable modems, DSL lines, and other fast-connection technologies, an entire Web page shouldn't weigh much more than 50–100k. A *k* is a kilobyte, and refers to the thousands of bits that make up an image.

Fortunately, when you save your files, Photoshop and ImageReady display how long a specific file will take to download at predetermined modem speeds, and even allow you to compare download times between different file format and color mode options. In Project 8, you'll learn more about the relationship between file size and quality relative to printing your images. For now, we're going to focus on preparing images for use on the Web.

In the following brief exercise, you compare different file types and see how those file formats impact the weight of an image when you prepare it for the Web.

Compare Image Sizes

1   **Open the file named ali_snow.psd from your Project_07 folder.**

2   **Save the file into your WIP_07 folder.**

From this point forward, use the WIP_07 folder whenever you save an image in this project.

3   **Choose Image>Image Size.**

The Image Size dialog box opens. This high-resolution image was taken with a digital camera. At this point, it weighs over 10 megabytes, which is not very big if you were going to use it in a color brochure; but it's far too big to use on the Web.

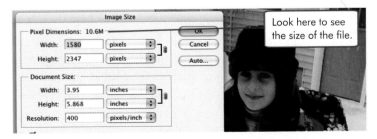

FIGURE 7.2

4   Click the Crop tool in the Toolbox. Draw a marquee selection around the girl's upper body and face. Press Return/Enter to crop the image.

FIGURE 7.3

5   Check the Image Size dialog box again.

Depending on exactly where you crop the photo, the file now weighs in at around 4 MB — still too big for the Web.

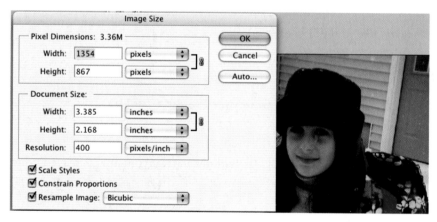

FIGURE 7.4

6   Save the cropped image in your WIP_07 folder and keep it open for the next exercise.

Optimize Images

Simply cropping an image clearly isn't sufficient to reduce the file size enough for downloading to a Web page. It takes *optimization* — the process of fine-tuning the size, file format, and color mode of an image — to arrive at the smallest possible size while maintaining the quality and appearance of the photo.

In the following exercise, you use Photoshop and ImageReady to optimize the size of this file so it downloads in a reasonable amount of time.

1 | **In the open file, choose File>Save for Web.**

The Save for Web dialog box appears. This dialog is actually from the ImageReady program.

2 | **Press Command/Control-minus (-) to reduce the size of the image until it fits in each of the four panes.**

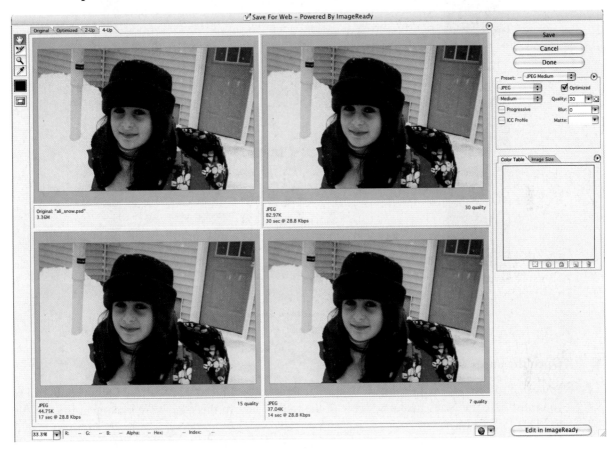

FIGURE 7.5

3 | **Look closely under the left- and right-bottom corners of each of the four images.**

File format setting with size and download times.

Quality setting.

FIGURE 7.6

4   Click Cancel to close the Save for Web dialog. Choose the Crop tool and draw a marquee selection around Alison's upper body and face. Press Return/Enter.

5   Save the image in your WIP_07 folder as a JPEG image.

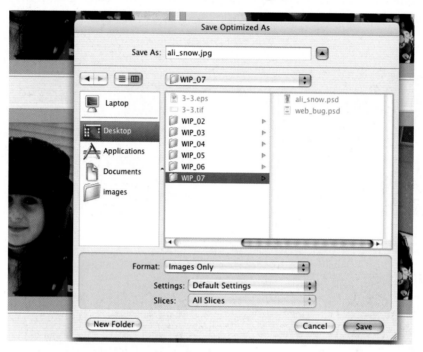

FIGURE 7.7

6   Open the image and check the file size.

You can also check the size of the file directly from the operating system on your computer. To do so, you must have the "size" attribute visible in the folder view. In this case, we're looking at the two files in Mac OS X Panther.

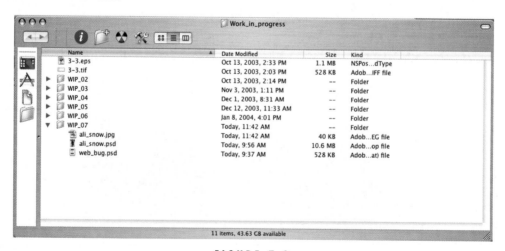

FIGURE 7.8

7   Keep the file open for the next exercise.

Save Optimization Settings

In the previous exercise, you used Photoshop and ImageReady to reduce the weight of the original file by a factor of 20. Starting out at more then 10 MB, cropping and optimization reduced the size of the final image you're going to use on the Web to less then 50k. Even on a slow modem, the file will download in an acceptable length of time.

In the next exercise, you learn how to save specific optimization settings so you can use them again later. When you save optimization settings, you can ensure that you use the same settings for each of the photographs you place on a site. Otherwise, you have to remember what settings you applied to the other images you saved for the site.

1　In the open document, choose File>Save for Web.

2　Select the image in the lower-right corner.

3　Choose Save Settings from the Preset pop-up menu.

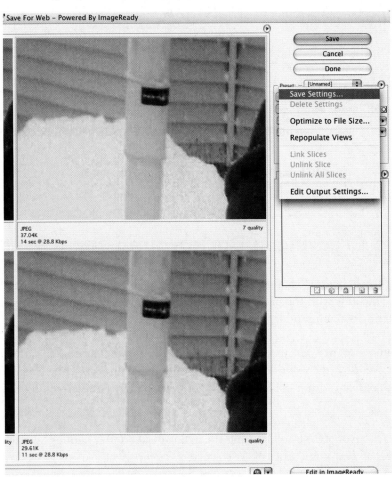

FIGURE 7.9

4 **Assign a name to the file in the Save As field. Save the file in the default folder.**

Photoshop and ImageReady use predetermined folders for the preset files, both for tools, as well as for optimization settings. Unless you have a good reason not to do so, save the file in the default folder location that appears in the Save Optimization Settings dialog box.

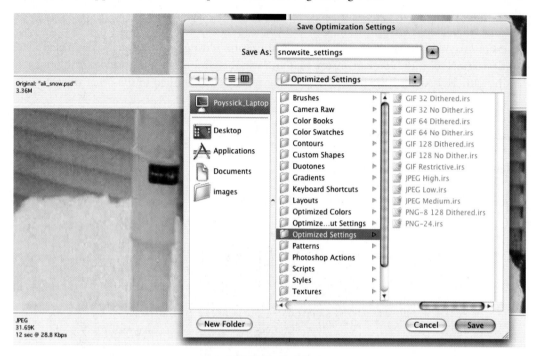

FIGURE 7.10

5 **Save the original file and close it when you're done.**

LESSON 2 Creating a Background for a Web Page

Over the years, designers have developed standard techniques for creating Web sites. One of these techniques is to dim an image and blend it with the background colors. Combined with smaller images in the foreground, this creates an interesting dynamic and lends visual depth to a page.

Backgrounds have other uses in Web site design, but they're images, the same as any other. If you want to use solid colors for your Web site, then you don't need to use Photoshop to create the background — you can fill the page with solid color from within HTML code. If you want patterns or pictures, however, Photoshop is the tool of choice.

In the following exercise, you define colors using the Color Picker and a naming system called ***hexadecimal notation***. Also known as ***hex***, it is a series of six characters, ranging from AA to FF and from 00 to 99. As an example, a yellow color might be named FFCC66. This notation system is necessary for proper color interpretation by today's browsers. You can enter these hex codes directly into the Color Picker dialog box.

Pick Colors for Web Objects

1   Create a new 72-ppi RGB document with a 600-pixel Width and 600-pixel Height.

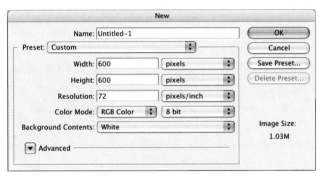

FIGURE 7.11

2   Click the foreground color chip at the bottom of the Toolbox.

The Color Picker opens.

3   In the Color Picker, enter "FFCC66" into the hexadecimal (#) field.

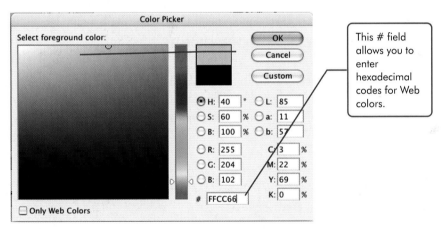

FIGURE 7.12

4   Press Option/Alt-Backspace to fill the background with the new color.

5   Save the image in your WIP_07 folder as "my_first_site.psd".

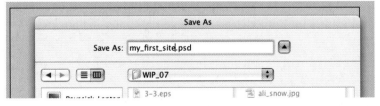

FIGURE 7.13

6   Keep the image open for the next exercise.

To Extend Your Knowledge...

LIMITED TEXT FORMATTING

Arguably the worst limitation from a design standpoint is that HTML doesn't handle text very well. Formatting is limited to basic attributes such as style (bold, italic) or color. Text size is measured not in points or pixels, but in relation to other text characters, and the browser determines the actual appearance of the text on screen. The use of Cascading Style Sheets (CSS) is an extension to HTML that was supposed to solve most of these issues, but CSS is not implemented consistently across browser platforms. This inconsistency means that some of the features are missing in some browsers, or they don't produce the same results; however, the most basic CSS features are reliable and allow the user to perform certain operations, including precisely setting the font size.

HTML is not capable of embedding fonts, a feature that Adobe Acrobat possesses. To display correctly, all fonts that you use in your design must be installed on the user's computer. This drawback limits you to using Arial/Helvetica and Times/Palatino — cross-platform fonts that are present on both Windows and Macintosh systems. If your design requires a headline to appear in a special font, you must rasterize the type and turn it into an image to ensure that it will be viewed as designed.

LESSON 3 Creating Graphic Assets

You can use Photoshop's Save for Web command to generate HTML documents directly from within the program. Whenever you save an HTML document, a number of different options are available to you, depending on exactly what the image contains (type, images, line art) and what you want to do with it once you're ready to publish it on the Web.

In the following exercise, you add another image to the color background you created in the previous lesson.

Create a Composite Image Background

1 Make sure that my_first_site.psd is open.

2 Open the players.jpg file from the Project_07 folder.

3 Use the Move tool to drag the players.jpg image onto my_first_site.psd.

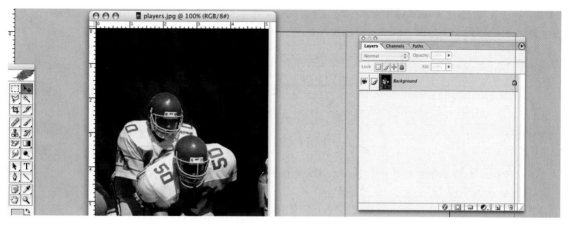

FIGURE 7.14

4 Close the players image and save your work.

5 Rename Layer 1 to "players".

FIGURE 7.15

6 Set the Opacity of the players layer to 30%.

7 Add a layer mask to the players layer.

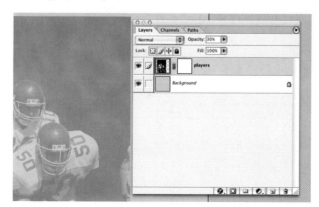

FIGURE 7.16

8 Choose the Brush tool in the Toolbox and reset the default colors. Set the Brush Size to 100. Make sure the Opacity of the brush is set to 100%, and that it has a soft edge.

FIGURE 7.17

9 Select the layer mask and paint away the edges of the players.

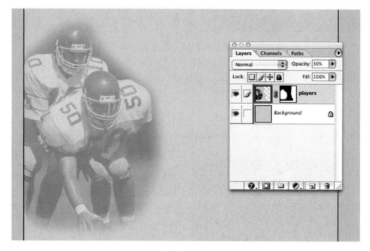

FIGURE 7.18

10 Choose Filters>Blur>Gaussian Blur and set the Radius value to approximately 1.5 pixels.

This softens the image a bit further and tones it down. Remember, no design should ever be so busy that one element distracts from another. Be sure to balance the relative dominance of each component in an image to create a visually pleasing overall effect.

FIGURE 7.19

11   **Save the file and keep it open for the next exercise.**

Note that you're still working on the original Photoshop file. There's a good reason for this: you should always try to keep your working files in native format. This way, all your layers and other attributes remain intact. When you apply the Save for Web command, the program generates the necessary JPEG or GIF image data along with, as you'll see in a moment, the HTML required to display the page properly when viewed in a browser.

Add Solid-Color Page Regions

In this exercise, you continue to develop the page by adding solid-color areas that help define different *regions* of the page — areas that are designed to hold specific content, such as navigation elements, advertisements, or other information.

1   **In the open file, change the foreground color to hexadecimal #996633.**

2   **Choose the Rectangle tool in the Toolbox.**

FIGURE 7.20

3   **Draw a rectangle across the top of the image that spans the left and right margins and stretches from the top of the image to just above the players' heads.**

You'll probably find that the best way to create flat-color objects is to use shape layers. This way, if you need to change the color of a page asset, you can simply click the color swatch that appears on the shape layer in the Layers palette. *Flat colors* are areas of color that do not contain any tonal gradations; they're simply solid-colored regions.

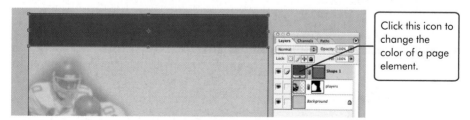

FIGURE 7.21

4   **Save the file and keep it open for the next exercise.**

LESSON 4 Adding Text

Up to this point in the book, you've only worked with graphic elements. In the real world, however, sites aren't comprised solely of images; they all provide information in the form of text. Many graphics also contain text as one of their design components. Examples of graphics that incorporate text include corporate logos, navigation buttons, banners, and other assets.

Although it's been said that a picture is worth a thousand words, words are critically important. Not only is the actual message important, but tasteful use of typefaces help set the mood and feel of your designs. Another consideration to keep in mind is the fact that most type objects you see on the sites you visit — most notably page titles, button text, headlines, and other elements — are actually graphics that start out as text and are rendered using Photoshop. This technique ensures that viewers see the site exactly as it was designed, even if they don't have a particular typeface installed on their systems.

In the following exercise, you add a logo to your football image using standard text objects and layer effects.

Create a Logo for the Site

1   **Continue in the open file. If necessary, reset the foreground color swatch to FFCC66.**

2   **Set the Font to 29- or 30-pt Comic Sans MS. Type the words "Sports zine". (Make sure there's a space between the two words.)**

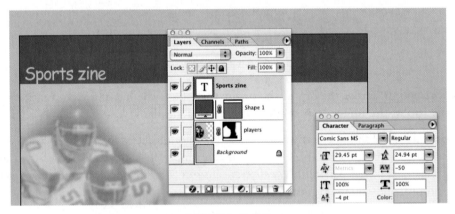

FIGURE 7.22

3   **Create another type layer containing just the letter "E".**

4   Select the letter "E" and change the Font to 60-pt ATC Oak colored #6EC3EE, which is a light blue.

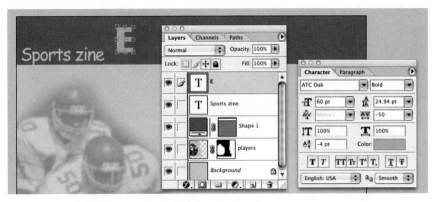

FIGURE 7.23

5   Place the letter "E" in the space between the two words.

6   Change the Opacity of the "E" to 50%.

FIGURE 7.24

7   Save the image and keep it open for the next exercise.

Create Text Buttons

So far, you've learned how to create a simple graphic element using nothing but text elements. Next, you're going to learn how to create the basic navigation object — the button. Buttons are most effective when they contain text that tells the viewer what they do. The ability to design and implement buttons and other navigational elements is a must-have skill for the professional graphic artist.

Unless all of your clients' sites have only one page (which is rare), you must provide a way to move (jump) from page to page. Buttons are special elements because they provide access to *links* — specific Web page addresses found either within the same site or on an external site — that allow viewers to jump from one section or page to another. In this exercise, you create a button comprised of a shape and text.

1 | **In the open file, draw a rounded-corner rectangle and fill it with the same blue (#6EC3EE) that you used for the "E" in the SportsEzine logo.**

The size of the rectangle doesn't have to be exact at this point; once you put some type into it, you can easily resize it to fit.

FIGURE 7.25

2 | **Create a type element using a Font of 12-pt ATC Maple Ultra colored Black. Enter "BUTTON1" for the text.**

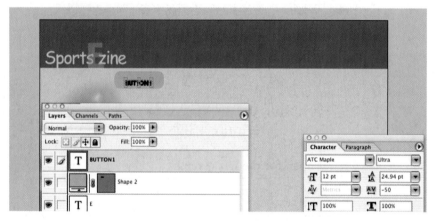

FIGURE 7.26

3 | **Save the file and keep it open for the next exercise.**

Before you go any further, you should organize the elements that make up this Web page. When you learned about layers and the Layers palette, we mentioned that organization of your layers becomes a critical issue when you develop and manage complex images. Using layer sets and properly managing layers is particularly important when you're developing and designing a Web site.

It's now time to apply what you learned about layer management. Soon, you will have so many related layers in this design that making changes will prove very cumbersome; it will also become difficult to navigate within the image. If you can't move around within your own document, imagine how hard it would be for someone else to make changes to this image. Remember, when you're working with Web sites, one thing is certain: changes are guaranteed. Make the editing process easy on yourself (and others) by organizing your assets.

Organize and Duplicate Related Assets

1   In the open file, link the shape and text layers. Rename the shape layer "button_shape".

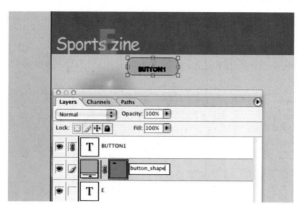

FIGURE 7.27

2   Add a drop shadow to the button shape.

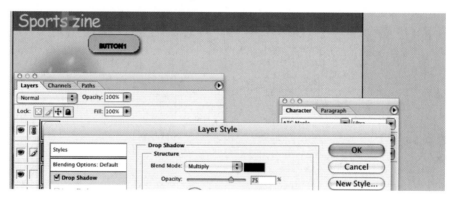

FIGURE 7.28

3   Create a new layer set and name it "buttons".

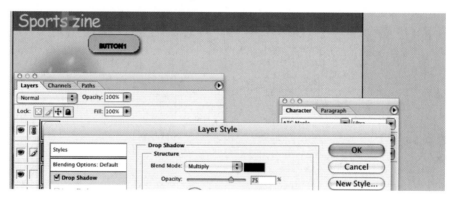

FIGURE 7.29

4 Drag the linked Button1 layer into the buttons folder.

5 Create another layer set inside the buttons set. Name it "button1". Move the two elements into this nested folder.

Nesting is the process of putting folders inside one another. You can also nest a table within the cell of a larger table. Think of nesting as the old-fashioned Russian dolls that fit inside one another, with smaller and smaller versions within each doll you open.

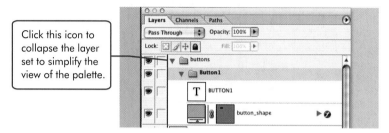

FIGURE 7.30

6 Collapse the Button1 set.

7 Drag the set to the New Layer icon at the bottom of the Layers palette.

A duplicate layer set is created.

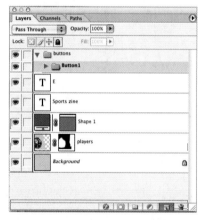

FIGURE 7.31

8 Create three more copies of the layer set.

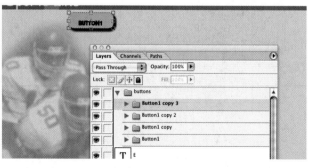

FIGURE 7.32

9 Rename the layer sets "Button1" through "Button4".

10 One at a time, select the sets and arrange them across the top of the image as shown below.

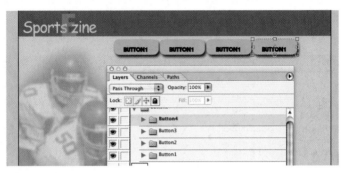

FIGURE 7.33

11 Collapse the view of the buttons sets. Move them all up and to the right, so all the buttons sit on the solid brown bar with their bottoms hanging onto the tan background, as shown below.

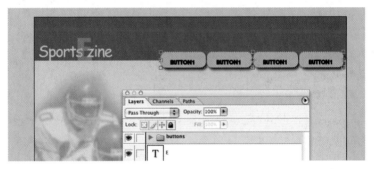

FIGURE 7.34

12 Move the entire buttons set underneath the brown shape.

This change in stacking order makes it look as though the buttons are cut in half, but they're actually still there. Their tops are simply hidden by the brown bar, which is now above them in the Layers palette.

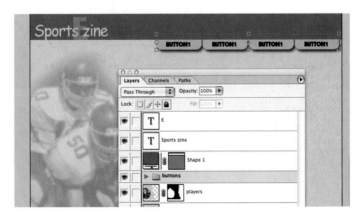

FIGURE 7.35

13   **Rename the buttons to "Home", "Events", "About Us", and "Contact", in that order.**

To make it easier to rename the buttons, open the layer sets and select each button in turn. While it isn't necessary for the integrity of the site, it's a good idea to rename the sets that contain each button, as well. We highly recommend that you keep all of your assets named and properly organized. In the long run, this practice saves more time than it takes to keep on top of all the assets in your sites.

FIGURE 7.36

14   **Save the file and keep it open for the next exercise.**

Import Large Text Blocks

Now you can see how important it is to create layer sets for Web designs. Not only do they make it easier to manage the entire collection of graphic assets (and there could be hundreds in a complex site), it makes it simpler to both create and position the assets once you've decided what you need to do.

In this exercise, you grab three blocks of copy from external files and import them into your Web page.

1   **Continue in the open file. Display your desktop and navigate to the Project_07 folder.**

2   **Sort the file list by "Kind" or "Type".**

The following image was captured on a Macintosh running OS X. If you're using Windows, your display looks different, but the concepts are the same, as are the individual processes.

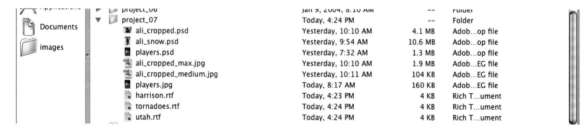

FIGURE 7.37

3   **Double-click the file named harrison.rtf.**

This is one of three files that were saved in Rich Text Format (RTF). **_RTF_** is a standard cross-platform file format used to save word-processing documents. Depending on your specific system configuration, the files will open in one of several different text-processing programs. The following screen image is from a Macintosh and shows the copy in the TextEdit application; the program you're using may look different on your screen, but will not adversely affect the process.

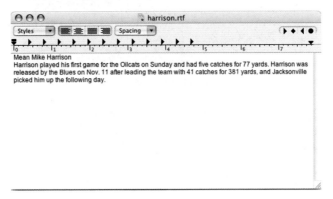

FIGURE 7.38

4   **Select all the copy in the file and press Command/Control-C to copy it to the clipboard.**

You can choose Edit>Select All or use the Command/Control-A shortcut. All of the major text editors use the same command.

5   **Return to Photoshop.**

6   **Activate the rulers if necessary.**

You can press Command/Control-R or select View>Show Rulers.

7   **Drag two vertical guides onto the page at the 1/2-inch and 3-inch marks.**

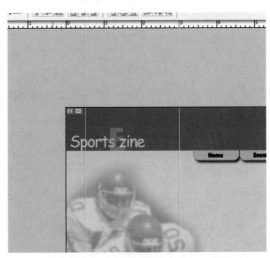

FIGURE 7.39

8   **Place a horizontal guide at the 2-inch mark on the left ruler.**

Guides on the page ensure consistent placement of repeating elements.

FIGURE 7.40

9   **Set the Font to 12-pt ATC Laurel with 14-pt Leading. Left Justify the paragraph.**

10   **Choose the Type tool. Draw a rectangle within the guides you created in Steps 7 and 8.**

11   **Paste the text into the block.**

You can choose Edit>Paste or press Command/Control-V to paste the text.

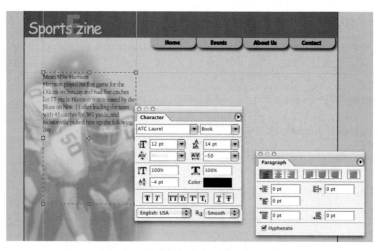

FIGURE 7.41

12   **Select only the "Mean Mike Harrison" headline. Set the Font to 14-pt ATC Maple Medium with 16-pt Leading.**

FIGURE 7.42

13   **Place the cursor at the end of the first paragraph and press the Return/Enter key.**

A blank line is inserted.

14   **Go back to the Project_07 folder. Copy all the text from utah.rtf.**

15   **Paste the text into the text block on your Web page.**

16   **Repeat Steps 14 and 15 for the tornadoes.rtf file.**

17   **Format the "Mountain" and "Back to Business" headlines to match the "Mean Mike Harrison" headline.**

If necessary, drag the bottom handle of the text block to make room for the additional text and headlines. When you're done, the page should resemble Figure 7.43.

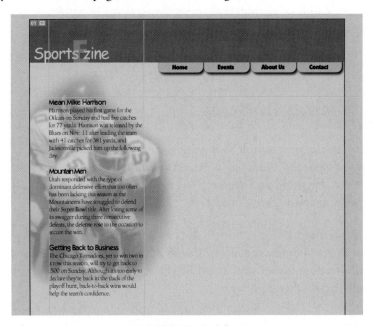

FIGURE 7.43

18   **Save the file and keep it open for the next exercise.**

At this point, you can see the page beginning to take shape. As your knowledge of Photoshop and general Web design grows, you'll learn more effective ways of building actual pages; but from a design standpoint, you're already well on your way to using the world's most powerful image-editing application as a Web page design tool.

To Extend Your Knowledge...

PHOTOSHOP AND SITE DEVELOPMENT

It's important to recognize that Photoshop is an excellent tool for some tasks and not the best choice for others. The program is critically important for developing assets such as buttons, backgrounds, and other assets — 99% of all professional Web site designers use it on a daily basis; however, Photoshop is *not* a site development and management program. To manage all the pages, links, animations, sounds, and other content commonly found on today's Web sites, you need an industrial-strength application that offers specialized functionality targeted at site management.

In this project, you are *designing* a site, not *building* a site. Most designers build a page or two in Photoshop — much as you're doing now — and either hand off the work to dedicated page-layout specialists or use Adobe's GoLive or Macromedia's Dreamweaver MX to actually build pages and manage sites. All of the Photoshop images you're creating in this project would be imported into one of those applications as part of the page-layout and site-construction process.

LESSON 5   Slicing Images

Although by no means complete, your sample Web page already offers a passable version of the design. It contains navigation elements, a logo, and some text blocks. You could spend some time placing more text on the page, but it's best that you jump ahead and explore your options for turning a Photoshop design into a functional Web page — and that includes slicing images.

Slicing an image refers to a technique that essentially cuts a Photoshop document into discrete pieces. The reason you slice images is to better optimize them. The slicing process allows you to keep some parts of the image at higher resolution, and therefore higher quality, while you can maximize compression in other areas where details and color range aren't critically important.

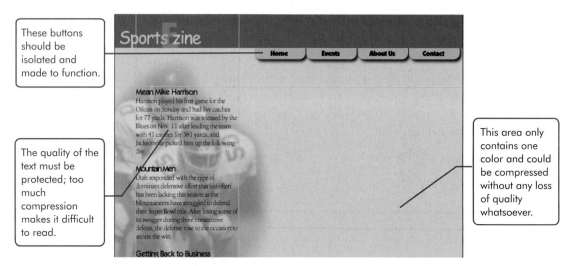

FIGURE 7.44

Slice Your Page

1 Open my_first_site.psd from the WIP_07 folder (if it's not already open).

? If you have problems...

When you use the Slice tool to slice an image, Photoshop automatically assigns a number to each slice. In the following exercises, you should be able to see the numbers. At first, they can be a little distracting, but they help you to conceptualize what's going on when you slice your documents into little pieces. If you can't see the numbers when you first use the Slice tool, choose View>Extras to turn on their display.

2 Choose the Slice tool in the Toolbox. Draw a rectangle over the sportsEzine logo.

FIGURE 7.45

3 In the Layers palette, select the layer containing the text for the stories on the left.

4 Choose Layer>Make Layer Based Slice.

This command turns the text block into its own slice.

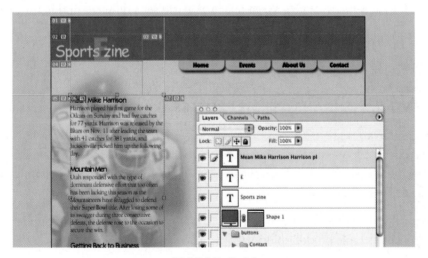

FIGURE 7.46

5 **Use the Zoom tool to take a closer look at the slice.**

You can see the numbers on the slices (if you can't, choose View>Extras to turn on the display). Slice 01 is the top rectangle; 02 is the region containing the logo; 03 is the region to the right of the logo. Creating the layer-based slice automatically generated Slice 06; doing so also sliced the region directly above the text blocks, creating Slices 04 and 05.

Equally important is the fact that the process automatically generated Slice 07, which contains nothing but a big flat area of a single color. This area can be significantly compressed in the final output.

FIGURE 7.47

6 **Save the file and keep it open for the next exercise.**

Select and Optimize Slices

1 **In the open file, choose File>Save for Web. Click the 2-Up Tab.**

Choosing this view option shows the original native Photoshop image on the left side of the Preview pane. On the right is the same image showing how the output will look based on current compression and image format settings. With a sliced image, you can set a different option for each of the slices.

To Extend Your Knowledge...

ZOOM PERCENTAGES AND THE DESIGN PROCESS

When you design a Web page, it's important that you work at 100% magnification as much as possible. This magnification allows you to see the page as your viewer will see it (the vast majority of viewers can only see the page at 100%). Even when you work at higher magnification to fine-tune small details, always keep the site visitor in mind.

Some programs (Macromedia Flash) and formats (SVG) provide for zooming on the Web, but that's outside the scope of this topic on designing Web assets with Photoshop.

2 | Choose the Slice Select tool in the Toolbox. Click the logo slice in the right-most image.

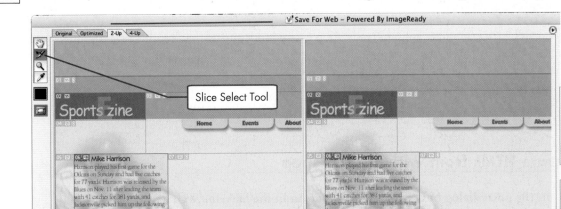

FIGURE 7.48

3 | Change the output settings for the logo slice to JPEG Maximum.

FIGURE 7.49

4 | One at a time, select additional slices and adjust the optimization settings for each one.

For the slices containing large areas of flat color, increase the compression by lowering the quality setting. For the text areas, keep the quality high to ensure viewers can read it.

5 | Keep the dialog box open for the next exercise.

LESSON 6 Saving an Image as HTML

Once your design is complete, you are ready to generate a document that can be properly interpreted by a browser — which, as you know, is the standard application used for surfing the Web. For a document to be interpreted by a browser, it must be generated as HTML.

In the following exercise, you generate the images and HTML code required to display your page in a Web browser.

Generate HTML from within Photoshop

1 In the open dialog box, click the Save button in the Save for Web dialog box.

2 Choose HTML and Images from the Format menu at the bottom of the dialog box.

FIGURE 7.50

3 Create a new folder inside your WIP_07 folder. Name it "site_folder".

4 Save the files into the new site_folder.

The reason we use the word "files" instead of "file" is because when you select the HTML and Images option, Photoshop generates a number of files; HTML for the actual page, as well as image files. In addition, if you've sliced an image, each individual slice is saved as a unique file.

5 Leave the file open for the next exercise.

Preview a Page in Your Browser

In this exercise, you look at the actual HTML code that was generated in the previous exercise.

1 From your desktop, look into the site_folder that you created. Make sure that you can see the file names, as well as their comparative sizes.

We set the view options so you could see that saving the image resulted in the creation of a folder named "images" and an HTML document named "my_first_site.html". The images folder contains the individual images generated by each slice.

If you double-click a slice with the Slice Select tool, you can rename the slice. Renaming slices gives you more control over the file names that are generated when the documents are saved as HTML.

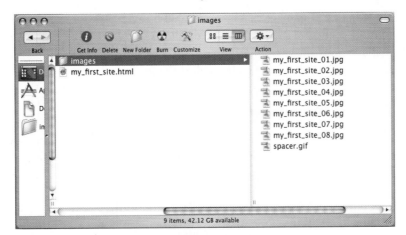

FIGURE 7.51

2 **Double-click my_first_site.html in the file list.**

The file opens in your browser. This example shows the page in Safari, the new browser Apple developed for OS X. The page should display correctly, however, regardless of the default browser on your system.

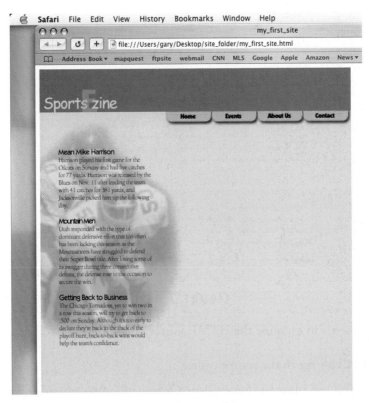

FIGURE 7.52

3 Keep the file open for the next exercise.

LESSON 7 Editing HTML Code

As you know, HTML is a markup language that is interpreted by Web browsers. HTML files are displayed in a browser according to the settings and codes found within the HTML code. The code contains all the instructions required to load the various images generated by a sliced document. Remember, each slice has its own optimization settings, so Photoshop generates an individual file for each slice.

Examine and Modify the Source Code

This book certainly isn't designed to help you learn HTML; but you can still do a lot to a Web page simply by changing a few lines of text. For the sake of instruction, however, the following exercise shows you how to change the title displayed at the top of the page when it's opened in a browser.

1   Open your text editor and use it to open my_first_site.html.

The text editor installed on your machine depends on the system's configuration. In our examples, we used BBEdit, installed on the Macintosh running Panther OS X.

FIGURE 7.53

2   Take a few moments to examine the HTML source code.

3   Locate the **`<title>`** tag in the source code.

An HTML *tag* is a special set of characters that is recognized by a browser when it's interpreting an HTML page. The **`<title>`** tag is only one example of an HTML tag. You can see many more tags in the document.

4   Change the words "my_first_site.html" to "sportsEzine: America's Leading Voice on Pro Sports".

FIGURE 7.54

5   Save the file and preview it in your browser.

Look at the top of the window. The change you made to the HTML file is reflected in the interpreted HTML document.

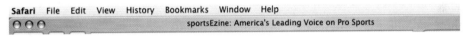

FIGURE 7.55

6   Close the browser and keep the image open for the next exercise.

LESSON 8   Creating Image Maps

You can use the separate image slices you generate when you split an image into separate pieces to create an image map. An ***image map*** is a graphic that contains ***hot spots***, which are HTML links to other pages, animations, sounds, graphics, or external sites. As a visitor moves his mouse over a hot spot, the cursor turns into a little pointing finger, indicating that he is hovering over a link.

Hot spots are used to provide navigational control. The buttons you created earlier are good candidates for becoming an image map; so, too, is the sportsEzine logo.

Create Slices for Buttons

1   In the open document, use the Slice tool to create a slice on top of the Home button.

FIGURE 7.56

2   Create slices for the other three buttons.

3   Choose the Slice Select tool in the Toolbox.

FIGURE 7.57

4   Use the Slice Select tool to double-click the Home button.

The Slice Options dialog box opens.

5   Rename the slice "home_button".

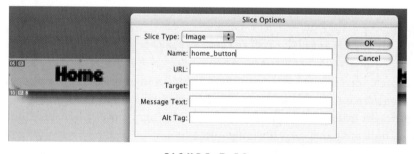

FIGURE 7.58

This has a marvelous effect. When you generate the HTML and images from the Save for Web dialog box, the slice becomes an independent file named home_button.jpeg.

As an experiment, you might want to save the buttons as GIF files. Simply select a slice and change the format options in the Save for Web dialog box. Make sure you make all the buttons the same — either all GIFs or all JPEGs.

6   Leave the dialog box open for the next exercise.

Link Buttons to Other Pages or Sites

Now you are ready to link your buttons to actual pages. Since we haven't built an entire site (yet), this exercise shows you how to link a button to any working Web site address.

1 | **In the open dialog box, enter what you know to be a functional URL into the URL field.**

URL is short for ***Uniform Resource Locator***, better known as a Web address. Fortunately, many designers now show a Web address as name.com, instead of writing http://www.name.com.

2 | **Enter descriptive text about the button in the Alt Tag field.**

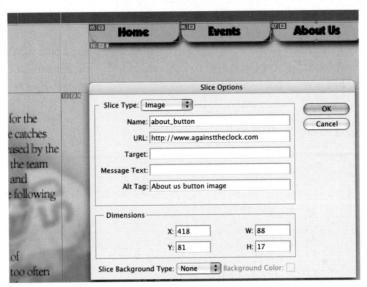

FIGURE 7.59

Alt text is used to describe the image if the graphic fails to download; more importantly, Alt text allows visually impaired visitors to "hear" the site instead of see it. Including Alt text for your Web elements comes under the broad heading of ***accessibility***. Paying attention to accessibility is critically important to people who are visually impaired, or those who are working on systems capable of displaying only text.

3 | **Preview the page in your browser and check the button.**

If you're online, everything should work perfectly. If not, you can still see that the link worked because clicking it generates an error that says, "Server Could Not Be Found."

4 | **Save the file and close it when you're done.**

SUMMARY

Project 7 provided you with a glimpse of how you can use Photoshop to design Web pages and sites. Although you only scratched the surface of what can be accomplished, you should now understand how to build a background, how to add graphics and text elements to a page, and how to create simple navigation elements.

You also learned the importance of download times, and how different file formats impact the size — also known as the weight — of each page you create. You learned how to optimize images using the Save for Web feature, and how to apply different compression levels to juggle the quality of an image with its size. You learned that certain images are better suited for specific file types — JPEG for photographs, and GIF for flat objects, such as buttons.

You also learned how to slice a large Photoshop image into manageable pieces, each of which can be individually optimized for quicker download. You explored how to generate HTML and discrete images from a single document. Finally, you learned how to create functional links from individual image slices to create an image map.

KEY TERMS

Accessibility	GIF	Link
Alt text	Hexadecimal/Hex	Nesting
Asset	Hot spot	Optimize
Browser	HTML	Page regions
CSS	Image map	Quality level
File size	Image slice	RTF/Rich Text Format
File weight	JPEG	Tag
Flat color	K/Kilobyte	URL

CHECKING CONCEPTS AND TERMS

MULTIPLE CHOICE

Circle the letter that matches the correct answer for each of the following questions.

1. The term URL stands for _____.
   - **a.** Unique Resource Locator
   - **b.** Unlinked Resource Locator
   - **c.** Unique Resource Link
   - **d.** None of the above.

2. A link connects _____.
   - **a.** one page to another
   - **b.** one site to another
   - **c.** a button to another page
   - **d.** All of the above.

3. You should always check your Web pages at _____ magnification.
   - **a.** 100%
   - **b.** 50%
   - **c.** 200%
   - **d.** All of the above.

4. To select a slice, you need to use the _____.
   - **a.** Move tool
   - **b.** Slice tool
   - **c.** Crop tool
   - **d.** None of the above.

5. You can design all aspects of a Web site using only Photoshop.
   - **a.** True
   - **b.** False

6. Alt text is important because _____.
   - **a.** it allows sight-impaired people hear what images are being loaded
   - **b.** it keeps you from having to download images
   - **c.** sites don't work if you don't download images
   - **d.** All of the above.

7. You should always _____.
   - **a.** preview your pages in more than one browser
   - **b.** check the pages on more than one computer platform
   - **c.** allow your service provider to check links on his servers
   - **d.** None of the above.
   - **e.** All of the above.

8. Shape layers allow you to _____.
   - **a.** change the name of the layer
   - **b.** easily change the color of solid objects
   - **c.** animate a Web page
   - **d.** None of the above.

9. The _____ file format is the best choice when saving photographic images.
   - **a.** GIF
   - **b.** JPEG
   - **c.** PRF
   - **d.** PDF

10. Flat objects benefit from the smaller file sizes offered by the _____ file format.
    - **a.** GIF
    - **b.** JPEG
    - **c.** PRF
    - **d.** PDF

DISCUSSION QUESTIONS

1.   Why is Alt text important to your designs?

2.   Why is a page's weight a significant consideration?

3.   Why is it a good/bad idea to completely manage a Web site using only Photoshop?

4.   What are links, and how do they help make a Web site more useable?

SKILL DRILL

Skill Drills reinforce project skills. Each skill reinforced is the same, or nearly the same, as a skill presented in the lessons. Detailed instructions are provided in a step-by-step format. You should work through the exercises in the order provided.

1. Create a Simple Page

In this Skill Drill, you begin the process of building a small site by creating the first page, which you'll use as a template for the rest of the site.

1.   Create a new 800 by 800-pixel RGB document.

2.   Create a background for the site using filters and other imaging techniques.

3.   Create a graphic for the page. Use your name or some derivation of your name.

4.   Save the page as "home.html" into a new folder named "mysite".

5.   Keep the file open for the next exercise.

2. Optimize Images

1.   In the open file, select an image for the home page.

2.   Complete any other solid or background graphics.

3.   Optimize all the images using the Save for Web command.

4.   Click Done and save the file in its original native format.

5.   Save the file and keep it open.

3. Add Text

1.   In the open file, write two paragraphs of copy about yourself.

2.   Place the text on the home page.

3.   Create four buttons for navigating around the site.

4.   Change the text on the buttons to read "Home", "Childhood", "Teen Years", and "Here and Now".

5.   Save the document and keep it open.

4. Generate Additional Pages

1. In the open file, use the Save for Web option to generate three additional copies of the home page.

2. Name the first copy "childhood.html".

3. Name the second copy "teenyears.html".

4. Name the fourth copy "currentlife.html".

5. Save the files and keep them open.

5. Modify the HTML Code

1. Open the HTML documents in a text editor.

2. Change the title of the home page to "All about [Your name here]".
   For example, All about Jane Doe.

3. Change the title of the childhood page to "[Your name here] in my Childhood Years".

4. Change the title of the teenyears page to "[Your name here] in my Teen Years".

5. Change the title of the currentlife page to "Living with [Your name here] today".

6. Save and close the text files.

7. Check the files in your browser to make sure the title changes took effect.

8. Leave the HTML documents open.

6. Create Image Maps

1. In the open image file, use the Slice tool to create separate slices for each of the four buttons.

2. One at a time, use the Slice Select tool to double-click each button slice. Name each button appropriately.

3. Add an appropriate file name into the URL field for each button.

4. Add Alt text for each button.

5. Leave the HTML files open.

7. Preview and Check the Site

1. Double-click the open home.html file to launch your browser.

2. Check all the links.

3. Go back to Photoshop to correct any linking problems.

4. Regenerate the HTML.

5. Save and close the file.

CHALLENGE

Challenge exercises expand on, or are somewhat related to, skills presented in the lessons. Each exercise provides a brief introduction, followed by instructions presented in a numbered-step format that are not as detailed as those in the Skill Drill exercises. You can work through one or more exercises in any order.

1. Create a Gallery Site

In this Challenge, you create a small gallery site that offers the viewer thumbnail versions of six different images that you generated in previous lessons. Remember that a thumbnail is a small image that shows the content of a larger image. Clicking one of the small thumbnails links the visitor to the larger version of the file; clicking the larger version should take them back to the thumbnail page.

1. Create a new folder to hold the site.

2. Create a new home page, including graphics and navigation elements.

3. Create a second (gallery) page to hold images. Make sure to leave enough space for at least six small images.

4. Create functional links between the home page and the gallery page.

5. Save all of your files and check the links in your browser.

6. Collect six images from the work you completed to this point in the book.

7. Resize the six images and save copies of each, keeping the originals intact.

8. One at a time, open each original, save it as a copy, and resize it to approximately 600 pixels wide. Depending on their aspect ratios, their relative height measurements will vary.

9. Save each copy as HTML and Images, with one large slice that links back to the gallery page.

10. Use the small images as thumbnails. Create slices that link to the larger versions you saved in Step 9.

11. Save all of your files and check the links to make sure they work properly.

12. Close the file.

2. Create Polygonal Image Maps

While rectangular shapes fulfill many navigation requirements, you will often be called upon to create irregular-shaped maps. An example is a (literal) map with county demarcations, where clicking on a specific county brings up information about that specific locale. In this exercise, you learn how to create an irregular-shaped map component using the Polygonal Image Map tool.

1. Open the file named cd_photo.tif from the Project_07 folder.

2. Choose File>Edit in ImageReady.

3. Choose the Polygonal Image Map tool in the Toolbox.

4. Draw a polygon around the CD.

5. Draw a polygon around the keyboard.

6. Draw a polygon around the monitor.

7. Find a Web site that offers monitors, keyboards, and CD-ROMs for sale.

8. Create links from your image map to the external retail sites.

9. Save and close the file.

3. Build a Catalog Page

Adding structure to your designs is critically important, as is consistency of layout. A perfect example is a catalog page where product images, navigational components, and related copy remain in the same position, regardless of how many pages the catalog contains. In the following exercise, you build a page that includes such structure.

1. Find a Web site that offers plants for sale. You might try Tropiflora.com, a major wholesaler of bromeliads and orchids based in Sarasota, Florida.

2. Pick six images and save them to your hard drive.

   You cannot simply download someone else's images and use them in your own work; you can, however, experiment with anyone's images, text, or other assets as long as you don't use them for a different project (without the express written permission of the owner of the rights to the assets).

3. Design a new site using the downloaded images.

4. List four reasons why your site is better than the original.

4. Filters on Multiple Images

In this Challenge, you create a mini-catalog of filter effects. For the sake of time, we're only instructing you to use four images and six filters, but it would be a good idea to make this an ongoing process, adding filters and effects whenever the mood strikes. It's an excellent way to familiarize yourself with the behavior of various filters before you actually need to use them on a live assignment.

1. Build a new folder, home page, and basic site design for an online resource that shows visitors what the Photoshop filters can do.

2. Pick four images from the Resource folder, or from your own collection of images.

3. Select six different Photoshop filters, and apply them to the images.

4. Use the File Browser to organize and manage the multiple images.

5. Create a thumbnail for each image.

6. Create a Filter Gallery page.

7. Use the thumbnails to populate the Gallery page.

8. Link the thumbnails to the higher-resolution versions of the images.

9. Save and close the file.

PORTFOLIO BUILDER

Build an Historical Web Site

The historical committee in your city asked you to prepare a small Web site that highlights and discusses six different historical locations that are going to be featured in an upcoming bicentennial exposition. Your job is to pick the six locations and build a site that meets the needs of the client.

1. Find six historical items of interest in your hometown.

2. Go to the library or use the Web to find at least one image for each of the six categories.

3. Build one page that contains navigational elements and common graphics. It should also contain a spot for the individual images.

4. Write a brief paragraph for each of the six pages.

5. Built the individual pages with their own unique graphics and text.

6. Build a simple home page that discusses the bicentennial celebration and contains links to the six individual events pages.

7. Test the site in at least two different browsers to make sure it works properly.

Printing and Publishing

OBJECTIVES

In this project, you learn how to

- Calculate proper image resolution

- Work with image size and page orientation

- Print images from within Photoshop

- Output color images

- Add solid spot colors to an image

- Manage print options during output

- Save images in proper formats for use in other applications

WHY WOULD I DO THIS?

One of the many unfulfilled prophesies concerning the impact of computer technology on our daily lives was the notion that using computers would result in a so-called "paperless office." Another unfilled prediction was the impending demise of the printing industry. After all, if you can access information on the Internet, why bother spending time and money putting ink on paper? Printing, the industry experts said, was doomed to join the dust heap of technological history, along with the abacus and manual typewriter.

As we know, offices are far from paperless and printing is still a viable way of delivering information. The Internet and other digital distribution methods have their benefits, and they have certainly resulted in a reduction of certain kinds of printing; but all you have to do is look at the magazine racks in the check-out lines in your favorite grocery store to know that there is a lot of color printing still being done.

What does this shift in the print industry mean to the graphics professional? Simply that you must know how to prepare Photoshop images for the printing process. In some limited cases, you'll print from within the program; in the majority of situations, however, your Photoshop images will be *placed* (used) in page-layout applications. These applications include QuarkXPress and Adobe InDesign, both of which are used to assemble pages before they're sent to the printer for output and reproduction.

VISUAL SUMMARY

Completing your potentially award-winning designs is only part of the publishing equation; getting them in front of the targeted audience is the other. In Project 7, you learned the basics of preparing images for viewing and distribution on the Web. In this project, you learn how to prepare your Photoshop documents for printing.

The printing process has existed for a long time: Gutenberg printed his Bible more than 400 years ago, and the Chinese invented moveable type long before that. Color printing, however, is a relatively new technological advance. The black-ink-on-white-paper technique of the middle ages assumed color only when someone with a great deal of patience hand-painted the pages. Color printing, as we know it today, was introduced approximately 70 years ago.

A photograph, transparency, or the image you see on your monitor is said to be a *continuous-tone image*; that is, the tonal values for each pixel blend seamlessly into the adjoining pixels. When an image is reproduced on a commercial press, however, this is not the case. Since there can either be ink or no ink on any given spot on the paper, a press cannot make one tiny spot on the paper one color and the spot directly adjacent another color. The only way a press can produce an image that appears to be in full color is by fooling your eye.

Let's take a moment to explore what you actually "see" when you look at a color picture in printed form. For example, you might think that the beautiful picture of a rainbow in Figure 8.1 includes all the colors of the rainbow.

FIGURE 8.1

If you were to look closely enough, however, you would see that the image is actually comprised not of a wide range of colors, but only four different tones — each positioned on the paper as a small dot. These dots are called **halftone dots**, and the process of converting an image from a continuous-tone image into a halftone image is called **screening**, and the number of dots per inch reproduced on the paper is called the **line screen**.

If an area of an image is yellow, for example, there would be a predominance of yellow halftone dots in that area, and very few cyan, magenta, or black dots. If an area were green, the majority of the dots in the area would come from the yellow and cyan plates. For purple, magenta and cyan would be the dominant colors.

To vary intensity or solidity of a color in a given area of an image, the screening process varies the size of the actual dots. Very tiny yellow dots show up as light yellow; mix large cyan dots and a few black dots with the tiny yellow dots and you end up with a dark green.

This is, naturally, a simplification of the process. A continuous-tone image can easily contain millions of different tonal values that must be interpreted into an image, and then printed on a press. It's for this reason that many colors are difficult to achieve on press, including very deep reds and rich greens. (When a press operator or prepress professional matches a color perfectly, it is called **hitting** the color.)

Professional printers employ certain tricks to make up for the lack of range imposed by halftone technology. Good commercial printers know all about the issues surrounding full-color printing; they will guide you through the process and help you achieve excellent results from print projects.

FIGURE 8.2

When you're outputting **hard copy** (a physical document; something you can actually hold in your hands and read), you face several basic choices:

- You can print the image directly from Photoshop. If you want to produce high-quality prints, you can do so using inexpensive printers and expensive paper. Check with Epson, Hewlett Packard, and Kodak for more information on printers and paper.

- You can export the file and place it into an illustration or page-layout application. The image becomes a page component, and the printing is done from there.

- A third option is saving the image for use on the Web — which you learned in Project 7.

- Saving images in Acrobat PDF (Portable Document Format) is often used in today's professional environments as a way to produce soft proofs. A **soft proof** is a color-corrected and calibrated image that's used for client approval. PDF files can contain written and verbal annotations and notes, and is increasingly gaining popularity as a method of saving images for use in CD presentations and digital workflows.

LESSON 1 Image Resolution

Using various Photoshop techniques, you can change the resolution of an image simply by changing its size. Being able to do this, however, does not make it the correct procedure to modify an image's resolution. Experience will tell you that using this technique to change the resolution of an image is, in fact, the wrong choice.

The Quality Factor

To ensure that your images reproduce properly when printed, you must have at least two pixels for each line screen dot that's required for the project. First, contact your printer and determine what line screen will be used for the job; then, multiply that number by two.

For example, let's say your project is being printed at a 150 line screen. Multiply 150 × 2 to arrive at the required resolution for the image you are working on — or the resolution at which you need to scan or capture with a digital camera. In this case, the proper resolution for the image is 300 ppi in Photoshop.

If you perform the quality calculation and determine that you need an image 4 inches wide by 5 inches high for printing in color at 150 line screen, quick math tells you that you need a 4 × 5-inch image at 300 ppi to meet the quality requirements.

What if your existing scan is only 2 inches wide by 2.5 inches high? You could place the image as-is in a page-layout program and simply drag to enlarge it to twice its original size; this stretches the pixels in the image to accommodate the increased size. In doing so, you reduce the resolution by 50%, with 150 ppi of resolution in a space where there should be 300 ppi. A better answer to this problem is to rescan the image — whenever possible — at the correct resolution. Remember, your goal when resizing an image is to protect the quality.

In the following exercise, you compare two different scans of the same original photograph. The model is Mike O'Donnell. You might remember him from the genie-in-the-bottle exercise from an earlier project.

Compare Images with Different Resolutions

1	**Open mikey150ppi.psd and mikey300ppi.psd from the Project_08 folder.**

2	**Choose Window>Arrange>Tile.**

You can see both images on your screen at the same time.

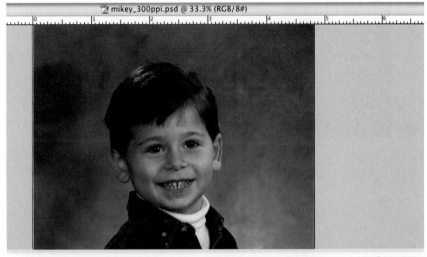

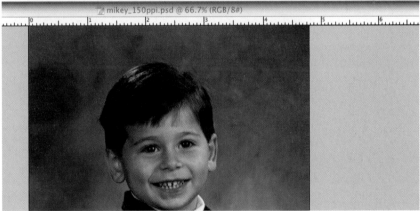

FIGURE 8.3

3   **Select the 150-ppi image. Choose Image>Image Size.**

The Image Size dialog box opens. Examine the values in the dialog box. Most noticeably, the width of the image (assuming it's output at 100%, and not resized in a page-layout application) is just under 5 inches, with a height of just under 7 inches. It weighs in at around 2 megabytes. Note the width and height measured in pixels.

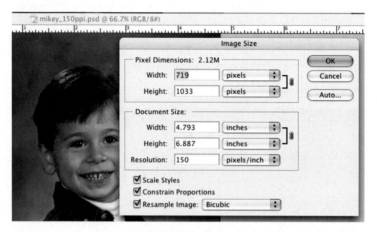

FIGURE 8.4

4   **Click OK. Select the 300-ppi image. Open the Image Size dialog box again.**

This file weighs 8.5 megabytes, and has twice the pixel width of the lower-resolution version: 1445 compared to 719. Despite the considerable increase in resolution and file size, the width and height remains the same. Two files of differing resolution can often appear the same — until you examine them closely.

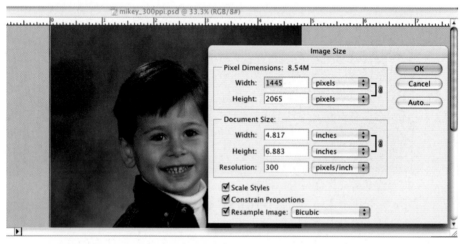

FIGURE 8.5

5   **Click OK to close the dialog box. Keep both files open for the next exercise.**

Besides the obvious fact that the 300-ppi image is almost 4 times heavier than the low-resolution version, the increase in resolution has a dramatic impact on fine detail. In the next exercise, you compare fine details in the two apparently identical images.

Examine Details

1 Select the 300-ppi image.

2 Look closely at the image. In the lower-right corner is a game board.

FIGURE 8.6

3 Zoom into the game board.

4 Zoom into the two images so they're both showing the same region. Arrange the two images until you can see the details of the word "Wild" on the game board.

You can clearly see the difference in detail between the two images. Besides the word "Wild," the lines and details of the other elements are much more defined and clear in the 300-ppi image.

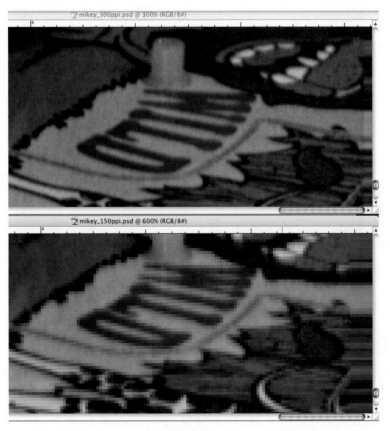

FIGURE 8.7

5 Position the two images so you can see the model's left eye.

Remember, the model's left eye is on the right side of the image.

Again, there are twice as many pixels available to render the details in the high-resolution image. The same details, rendered with half the pixels, clearly suffer in terms of quality.

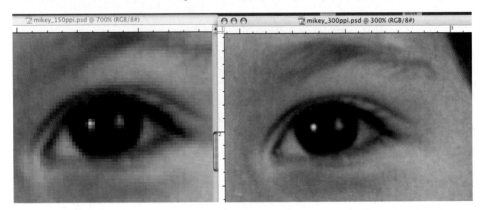

FIGURE 8.8

6 Keep the files open for the next exercise.

Resize and Resample

You can resize images directly in Photoshop. The effects of resizing, however, must be considered whenever you need a larger or smaller original. In some cases, you achieve better results when you rescan or reshoot the image; in others, you can use sharpening and softening techniques to overcome problems associated with resizing.

In this exercise, you examine the result of resizing a low-resolution image.

1 Select the 150-ppi image. Open the Image Size dialog box.

2 Enter "300" in the Resolution field. Don't change any other values. Click OK.

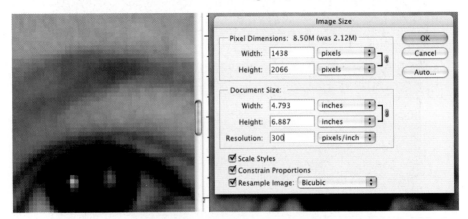

FIGURE 8.9

The image on the right is resized to twice its original resolution.

3 | **Look at the two eyes again.**

Resizing the 150-ppi image added data to increase the resolution. The program interpolated the information it needed from what was already there. *Interpolation* is the mathematical process of adding or subtracting pixels from an image when it's being enlarged or reduced in size. The process is also called *resampling* because the program samples the pixels in each area and uses that information to determine where and how to enlarge or reduce an image.

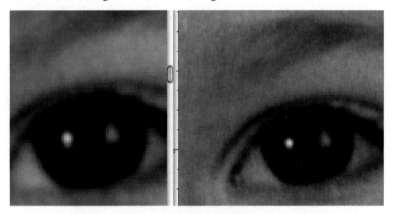

FIGURE 8.10

4 | **Use a Sharpening filter to improve the details of the now-resized image.**

Unsharp Mask is the best choice, but feel free to experiment. Remember, the data wasn't available in the lower-resolution image; the program simply made it up for the higher-resolution image.

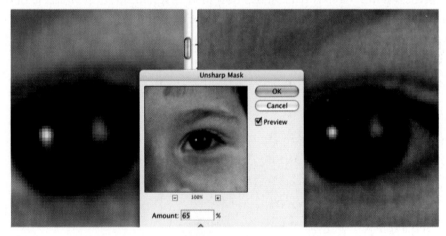

FIGURE 8.11

5 | **Examine the result carefully.**

You should note that the resized image is lacking in some very important details — specifically the eyebrows and lashes. Since these details couldn't be resolved in the original low-resolution scan, the program didn't know they were there. In the high-resolution scan, the details in lashes, highlights in the eyes, and the game board graphics will all reproduce much better.

6 | **Close the images without saving.**

To Extend Your Knowledge...

SCREENING

Printed materials are reproduced by converting the digital image (measured in pixels per inch) into a pattern of dots on the paper. The dots vary in size; where an image is lighter, the dots are smaller. Where the image is darker, the dots are larger. This process of converting pixelated images into lines of dots on a printed page is called screening, and the number of dots per inch reproduced on the paper is called the line screen.

FIGURE 8.12

Pick up a newspaper, a quality magazine, and a magnifying glass — or better yet a ***printer's loupe***, which is a specialized magnifying glass that's designed to count threads in fabric and to examine printed materials very closely. If you're doing a lot of color printing, it's a good idea to own one or more printer's loupes. The following images are from the Triplet loupe and optics company.

FIGURE 8.13

Newspaper images, particularly the black-and-white ones, are excellent examples of the screening process. Next, look closely at the magazine images. Notice that the dots that make up high-quality color images in a magazine are much smaller then the dots that make up black-and-white images in a newspaper. Note the four different colored dots on the paper, as we mentioned earlier.

LESSON 2   Image Size and Page Orientation

The Page Setup dialog box — common to virtually every application you'll work with — is used by the operating system to determine various attributes of a printed document. Included among these attributes is the ***orientation*** of the page, specifically whether it's wider than it is high (***landscape orientation***) or taller than it is wide (***portrait orientation***). The size and orientation of your image must match the orientation of the page, or else portions of the image will be ***clipped*** (cut off) in the final output.

In the following exercise, you explore some of the basic requirements for outputting an image to a printer directly from within Photoshop.

Work with Page Setup

1   **Open the image named revolucion.psd from the Project_08 resource folder.**

Well-known Tampa photographer Chris Dunn shot this black-and-white image in Cuba in early 2000.

2   **Choose Image>Image Size. Note the size and resolution of the image in the Image Size dialog box.**

The 200-ppi image is just under 8-1/2 inches wide and 6 inches high. When the aspect of an image is wider than it is tall, the image is said to be of landscape orientation.

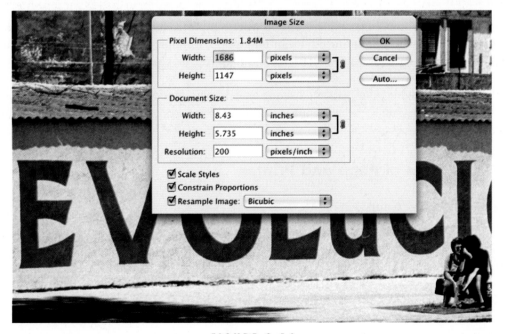

FIGURE 8.14

3   **Click Cancel when you're done looking, and keep the file open for the next lesson.**

To Extend Your Knowledge...

MEASURING RESOLUTION

No matter what kind of printer you use to print an image, it reproduces your images by converting the square pixels you see on screen to dots of ink on paper.

The resolution determines how many pixels make up an image. If you're using a scanner to capture your image, then the maximum resolution is determined by the device's specific model and type. Scanners often have two stated resolutions. The first is the physical resolution of the device, which is called the *optical resolution*. This attribute is often referred to in *dots per inch*, or *dpi*. If a scanner is said to offer an optical resolution of 1200 dpi, it means it can break a linear inch of an image into 1200 unique values (dots).

The second type of resolution is called *interpolated resolution*. In this case, the software packaged with (or actually built into) the scanner takes the optical resolution and enlarges the result. The important value is the optical resolution because that's what the scanner can actually record on its own.

Generally, resolution is measured in dots per inch (dpi), or more accurately, pixels per inch (ppi).

LESSON 3 Printing from within Photoshop

While most of the images you generate in Photoshop will be imported into other applications for final output, many projects are suitable for output directly from Photoshop. Examples include posters, photographs for an album or portfolio, greeting cards, package designs, and silkscreen graphics.

The first thing to learn about printing is the need to match the orientation of the page to the orientation of the paper. In this exercise, you see what happens when you print a document with mismatched orientation and size settings.

Match Orientation of Page and Printer

1 Choose File>Page Setup.

The Page Setup dialog box opens. Unless you've already been printing your images, it's likely that you'll see the generic Print Dialog box, which is part of your computer's operating system. The Paper Size is likely set to Letter (8.5 by 11 in) and the Orientation set to Portrait (tall).

2 Set the Paper Size to Letter and the Orientation to Portrait (if necessary).

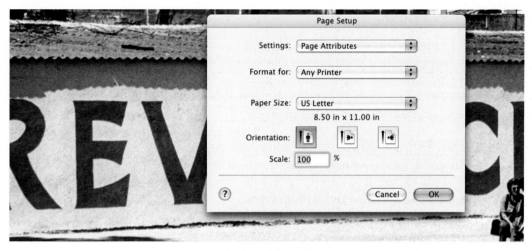

FIGURE 8.15

? ## If you have problems...

Several of the following exercises require that you connect to an output device. It's not important whether the printer is directly connected to your personal computer or part of the network on which you're working, but you will be unable to follow every instruction if you don't have access to an output device.

---

3 | **Click OK. Choose Print from the File menu.**

The width of the image is wider than the paper, so you receive a warning that the image is going to be clipped. Click Proceed and send the document to the printer anyway. When it prints, look at what happened during the clipping.

FIGURE 8.16

4 | **Return to the Page Setup dialog box.**

5 | **Leave the file open for the next exercise.**

Use Print with Preview

Photoshop includes an option that allows you to see what's going to happen when you print an image. It's called the Print with Preview option, located in the File menu. Using this option is the easiest way to eliminate any unexpected problems with your output. When outputting to a regular black-and-white laser printer, this isn't a significant issue. When outputting to a color printer or using expensive photographic print media, however, each mistake costs a considerable amount of money.

In this exercise, you preview the image you worked with in the previous exercise before you click the Print button — making sure that the orientation of the paper matches the dimensions of the image itself.

1   **In the open file, choose File>Print with Preview.**

The Print dialog box opens; but this time, it includes a preview of the image.

2   **If the Show More Options box is checked, uncheck it.**

From this dialog box, you can access the Page Setup dialog box to correct what is now an obvious problem: the preview shows that the orientation of the image doesn't match the size of the paper it's going to be printed on.

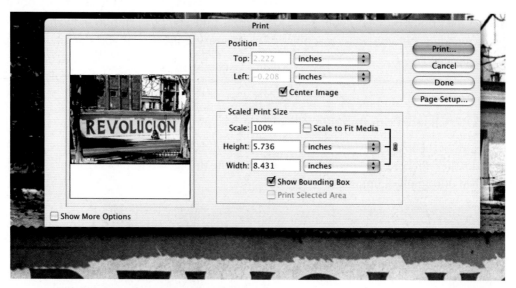

FIGURE 8.17

To Extend Your Knowledge...

MORE ON LINE SCREENS

Typical line screens used in commercial printing range from between 85–150 lpi for general color printing. Certain technologies often push the upper limit of the line-screen factor beyond 200 lpi. Waterless printing (a recent advance in the actual printing process) can reach line screens as high as 300 lpi.

3 **Click the Page Setup button. Change the page's Orientation to Landscape.**

The preview changes to reflect the new (correct) orientation. As an experiment, press the Option/Alt key. The buttons change and you have the option of either resetting the original values or remembering the settings you're using now.

You can manually size the image by pulling on the handles. These handles show the image's "bounding box."

Check this box to automatically size the image to the paper available in the printer.

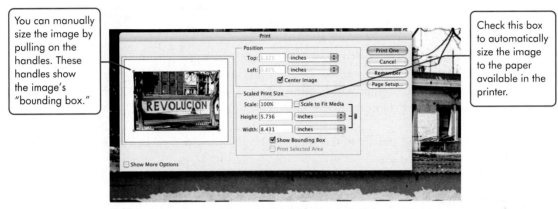

FIGURE 8.18

4 **Click the Scale to Fit Media check box.**

The image automatically fills as much of the paper as possible. Some printers are capable of using larger sheets of paper, most commonly called *tabloid-size pages*. These pages are the same size as two letter-size pages put together on their long sides to measure 11 by 17 inches.

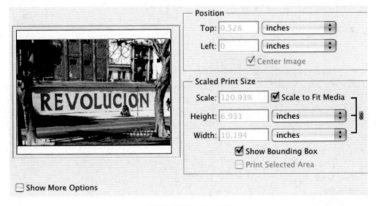

FIGURE 8.19

5 **Print the page again to make sure everything worked properly.**

6 **Save the file in your WIP_08 folder. Close the file when you're done.**

LESSON 4 Color Printing

When you're printing from within Photoshop, you have two primary choices. The first is to print a ***composite*** image, one what combines any and all color channels in the image into a single output stream. If you're lucky enough to have access to a color printer, then you can print color composites. If not, a color image prints as grayscale when output to a more common black-and-white device.

The second choice is to print what are called ***color separations***, where each channel in the document is printed on a different piece of paper. When a commercial printer prepares to print your document in color, he generates four different sets of negatives from which printing plates will be generated. Each of these plates corresponds to one of the four process colors (cyan, magenta, yellow, and black).

In the following exercise, you see exactly how a four-color separation works when an image is reproduced in process color inks.

View Separations

1. **Open the file named florida_pompano.psd from the Project_08 folder.**

2. **Activate the Channels palette.**

   You know that this is a CMYK image because it has four channels — one channel for each of the four process ink colors — as well as a composite channel that displays all of the colors to simulate what will happen when they're overlaid during the printing process.

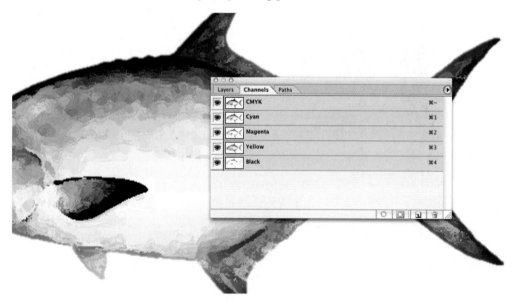

FIGURE 8.20

3   **Choose Preferences>Display & Cursors. Make sure the Color Channels in Color box is not checked.**

Actual separation plates are grayscale, not color. The process color inks aren't applied until the actual press is running. A channel carries the specific density of color (called ***color density***) at a specific location in the image. When the four tonal values are combined on press, the result fools the eye into seeing many more colors than are actually there.

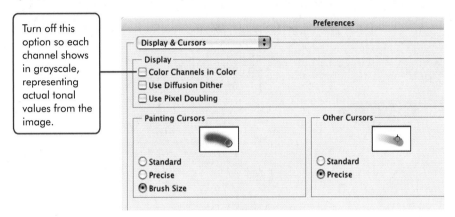

Turn off this option so each channel shows in grayscale, representing actual tonal values from the image.

FIGURE 8.21

4   **Look at the image closely. Hide all but the Cyan channel.** →

The channel displays only in grayscale, which is expected. The combination of process inks begins to show in the result when you mix more than one color.

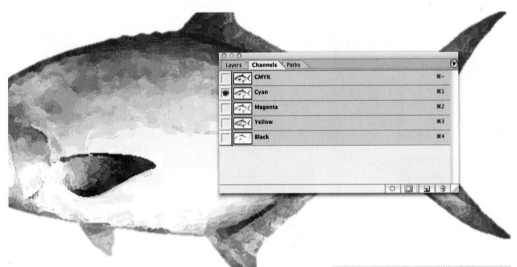

FIGURE 8.22

5   **Turn on the Yellow channel.**

You see the color in the fish's belly. This species has a yellow stomach, which is very bright in real life, and apparent even in this watercolor rendition.

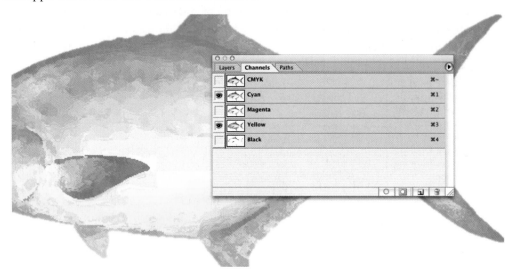

FIGURE 8.23

6   **Turn on the Magenta channel.**

At this point, you can see that the image is largely comprised of the three color channels. In fact, CMY are enough to render an image quite well, except for one fatal flaw: the impurity of process inks.

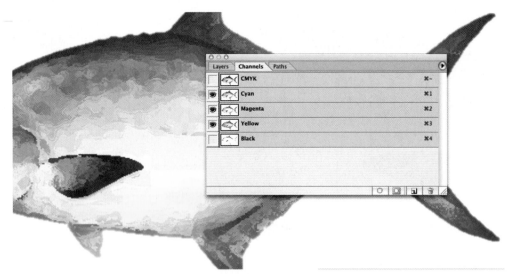

FIGURE 8.24

7   **Toggle the Black channel on and off.**

If cyan, yellow, and magenta inks were chemically and optically pure, you wouldn't need black — the combination of CMY would produce solid black. Impurities do exist, however, so the CMY combination renders a dark, dull, brownish gray.

These impurities result in some loss of details (**key details**). The addition of the **blacK**, or **Key plate,** supplies the pure black to keep the details and edges crisp. Another theory for why the channel carrying the black tones is called "K" instead of "B" (for black) is that the letter "B" could be mistaken for blue, which is actually the cyan ("C") channel.

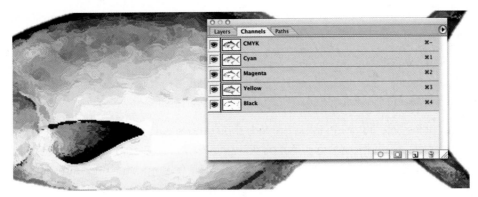

FIGURE 8.25

8   Look only at the Black channel.

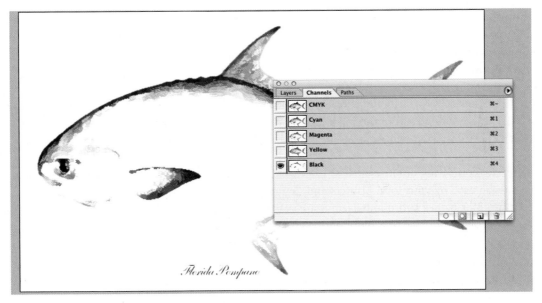

FIGURE 8.26

9   Close the file without saving it.

In the world of commercial printing, process inks aren't opaque; they're translucent, allowing underlying colors to show through to the viewer. This exercise shows how the combination of inks on press results in the appearance of a wide range of colors that aren't actually there.

Think of what happens when you draw with a yellow crayon on a piece of white paper, and then draw on top of the yellow with a blue crayon. The areas where the colors overlap are green. The same theory is used when process inks are applied to paper during commercial printing; you might see green, but it was actually created with blue and yellow.

To Extend Your Knowledge...

THE EFFECT OF IMPROPER RESOLUTION

If you fail to keep the quality factor in mind, your image will have either too much resolution or too little. Either way, the printed result would be better if you scanned the image at the correct resolution.

You also must remember that if the image is resized in a page-layout program, which is very easy to do, the effective resolution changes accordingly. If the image is reduced by 50%, the effective resolution doubles; if the image is enlarged by 100%, the effective resolution is halved.

The final image, at the size it's going to be printed, should have twice the ppi as the lpi at which the job is going to be printed. Sounds confusing, but as you gain experience outputting images, the calculation will become second nature. You also don't have to be perfect. A few ppi in either direction aren't critical.

LESSON 5   Spot Color Printing

Although four-color process printing can reproduce a vast number of shades (approximately 9,000), there are times when you need to reproduce a color that's simply not available from current technology on printing presses. A perfect example is a corporate logo that requires a specific color (usually trademarked) of ink. This special color is known as a *spot color*.

Besides four-color process printing inks, printers have access to an enormous library of solid-color inks (spot colors). These inks are the result of mixing a little of this color with a little of that color — much the same as when you buy custom-mixed paint at your local home improvement center.

There are several competing libraries of these pre-mixed ink colors. The most popular library, as well as the one most likely to be used by your local printers and design companies, is the Pantone library. Pantone colors are represented by color names and numbers, and are available as swatches in Photoshop. There are two different libraries of Pantone colors — one represents colors that can be created by using various combinations of process colors, and another that allows you to specify solid inks.

Create a New Spot Color Channel

1   **Open the file named east_river.psd from the Project_08 resource folder.**

2   **Open the Channels palette. Command/Control-click the New Channel icon in the Channels palette.**

Using the Command/Control key to create the new channel tells Photoshop you want to produce a spot color channel. You can also create a spot color channel from a regular (extra) alpha channel. Simply add the channel, and then designate it as a Spot Color from the Channel Options dialog box.

3   Double-click the Color chip, and then click the Custom button. Choose Pantone 171 C from the color swatches on the left.

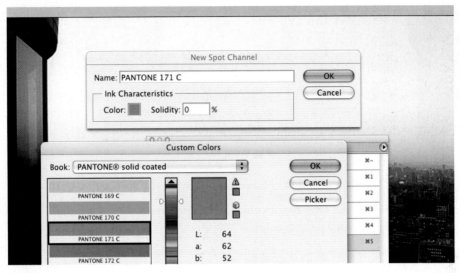

FIGURE 8.27

4   Select a typeface that you like, and enter the text "New York State" on a line at the top of the image, as shown below.

When you create type on a spot color channel, Photoshop assumes that you want the type to be the color of the channel, and creates a type mask accordingly. You can see the mask as you enter the text. We used American Typewriter as the typeface for this example, but you can use any font you prefer.

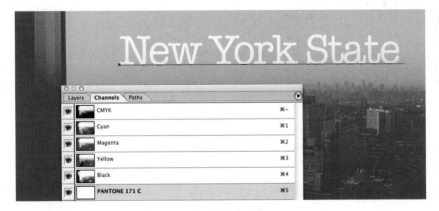

FIGURE 8.28

5 Choose the Move tool in the Toolbox. Use the Move tool to deactivate the mask and reposition the text slightly to the right.

FIGURE 8.29

6 Turn on only the Yellow and Black channels along with the spot color channel.

Notice that the color of the type is not comprised of process color inks; rather, it is a solid red shade that isn't affected by the four process colors.

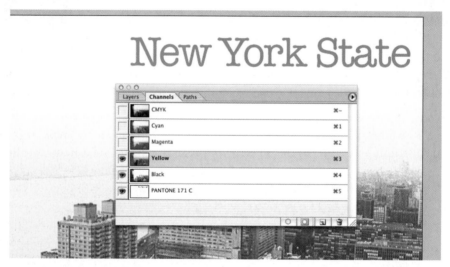

FIGURE 8.30

7 Close the file without saving your changes.

To Extend Your Knowledge...

COMMUNICATING WITH YOUR SERVICE PROVIDERS

When you're working with spot colors, make sure that you tell your printers and other service providers (such as output service bureaus) exactly what you want. First, you must make sure that both you and they understand how the spot color is supposed to look. In addition, it's always a good idea to talk with your printer before you actually send him a specific project. Printers have extensive experience reproducing digital images and can help you as you gain experience with the complexities surrounding color technology.

LESSON 6 Working with Print Options

Many options are available to you when you're outputting an image directly from Photoshop. These print options are available from the Print with Preview dialog box that you worked with in Lesson 3.

A few of the options are straightforward and apply primarily to images that you're outputting directly from Photoshop to a local or networked printer. Others are more technical and designed to alter the screening and tonal information stored in the file when it's saved in a format for external use. In addition, print options are organized into two groups; one controls output functions, and the other provides controls over color management and separation settings.

In the following exercise, you work with some of the more basic output options available from the Print Options dialog box.

Use Basic Output Options

1 Open the file named beau_rivage.psd from the Project_08 resource folder.

2 Review the Resolution and Document Size values in the Image Size dialog box.

This well-composed and compelling image is the work of a Tampa photographer named Wynn Wollof. Notice that the resolution is 240 ppi — appropriate for output at 100% in a project printed using a 120 line screen. It weighs in at 11.6 megabytes.

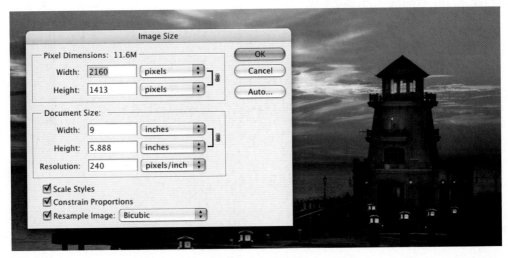

FIGURE 8.31

3 Click OK to close the Image Size dialog box.

4 Choose File>Print with Preview. Click the Page Setup button. Change the Page Orientation to Landscape. Click OK to see the change.

When you first preview the image, the page orientation is probably incorrect. Changing the page orientation corrects the problem and shows the image centered on the paper.

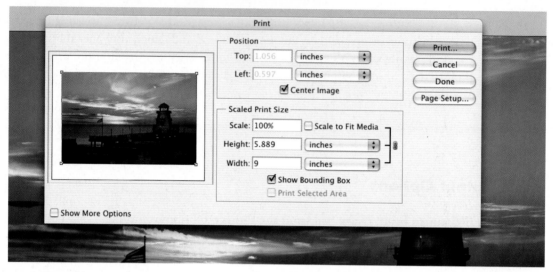

FIGURE 8.32

5 Check the Show More Options check box. If necessary, select Output from the pop-up menu at the left of the expanded dialog box.

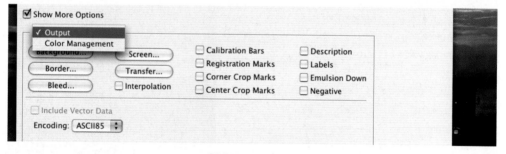

FIGURE 8.33

To Extend Your Knowledge...

UNDERSTANDING WORKFLOW

A high level of communication is required up and down the entire workflow to complete any project. *Workflow* is a term that describes all of the various processes, tasks, milestones, and deadlines that occur throughout the life cycle of a typical assignment. Workflow doesn't include only processes; there are people — many with unique skills and most with specific and unique responsibilities — at each point in the cycle. The life of a project is often mapped out on a *timeline* that starts with the initial assignment and ends when the client approves the finished *creative* (design).

6   **Turn on some of the check boxes on the right side of the dialog box.**

These options help align the four negatives (called *registration* in the trade), put color bars on the page, and add *crop marks* for cutting the image from the surrounding paper.

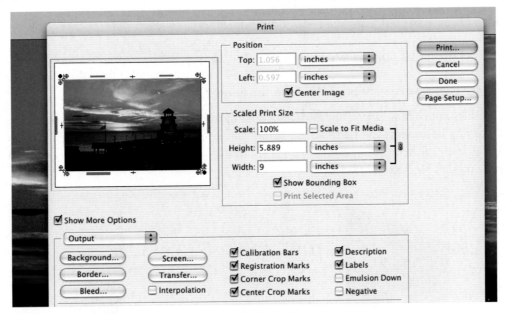

FIGURE 8.34

7   **Print the document and examine the items placed on the page.**

You can also experiment with different backgrounds and borders by clicking the appropriate buttons on the Print Options dialog box. The Screen and Transfer options are best left for your printer or output service provider to adjust.

8   **When you're done, close the file without saving the changes.**

LESSON 7   Preparing Images for Use in Other Applications

As we already mentioned, the majority of the images you create with Photoshop aren't output directly from within the program. Most workflows require that images prepared in Photoshop be used as components within the context of a page-layout application.

While some programs can directly import native Photoshop (.psd) files, most workflows call for other, more compatible formats. This means that in the majority of cases, you will export your images into one of these print- and workflow-compliant formats.

In the following exercises, you use Photoshop to create several images using different file formats.

Save TIFF Images

TIFF files are among the most common types of images used for print purposes. As a result, you will save your Photoshop images as TIFF files more often than any other type.

1　Open citrus_park.psd from the Project_08 folder.

2　Save the file (as is) into the WIP_08 folder.

3　Choose File>Save As. Choose TIFF from the Format pop-up.

TIFF files can contain layers; but in the majority of cases, you should keep your layered files as native Photoshop documents and flatten them before you save them as TIFF files. TIFF's support for layers doesn't really mean much, since the native PSD format offers a full range of features without having to go to another file type.

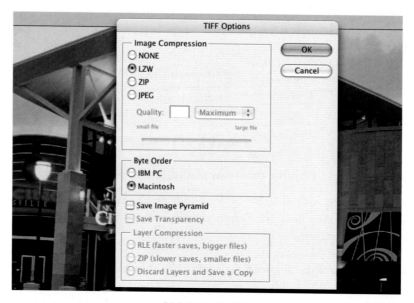

FIGURE 8.35

4　Close the file when you're done saving it.

5　Go to your desktop and compare the size of the two files.

When you're saving TIFF files, you can usually save some space by applying the LZW compression method, available from the TIFF Options dialog box that appears whenever you save a file into TIFF format.

We used a Macintosh while writing this book, and you can see that we used the LZW compression scheme and the Macintosh Byte Order. This byte order simply determines how the information is written to the disk, and has no impact whatsoever on your ability to use the file, whether you're working on a Macintosh, Windows-based system, or a UNIX machine (a Silicon Graphics or Solaris workstation).

Save EPS Images

EPS files are particularly important when you're working with type or other vector objects that must maintain their crisp, clear edges, even when the rest of the image is comprised totally of pixels.

1   **Open the file named brick_house.psd from the Project_08 folder.**

2   **Place the words "Brandon Estates" in the upper-left corner of the image. Use the typeface of your choice.**

FIGURE 8.36

3   **Choose File>Save As. Choose Photoshop EPS as the Format.**

Notice that you have to save the file as a copy when you use this format. This is good practice; when you export one of your images for use in another program, you want to keep the original intact.

4   **When you click OK, the EPS Options dialog box appears. Choose Include Vector Data.**

This option keeps your type as vector objects, which means that the fonts will print at the maximum resolution available on the output device, instead of being pixelated or rasterized when you save the file. If you were to open this file in Adobe Illustrator, you would still be able to edit the type.

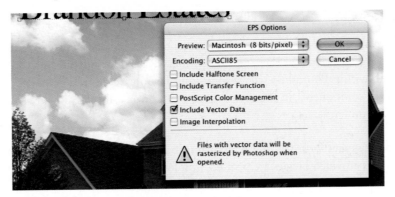

FIGURE 8.37

5   **Save the file and close it when you're done.**

6   **Compare the file sizes in the folder.**

It's always a good idea to look into the actual folders (from the operating system) that contain your images. The size of files is more accurately shown there than they are in the Photoshop Image Size dialog box.

C A R E E R S   I N   D E S I G N

WORKING WITH YOUR PRINTER

Getting a job from the Photoshop application onto paper is far more complex and difficult then it might appear. Many factors come into play when you're getting ready for the press. Unless you've worked in a commercial printing environment, some things are going to be beyond your knowledge — at least until you've had a dozen or more jobs go wrong.

There's an old adage that essentially says you never learn anything when everything goes as planned; you only learn from mistakes. We're definitely subscribers to that theory. You can fight back against Murphy's Law by visiting printers and discussing your jobs long before the project is scheduled to go to press.

Consider contacting several commercial printing or prepress companies; ask them if you can visit their facilities to discuss how they would like your work to be prepared. Many sites use different workflows, or series of processes to get their clients' work through the factory and out the door in a satisfactory manner. Since workflows differ, and are often based on specific equipment configurations at the service provider location, visiting the site and talking with various people who will be involved in getting your work done will prove invaluable.

In many cases, the salespeople working for the service provider are fountains of knowledge, since they handle work from many different types of creative locations. Talking with a sales representative about the kind of work you do is a logical first step in the process of learning how to avoid costly mistakes.

S U M M A R Y

In Project 8, you were introduced to the important aspects of printing your images once you have completed your Photoshop work. You learned that there are two primary ways to print your images. The first is to output an image directly from within Photoshop; the second (and far more common) situation is when your images are going to be used as components in the creation of publications, display advertisements, brochures, and many other types of documents.

You learned about color separations, and the relationship between the scanning resolution, the image resolution, and the line screens at which images are printed. You learned about the process of screening, which is the conversion of images containing pure tones into a simulation of that image that can be reproduced using current printing technologies (which haven't changed very much over the last 30 years).

Finally, you learned more about file formats and the implications that an image's format has on how it's going to be used in the publishing process.

KEY TERMS

Color density	Landscape orientation	Resampling
Color separation	Line screen	Resolution
Composite image	lpi	Sampling
Continuous tone	Optical resolution	Screening
Creative	Pantone color	Soft proof
Crop marks	Placed image	Specification
dpi	Pixel dimensions	Spot color
Halftone	Portrait orientation	Tabloid page size
Hard copy	ppi	Timeline
Interpolated resolution	Printer's loupe	Workflow
Interpolation	Process color	
Key plate	Registration marks	

CHECKING CONCEPTS AND TERMS

MULTIPLE CHOICE

Circle the letter that matches the correct answer for each of the following questions.

1. Your original 8 × 10-inch image is going to be used in a QuarkXPress or Adobe InDesign publication as a 4 × 5-inch image. The piece is being reproduced at a 120 lpi. What should you use as the scanning resolution?

   a. 120 ppi

   b. 240 ppi

   c. 300 ppi

   d. None of the above.

2. For use on the Web, the _____ file format is most appropriate.

   a. PDF

   b. EPS

   c. PSD

   d. JPG

3. For print-related projects, you probably should use the _____ file format.

   a. TIFF

   b. EPS

   c. PSD

   d. JPG

4. If you have type elements in your document, you might consider saving the file as _____.

   a. PDF

   b. EPS

   c. PSD

   d. JPG

5. To save space, you could use the _____ when saving a TIFF file.

   a. LZW compression method

   b. Macintosh Byte Order

   c. Windows Byte Order

   d. JPG file format

6. When you resize a file, Photoshop uses
_____.

   a. resampling

   b. interpolation

   c. LZW compression

   d. All of the above.

7. You should always _____.

   a. use the Image Size dialog box to change the resolution of your images

   b. scan images at the proper size

   c. let your service provider scan your images

   d. use a digital camera

   e. All of the above.

8. LPI refers to the _____.

   a. pixel resolution of an image

   b. pixel resolution of a scanner

   c. resolution of a printed project

   d. None of the above.

9. PPI refers to the _____.

   a. pixel resolution of an image

   b. pixel resolution of a scanner

   c. resolution of printed materials

   d. A and B above.

10. A scanner with an optical resolution of 1200 dpi and an interpolated resolution of 2400 dpi is better than a scanner with only an optical resolution of 1200 dpi.

   a. True

   b. False

DISCUSSION QUESTIONS

1. What color should result from a solid mix of cyan, magenta, and yellow? Why is the expected color not produced?

2. What is a spot color? Give an example of a spot color.

3. Define the term "orientation."

4. What is an EPS file and when is the format appropriate for an image created in Photoshop?

SKILL DRILL

Skill Drills reinforce project skills. Each skill reinforced is the same, or nearly the same, as a skill presented in the lessons. Detailed instructions are provided in a step-by-step format. You should work through the exercises in the order provided.

1. Create a Contact Sheet

A contact sheet is hard copy that presents a number of different images organized for review in the artistic and production workflow. For example, an artist might want to select several images for use in a cover design, but doesn't know exactly which ones she prefers. Rather than look through the images one at a time, she can use a contact sheet for the selection process. In this Skill Drill, you use a built-in function that prepares and produces professional contact sheets from the Gallery.

1. Use the File Gallery to organize all of the images you've created since the first project in the book. Place the images into categories.

2. From within the File Gallery, use the Automate>Contact Sheet command to create hard-copy output of each category's images.

3. Print the copy sheet to a color printer, if available.

4. Repeat the process for each of the projects. Close all the files when you're done.

2. Optimize Images

All images must be optimized for use on the Web if you want to ensure that they look good and download as quickly as possible.

1. Create a folder on your desktop called "web_portfolio".

2. Using the contact sheet you prepared in the previous exercise as a visual guide, go through each of the images and establish sizes for each one that will allow the horizontal measure to fit within 5 inches.

3. One at a time, open each image and use the Save for Web function to both resize them and establish a suitable format (usually JPG, but GIF could work for certain images, as well).

4. Use the Save for Web command to save copies of the files into the folder you created in Step 1.

5. Individually, drag each image onto a browser window to evaluate your choices when optimizing the images. Redo the images you're not satisfied with.

3. Create a Poster of Your Samples

1. Select five favorite images from the collection of contact sheets you created in the previous Skill Drill.

2. Compare the relative sizes and resolutions of each image.

3. Use the Image Size dialog box to match the Resolutions and Sizes of the five images.

4. Use sharpening techniques (if necessary) to enhance the quality of the resized images.

5. Create a poster large enough to hold the five images.

6. Arrange the images, however you prefer.

7. Add text and other graphics, as necessary.

8. Print hard copy of the poster to a color output device, if available.

9. Close the file when you're done.

4. Create a Postcard

In this exercise, you generate a file that can be used as a print-ready postcard.

1. Pick one of the five favorite images you identified in the previous exercise.

2. Save a copy of the file.

3. Convert all the images to CMYK.

4. Create a new CMYK document with a 4.5-in Height and 5.5-in Width.

5. Place non-printing guides 1/4 inch from the top, bottom, and both sides.

6. Drag the CMYK image into the new document.

7. Resize the image. The image might have to be cropped or clipped to fit the aspect ratio of the post-card. Be creative in positioning the image on the card. The image should stretch all the way to the edges of the document.

8. Flatten the image.

9. Use Saturation and Colorizing to enhance the postcard.

10. Apply filters, if necessary.

11. Add type and other elements.

12. Open the Print Options dialog box, and add Printer's Marks to the image.

13. Output the postcard on card stock to a color printer.

14. Trim off 1/4 in from each edge of the card. Your postcard is complete.

CHALLENGE

Challenge exercises expand on, or are somewhat related to, skills presented in the lessons. Each exercise provides a brief introduction, followed by instructions presented in a numbered-step format that are not as detailed as those in the Skill Drill exercises. You should work through the exercises in the order provided.

1. Create a Simple Page

In this exercise, you create two images with different resolutions, print them, and compare the impact that the image resolution has on the quality of the output.

1. Open the image named agave.psd from the Project_08 resource folder.

2. Convert the image from RGB to CMYK.

3. Save two different versions of the files: one for 100 lpi and another for output at 120 lpi.

4. Output each file to a color printer. Examine the difference in the details.

5. Close the file.

2. Optimize Images

1. Open each of the images you used in this project.

2. Create a new folder on your desktop. Name the new folder "output samples".

3. Change the Resolution and Size of each image so they're relatively equal.

4. Create a cloth texture background. Import each of the resized images onto its own layer.

5. Create a drop shadow for each of the images. Keep them all the same Angle and Size.

6. Save and output the file to a color printer.

7. Close the file when you're done.

3. Add Text

In this exercise, you add text in a spot color to an image.

1. Open the image named bishops_harbor.psd from the Project_08 resource folder.

2. Convert the image to CMYK.

3. Examine the separate color channels.

4. Create a spot color channel using Pantone 4745.

5. Select a large typeface for the poster headline.

6. Type "Live Aboard".

7. Check your color separations.

8. Output the image to a color printer.

9. Close the file when you're done.

4. Generate Additional Pages

In this Challenge exercise, you use one image to create several different pages.

1. Open the tampa_nightscape image from the Project_08 resource folder.

2. Use the font, style, and size of your choice to enter the word "TAMPA" somewhere on the image.

3. Create a copy for use on the Web. It should be no more than 4 inches wide.

4. Create another copy for use in an 85-line screen black-and-white newspaper.

5. Create another image at the original size for a 175-line screen color project.

6. Print and compare the images.

7. Close the files.

PORTFOLIO BUILDER

Build an Art Portfolio

You're about to interview for a job with a leading local ad agency. They want to see multiple examples of your work.

1. Use the Gallery to scroll through all of the jobs you completed in Project 8.

2. Pick nine of the best-looking jobs.

3. Use the painting tools to create a signature or other identifying mark. Apply a Transparent background. Create the signature in a separate file.

4. Open each of the nine files and drag the signature into them.

5. Change the resolution and size of each image so it fits within the boundaries of an 8.5 by 11-in page.

6. Create a single montage from all the images. Use layer masks, selections, gradient masks, and any other technique you feel will improve the appearance of the montage.

7. Find a friend or service company that has a high-quality color printer.

8. Output the montage and the nine images to the printer.

9. Purchase a folder or binder to hold the images under clear plastic, so they are protected, but totally visible. Consider a matte or flat plastic to reduce the shine.

INTEGRATING PROJECT

This integrating project is designed to reflect a real-world graphic design job, drawing on the skills you learned throughout this book. The files you need to complete this project are located in the RF_Photoshop_L1>Project_IP folder.

USA Poster

Your assignment is to create a high-resolution, high-quality poster for a local patriotic celebration being held in honor of military, fire, police, and rescue personnel. The client is the town's celebratory committee, whose members are known to be very demanding — and particular — about the quality of the artwork they commission.

CREATING REALISM

This project is unique in the sense that it relies on the realistic simulation of a physical object, namely an American flag. Starting with a line art illustration created in Adobe Illustrator (and saved as an EPS file), you're going to use advanced techniques such as displacement filters to convert a flat-colored graphic into believable linen.

Once the flag is complete, you'll incorporate a number of related images to produce a complex and compelling high-resolution poster.

Create the Image File

The first part of the project requires that you set up the file size and resolution, and then import artwork created in Adobe Illustrator and saved as an EPS (Encapsulated Postscript) file. The initial artwork is flat (it contains only solid colors and shapes). As the project develops, you add texture, depth, and very realistic shading.

1   Create a new 300-ppi RGB document named "flag.psd", 10 in by 10 in, with a Transparent Contents setting.

2   Save the file into the WIP_IP folder.

3   Choose File>Place. Choose the american_flag.ai illustration from the Project_IP resource folder.

4   Press Return/Enter to complete the process of placing the graphic.

5   Save the file and keep it open for the next stage of the project.

Use Channels to Develop a Texture

This is an RGB image, and as such, already has three channels reserved for the red, green, and blue tonal values. In this series of steps, you create two channels to store some noise, which you filter using motion blurs. You then combine the two channels into a third (new) channel, and delete them when you're done.

1   Add a new channel to the Channels palette.

By default, it is named Alpha 1, and appears at the bottom of the palette.

2   If the channel isn't automatically filled with black, reset the default color swatches and fill the channel with black.

3   Use the Add Noise filter to apply Monochromatic Gaussian noise with an Amount value of 100.

4   Apply a Motion Blur filter set at a 90-degree Angle with a Distance of 95 pixels.

5   Create another new channel.

It is named Alpha 2 by default.

6   With Alpha 2 selected, repeat Steps 3 and 4; but this time, change the Angle of the Motion Blur to 0 degrees.

7   Choose Image>Calculations.

This dialog box allows you to combine the tonal values of two different channels into a single new channel. You can also apply blending modes at the same time. This powerful, yet obscure, Photoshop function is one that most designers never use.

8   In the Calculations dialog box, Source 1 and Source 2 should use flag.psd. Both Layers should use americanflag.ai. Use the Alpha 1 channel for Source 1, and use the Alpha 2 channel for Source 2. Pick Hard Light from the Blending Mode pop-up menu. Click OK.

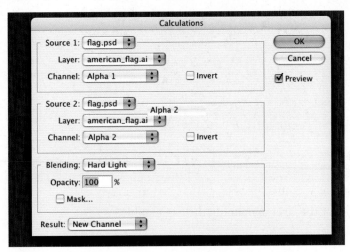

The calculation creates a third channel named Alpha 3.

9   Still working in the Channels palette, delete Alpha 1 and Alpha 2, and then select Alpha 3 (if necessary).

10   Choose Image>Adjustments>Brightness/Contrast.

11   Use the sliders to set the Brightness value to 40, and set the Contrast value to 70. Click OK.

      This brightens the channel and improves the visibility of the custom texture.

12   Select the RGB channel to see the entire image. Save the file, and keep it open for the next exercise.

Apply the Texture to the Flag

Now that you've created the texture, it's time to apply it to the flag. Since the flag occupies only a portion of the entire canvas, you need to mask the regions outside the flag itself. That way, you can apply the texture to the flag while ensuring that other areas are unaffected.

1   Still working in the Channels palette, select the entire Alpha 3 channel (Select>All) and copy it (Command/Control-C) to the clipboard.

2   Switch to the Layers palette. Press Command/Control-V to paste the linen texture into the document.

      If you feel it's easier to separate the Layers and Channels palettes, doing so will have no effect on the project; however, the screen captures we used to show you the progression of the project won't look exactly the same as what you will see on your screen.

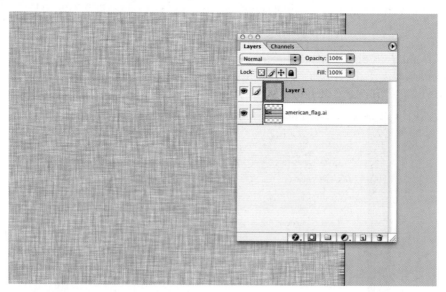

3   Hide Layer 1. Select the layer containing the flag graphic.

4 Use the Magic Wand tool with a Tolerance setting of 1 to select the transparent area outside the flag graphic.

5 Show and select Layer 1. Delete the content of the selection, then deselect by pressing Command/Control-D.

6 Set the Blending Mode of the layer to Luminosity and the Opacity of the layer to 25%.

7 Apply the Merge Visible command to merge the two layers. Save the image, and keep it open for the next exercise.

Create a Map to Shape the Cloth

In the real world, cloth isn't flat; unless it's pressed under glass, it shows folds, creases, and shadows. To better simulate the appearance of real cloth, you need to use a displacement map. In this series of steps, you use filters and channels to generate the texture for the map, and then save it into a new document so it can be used with the Distort>Displace filter.

1 Select the Alpha 3 channel.

2 Choose Filter>Render>Clouds.

3 Select all, and then press Command/Control-C to copy the content of the channel.

4 Choose File>New to create a new image.

The dimensions, color mode, and other values reflect the image you have on the clipboard.

The default Grayscale color mode is assigned because you used a channel to create the artwork. If you had used a layer, you would have incurred an additional step because the channel fill would have contained RGB values. This is one of the advantages of using channels to create elements — they don't contain any color values and allow you to create pure gray tones.

5 Paste the clouds into the new image by pressing Command/Control-V.

6 Save the image into the WIP_IP folder as "flag_dmap.psd", and then close it.

7 If necessary, deselect by pressing Command/Control-D. Select the flag layer, and then choose Filter>Distort>Displace.

8 Set both Scale values to 5. Click the Stretch to Fit and Repeat Edge Pixels radio buttons. Click OK.

An Open dialog box appears.

9 If necessary, navigate to the working folder and double-click the flag_dmap.psd file.

The random tonal values generated by the Clouds filter are used to distort the flag, adding realistic bumps and shapes to the cloth.

10 Save the file and keep it open.

Shade the Surface of the Cloth

In this series of steps, you add shadows to the surface shapes on the flag. To do this, you use the same file that you used for the displacement map. This way, the shadows follow the same shape and dimensionality that's already there.

1 In the Layers palette, select Layer 1. Use the Magic Wand tool to select the transparent areas outside the flag. Invert the selection.

2 Choose Select>Save Selection to save the selection as "flag" into a new channel.

3 Select the Alpha 3 channel. Copy the content of the flag selection by pressing Command/Control-C.

4 Select the RGB channel.

5 Switch to the Layers palette. Press Command/Control-V to paste the content of the clipboard.

A new layer is created.

6 Set the Blending Mode of the new layer to Darken and the Opacity to around 20%.

7 To reduce the size of the file, delete the Alpha 3 channel, and then select the RGB channel again.

8 Switch to the Layers palette. Merge the visible layers.

9 Save the file and keep it open for the following exercises.

? If you have problems...

Throughout these exercises, we refer to the handles that appear at the corners of images when they're brought into the flag project. If you can't see them, be sure to click the Show Bounding Box check box in the tool Options bar. If this option isn't checked, you won't see the handles. This will cause problems as you attempt to resize any of the images that you're using to create the final composite. You could, of course, still select the graphic and use the Edit>Transform command to accomplish the scaling that's required, but that adds an additional step for each of the images you're working with.

CREATING A MASKED COMPOSITE

Now that you have the flag, it's time to add the next major component to the artwork. The concept is to place the outline of a map that's floating on the center of the flag. You're going to start with a standard blackboard type of map, and use it to create a channel in the shape of the United States. Later, you will use this channel to create layer masks, which will allow you to drop images into the shape of the U.S. and move them around as if you were looking through a hole in a piece of black cardboard.

In this part of the assignment, you bring in the map and create the mask.

Add a Map and Create a Mask

1   Open usa_map.psd. Use the Move tool to drag the layer with the artwork onto the flag image. Close the usa_map.psd image.

2   In the flag image, handles appear on the map. Hold down the Shift key while you use the handles to resize the image until it fits comfortably inside the flag.

     If the handles don't appear, make sure to check the Show Bounding Box check box on the Move tool's Options bar.

3   Press Return/Enter to render and commit the transformed image.

4   Open the liberty_fireworks.psd image. Use the same process as you did in Step 1 to drag liberty_fireworks.psd onto the flag image above the map layer. Close the fireworks image.

5   Hide the fireworks layer. Use the Magic Wand tool to select the outline of the U.S.

6   Save the selection into a new channel (Select>Save Selection) named "usa". Press Command/Control-D to deselect the region.

7   Show the fireworks layer, and select it.

8   Choose Select>Load Selection to reload the usa channel. Click the Add Layer Mask icon.

9   Click the Link icon between the mask and the fireworks graphic to unlink them.

By default, a mask and the content of the layer on which it is created are linked and will move as a single object. When you unlink them, you can select and move the content of the layer within the mask, which is exactly what you need to do now.

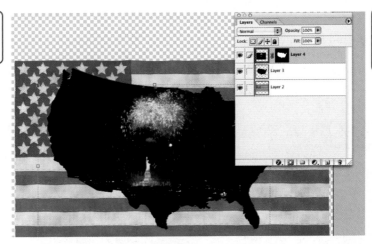

Once unlinked, select the layer, not the mask.

Click here to unlink the mask and the content of the layer.

10   Select the fireworks layer (click the icon displaying the content of the layer — not the mask). Use the Move tool to roughly center the fireworks within the map mask.

If you try to move the fireworks image and the mask moves along with it, you haven't selected the content icon. It's the icon on the left, directly next to the paintbrush icon. The picture should move within the mask, as if you were looking through a hole in the shape of the United States.

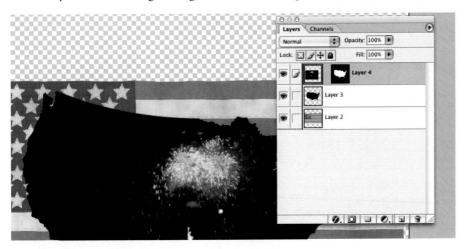

11   Save the file and keep it open.

Add the Balance of the Images

Now that you have a mask, you can use it to contain all of the other images. Apply your creativity while you decide where to position each image and how to mask it so it blends perfectly into the background of the shape of the United States.

1 Open sunset_silo.psd. Drag the image into the flag document.

2 With the new layer selected, load the usa selection (Select>Load Selection) and then add a mask to the layer.

3 Unlink the mask and image. Use the Move tool to position the sunset on the left side of the map.

4 Use the Eraser tool with a soft brush to help blend the image into the flag document.

5 Repeat the process with liberty_bell.tif, partriot_drummer.psd, soldiers.psd, wethepeople.psd, and space_shuttle.psd.

6 Vary the Opacity of each layer to improve the overall effect. You are free to reposition the stacking order to enhance the image, as well.

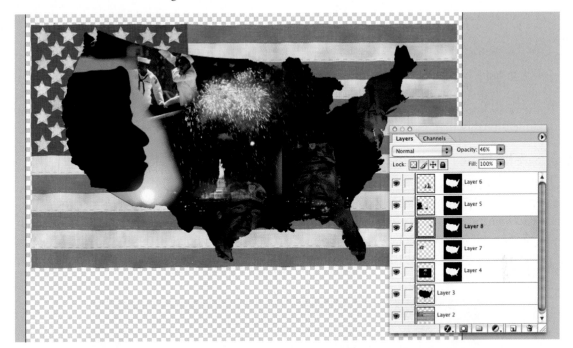

7 Save the file and keep it open.

Detail the Image

Now you're on your own. We do have a few suggestions for you, however.

1 Change the Canvas Size (Image>Canvas Size) to 10 inches wide by 8 inches high. Ignore the warning that you're going to clip the file.

2 Hide the map and flag layers, and then apply the Merge Visible command to simplify the image.

3 Show the map and flag layers. Add a layer underneath the flag layer.

4 Fill the area with noise, and create a texture using any of the filter methods you've already learned — or techniques you haven't tried yet.

5 Colorize the texture.

6 Create a rectangular selection area around the outside edge of the image. Invert the selection to create a frame.

7 Create a different texture in this area. You might want to try to simulate the appearance of wood.

8   Add two type layers to the image. The title should read "A Celebration of Freedom", and the tag line should read "June 1 – Freedom Park".

Use whatever typeface you prefer for the text elements. We used Papyrus and Impact for the two lines.

9   Add drop shadows to the flag and map layers.

When applying shadows, remember that light is directional, emanating from one or more sources; always keep the angles of shadows consistent. Pay particular attention to the frame you build around the outside edge of the image. Inside glows help because they create highlights that add excellent dimensionality to objects such as frames made of wood, metal, or even glass and plastic.

10   Save the file and keep it open.

The following image shows our final design; your flag and map outline should appear similar. Many other features, such as the layer effects you chose to use, the typeface, and (most notably) the placement of the images within the map masks, will undoubtedly result in a different appearance than the one you see here. If you're completing this project as part of an organized class, comparing each other's results and discussing the ideas behind individual creative decisions will prove very helpful and insightful.

PUBLISHING YOUR IMAGE

This project was created with high-resolution files. In reality, if this were a production poster, the size would have been 28 or more inches high by 40 or more inches wide — meaning you would have had to throw around almost a gigabyte of data (counting all the layers you created during the development process). We felt this would put too much strain on anything but real-life production workstations, so we sized down the file a bit.

Even so, this image contains a great deal of detail and depth; look closely at the weave, the quality of the type elements, and the subtlety of your composition.

You should first output the finished job to a good-quality color printer as a composite. That way, you can see the image as it would look if printed at a commercial printer. If you were to use a commercial printer, the printer and/or imaging service vendor would provide critical information about proper file formats, resolution, calibration, device profiles, and other production-related issues.

Color calibration of the various devices (your monitor, the color laser or die-sublimation printer, and the press on which you're going to print the job) is beyond the scope of an introductory training aid such as this one. The basic idea, however, is if you know exactly how each device is going to reproduce a specific color, you can make them all match and ensure that what you see on your monitor is exactly what you're going to receive from the press.

For the purposes if this book, you will get acceptable results from outputting the job yourself. By the time you are ready to enter the world of commercial reproduction, you will have finished *Essentials For Design: Photoshop CS Level 2*, and you'll know exactly how to reproduce predictable color.

Create Separations

1 Save a copy of the image as "flag_cmyk.psd".

2 Use the Layers palette Options menu to flatten the image and reduce it to a single layer.

3 Choose Mode>CMYK to convert the RGB data to four-color process.

You should see a noticeable change in color intensity; CMYK color is simply not as vibrant as what you see on your monitor while the image is still in the original RGB mode.

4 Delete any extraneous channels.

These channels were important while you were developing the artwork, but they are not needed in the image you send to the printer. They needlessly take up space and complicate the output process.

5 Save and close the file.

The printer or imaging service provider prepares the actual output of the separated channels. For now, simply separating the file into CMYK channels is enough to prepare it for output at a commercial site.

Save the Image for Use on the Web

1 Open the original flag.psd image from the WIP_IP folder.

2 Choose Image>Image Size. Reduce the Size of the image to 5 inches wide. The height measurement adjusts accordingly.

In its current state, this image is too large for the Save for Web feature.

3 Choose Save for Web.

Select the 4-Up option. Try several different JPEG quality settings until you find one that you like.

4 Click the Save button to complete the process.

5 Close the original flag.psd file without saving changes.

6 Drag the JPEG file that you created in Step 4 onto an open browser window. Preview the result.

7 Close the browser window.

If you followed the steps in this project, you successfully applied many — in fact most — of the critical skills you learned by completing this Essentials Series book. If you want to learn more, we suggest that you continue your education in the world's most popular and powerful imaging application by purchasing *Essentials For Design: Photoshop CS Level 2.*

TASK GUIDE

Task	Macintosh	Windows

Managing the Workspace

CONTROL THE SCREEN MODE

Task	Macintosh	Windows
Toggle between Standard screen, Full screen, and Full screen with menu bar	F	F
Toggle between Standard and Quick mask mode	Q	Q
Cycle through open documents	Control-Tab	Control-Tab

NAVIGATE IMAGES

Task	Macintosh	Windows
Fit image in window	Double-click Hand tool	Double-click Hand tool
Magnify 100%	Double-click Zoom tool	Double-click Zoom tool
Scroll up 1 screen	Page Up	Page Up
Scroll down 1 screen	Page Down	Page Down
Scroll left 1 screen	Command-Page Up	Control-Page Up
Scroll right 1 screen	Command-Page Down	Control-Page Down
Scroll up 10 units	Shift-Page Up	Shift-Page Up
Scroll down 10 units	Shift-Page Down	Shift-Page Down
Scroll left 10 units	Command-Shift-Page Up	Control-Shift-Page Up
Scroll right 10 units	Command-Shift-Page Down	Control-Shift-Page Down
Move view to upper-left corner	Home	Home
Move view to lower-right corner	End	End
Move marquee while dragging with Zoom tool	Spacebar-drag	Spacebar-drag
Apply and keep zoom percentage field active (Navigator palette)	Shift-Return	Shift-Enter
Zoom in on specified area (Navigator palette)	Command-drag over preview	Control-drag over preview

ACCESS PALETTES

Task	Macintosh	Windows
Show/Hide Brushes palette	F5	F5
Show/Hide Color palette	F6	F6
Show/Hide Layers palette	F7	F7
Show/Hide Info palette	F8	F8
Show/Hide Actions palette	Option-F9	F9
Show/Hide all palettes	Tab	Tab
Show/Hide all except Toolbox and Options bar	Shift-Tab	Shift-Tab
Highlight Options bar	Select tool and press Return	Select tool and press Enter

Task	Macintosh	Windows

Managing the Workspace (Cont'd)

MANAGE GUIDES

Task	Macintosh	Windows
Change measurement units	Click Crosshair icon	Click Crosshair icon
Make protractor (Measure tool active)	Option-drag end point	Alt-drag end point
Snap guide to ruler ticks (View>Snap active)	Shift-drag guide	Shift-drag guide
Convert between horizontal and vertical guide	Option-drag guide	Alt-drag guide

INTERACT WITH DIALOG BOXES

Task	Macintosh	Windows
Change Cancel button to Default	Command	Control
Change Cancel button to Reset	Option	Alt

Working with the File Browser

Task	Macintosh	Windows
Open file browser	Command-Shift-O	Control-Shift-O
Move up a folder (in folder view) or a row	Up Arrow	Up Arrow
Move down a folder (in folder view) or a row	Down Arrow	Down Arrow
Move up a level (in folder view)	Command-Up Arrow	Control-Up Arrow
Move left one item	Left Arrow	Left Arrow
Move right one item	Right Arrow	Right Arrow
Move to the first item	Home	Home
Move to the last item	End	End
Commit an inline renaming	Return	Enter
Refresh tree and thumbnail panes	F5	F5
Add an item to the selection	Shift-Arrow keys	Shift-Arrow keys
Rotate clockwise	Command-]	Control-]
Rotate counterclockwise	Command-[	Control-[
Open a file and close the File Browser	Option-Return or Option-double-click file	Alt-Enter or Alt-double-click file
Launch File Browser palette in maximized state and auto-hide palettes	Command-click Toggle File Browser icon in the Options bar	Control-click Toggle File Browser icon in the Options bar
Open a file and suppress open option and color warning dialogs	Shift-Enter or Shift-double-click File Browser thumbnail	Shift-Enter or Shift-double-click File Browser thumbnail
Apply a new filter on top of selected filter	Option-click on a filter	Alt-click on a filter
Open/close all disclosure triangles	Option-click on a disclosure triangle	Alt-click on a disclosure triangle

Task	Macintosh	Windows

Accessing Tools

If the Use Shift Key for Tool Switch option is *not* active in the General Preferences pane, you can simply press the appropriate key to access the desired tool. If the Use Shift Key for Tool Switch option is active in the General Preferences pane, you have to use the Shift key in combination with the following key shortcut.

Pressing the same key shortcut more than once cycles through the hidden tools (except for the Add Anchor Point, Delete Anchor Point, and Convert Point tools hidden under the Pen tool). In the following table, the top tool in a stack is indicated in **bold type**.

You can also press the Option/Alt key while clicking a tool in the Toolbox; this cycles through the hidden tools (except for the Add Anchor Point, Delete Anchor Point, and Convert Point tools hidden under the Pen tool).

STANDARD TOOLS

Task	Macintosh	Windows
Rectangular Marquee; Elliptical Marquee; Single Row Marquee; Single Column Marquee	M	M
Move	V	V
Lasso; Polygonal Lasso; Magnetic Lasso	L	L
Magic Wand	W	W
Crop	C	C
Slice; Slice Select	K	K
Healing Brush; Patch; Color Replacement	J	J
Brush; Pencil	B	B
Clone Stamp; Pattern Stamp	S	S
History Brush; Art History Brush	Y	Y
Eraser; Background Eraser; Magic Eraser	E	E
Gradient; Paint Bucket	G	G
Blur; Sharpen; Smudge	R	R
Dodge; Burn; Sponge	O	O
Path Selection; Direct Selection	A	A
Horizontal Type; Vertical Type; Horizontal Type Mask; Vertical Type Mask	T	T
Pen; Freeform Pen	P	P
Rectangle; Rounded Rectangle; Ellipse; Polygon; Line; Custom Shape	U	U
Notes; Audio Annotation	N	N
Eyedropper; Color Sampler; Measure	I	I
Hand	H	H
Zoom	Z	Z

Task	Macintosh	Windows

Accessing Tools (Cont'd)

EXTRACT FILTER TOOLS

Task	Macintosh	Windows
Edge Highlighter	B	B
Fill	G	G
Eraser	E	E
Eyedropper	I	I
Cleanup	C	C
Edge Touchup	T	T

LIQUIFY FILTER TOOLS

Task	Macintosh	Windows
Forward Warp	W	W
Reconstruct	R	R
Twirl Clockwise	C	C
Pucker	S	S
Bloat	B	B
Push Left	O	O
Mirror	M	M
Turbulence	T	T
Freeze Mask	F	F
Thaw Mask	D	D

TEMPORARY TOOL ACCESS

Task	Macintosh	Windows
Direct Selection (Path Selection, Pen, Add/Delete Anchor Point, or Convert Point active)	Command	Control
Convert Point (Pen or Freeform Pen tool active)	Option	Alt
Eyedropper (Any painting or shape tool active)	Option	Alt
Color Sampler tool (Eyedropper tool active)	Shift	Shift
Move tool (except when Slice, Path, Shape, or any Pen tool is selected)	Command	Control
Lasso tool (Magnetic Lasso active)	Option-drag	Alt-drag
Polygonal Lasso tool (Magnetic Lasso active)	Option-click	Alt-click
Hand tool (not in text-edit mode)	Spacebar	Spacebar
Zoom In tool	Command-Spacebar	Control-Spacebar
Zoom Out tool	Option-Spacebar	Alt-Spacebar

Task	Macintosh	Windows

Working with Selections

Reposition marquee while selecting	Spacebar-drag	Spacebar-drag
Add to a selection	Shift-drag	Shift-drag
Subtract from selection	Option-drag	Alt-drag
Intersect a selection	Shift-Option-drag	Shift-Alt-drag
Constrain marquee to square or circle	Shift-drag	Shift-drag
Draw marquee from center	Option-drag	Alt-drag
Constrain shape and draw marquee from center	Shift-Option-drag	Shift-Alt-drag
Feather Selection	Shift-F6	Shift-F6
Invert Selection	Shift-F7	Shift-F7
Move selection 1 pixel (any Marquee tool active)	Arrow keys	Arrow keys
Move selection 10 pixels (any Marquee tool active)	Shift-Arrow keys	Shift-Arrow keys
Move selection 1 pixel (Move tool active)	Arrow keys	Arrow keys
Move selection 10 pixels (Move tool active)	Shift-Arrow keys	Shift-Arrow keys
Move copy of selection (Move tool active)	Option-drag selection	Alt-drag selection
Fill selection/layer with foreground color	Option-Delete	Alt-Backspace
Fill selection/layer with background color	Command-Delete	Control-Backspace

Editing and Transforming Images

Cut	F2	F2
Copy	F3	F3
Paste	F4	F4
Revert	F12	F12
Fill Selection	Shift-F5	Shift-F5
Transform from center or reflect	Option	Alt
Constrain	Shift	Shift
Distort	Command	Control
Free transform with duplicate data	Command-Option-T	Control-Alt-T
Transform again with duplicate data	Command-Shift-Option-T	Control-Shift-Alt-T
Toggle crop shield off and on	Forward slash (/)	Forward slash (/)
Apply transformation or crop	Return	Enter
Cancel transformation or crop	Command-Period (.) or Esc	Control-Period (.) or Esc

Task	Macintosh	Windows

Working with the History

Undo/Redo	Command-Z	Control-Z
Step forward	Command-Shift-Z	Control-Shift-Z
Step backward	Command-Option-Z	Control-Alt-Z
Rename snapshot	Double-click snapshot name	Double-click snapshot name
Step forward through image states	Command-Shift-Z	Control-Shift-Z
Step backward through image states	Option-Shift-Z	Alt-Shift-Z
Duplicate any image state (except current state)	Option-click image state	Alt-click image state
Permanently clear history	Option-Clear History (palette pop-up menu)	Alt-Clear History (palette pop-up menu)
Fill from history	Command-Option-Delete	Control-Alt-Backspace

Working with Color

Change color readout modes	Click eyedropper icon	Click eyedropper icon
Select background color	Option-click with Eyedropper tool	Alt-click with Eyedropper tool
Delete color sampler	Option-click with Color Sampler tool	Alt-click with Color Sampler tool

USE THE COLOR PALETTE

Select background color	Option-click color in Color Bar	Alt-click color in Color Bar
Display Color Bar menu	Control-click Color Bar	Right-click Color Bar
Cycle through color choices	Shift-click Color Bar	Shift-click Color Bar
Select background color	Command-click swatch	Control-click swatch
Add current foreground color	Click New Color button	Click New Color button
Add current background color	Option-click New Color button	Alt-click New Color button

USE THE SWATCHES PALETTE

Select background color	Command-click swatch	Control-click swatch
Create new swatch from foreground color	Click in empty area of palette	Click in empty area of palette
Delete color	Option-click swatch	Alt-click swatch
Select multiple contiguous colors	Shift-click a second swatch	Shift-click a second swatch
Select noncontiguous colors	Command-click multiple swatches	Control-click multiple swatches

Task	Macintosh	Windows

Working with Layers

CREATE AND CONTROL LAYERS

Create new layer below target layer	Command-click New Layer button	Control-click New Layer button
Open Layer Comp Options dialog	Double-click layer comp	Double-click layer comp
Rename layer	Double-click layer name	Double-click layer name
Show/hide all layers/sets but current	Control-click eye icon	Right-click eye icon
Show/hide all other layers	Option-click eye icon	Alt-click eye icon
Load layer transparency as a selection	Command-click layer thumbnail	Control-click layer thumbnail
Add to current selection	Command-Shift-click layer thumbnail	Control-Shift-click layer thumbnail
Create new layer set below current layer/layer set	Command-click New Layer Set button	Control-click New Layer Set button
Create new layer set with dialog	Option-click New Layer Set button	Alt-click New Layer Set button
Display layer set properties	Control-click the layer set	Right-click on layer set

SELECT LAYERS

Select multiple contiguous layers	Shift-click	Shift-click
Select multiple noncontiguous layers	Command-click	Control-click
Select next layer down	Option-[	Alt-[
Select next layer up	Option-]	Alt-]
Activate bottom layer	Shift-Option-[	Shift-Alt-[
Activate top layer	Shift-Option-]	Shift-Alt-]

CONTROL POSITION AND STACKING ORDER

Move layer 1 pixel when nothing is selected	Command-Arrow keys	Control-Arrow keys
Move layer 10 pixels when nothing is selected	Command-Shift-Arrow keys	Control-Shift-Arrow keys
Move target layer down	Command-[	Control-[
Move target layer up	Command-]	Control-]
Bring target layer to back of set	Command-Shift-[	Control-Shift-[
Bring target layer to front of set	Command-Shift-]	Control-Shift-]
Merge layer down	Command-E	Control-E
Merge visible layers	Command-Shift-E	Control-Shift-E
Merge a copy of all visible layers into target layer	Command-Shift-Option-E	Control-Shift-Alt-E
Copy current layer to layer below	Option-Merge Down (palette pop-up menu)	Alt-Merge Down (palette pop-up menu)
Copy all visible layers to active layer	Option-Merge Visible (palette pop-up menu)	Alt-Merge Visible (palette pop-up menu)
Copy visible linked layers to active layer	Option-Merge Linked (palette pop-up menu)	Alt-Merge Linked (palette pop-up menu)

Task	Macintosh	Windows

Working with Layers (Cont'd)

CONTROL LAYER STYLES

Edit layer effect/style, options	Double-click layer effect/style	Double-click layer effect/style
Hide layer effect/style	Option-double-click layer effect/style	Alt-double-click layer effect/style
Reveal/hide all layers and effects	Option-click layer set expansion triangle	Alt-click layer set expansion triangle
Edit layer style	Double-click layer thumbnail	Double-click layer thumbnail
Select all type; temporarily select Type tool	Double-click type layer thumbnail	Double-click type layer thumbnail

MANAGE LAYER MASKS

Disable/enable vector mask	Option-click vector mask thumbnail	Alt-click vector mask thumbnail
Toggle vector mask on/off	Shift-click vector mask thumbnail	Shift-click vector mask thumbnail
Open Layer Mask Display Options dialog	Double-click layer mask thumbnail	Double-click layer mask thumbnail
Toggle layer mask on/off	Shift-click layer mask thumbnail	Shift-click layer mask thumbnail
Toggle between layer mask/composite image	Option-click layer mask thumbnail	Alt-click layer mask thumbnail
Toggle rubylith mode for layer mask on/off	Backslash (\), or Shift-Option-click	Backslash (\), or Shift-Alt-click
Create a clipping mask	Option-click the line dividing two layers	Alt-click the line dividing two layers
Create layer mask that hides all/selection	Option-click Add Layer Mask button	Alt-click Add Layer Mask button
Create vector mask that reveals all/selection	Command-click Add Layer Mask button	Control-click Add Layer Mask button
Create vector mask that hides all/selection	Command-Option-click Add Layer Mask button	Control-Alt-click Add Layer Mask button

Working with Paths

Select multiple anchor points (Direction Selection tool active)	Shift-click	Shift-click
Select entire path (Direction Selection tool active)	Option-click	Alt-click
Duplicate a path (Pen tool active)	Command-Option-drag	Control-Alt-drag
Close path (Magnetic Pen tool active)	Double-click	Double-click
Close path with straight-line segment (Magnetic Pen tool active)	Option-double-click	Alt-double-click
Add path to selection	Command-Shift-click path name	Control-Shift-click path name
Subtract path from selection	Command-Option-click path name	Control-Alt-click path name
Retain intersection of path as a selection	Command-Shift-Option-click path name	Control-Shift-Alt-click path name
Hide path	Command-Shift-H	Control-Shift-H
Load as a selection	Command-click path thumbnail	Control-click path thumbnail
Add to current selection	Command-Shift-click path thumbnail	Control-Shift-click path thumbnail

Task	Macintosh	Windows

Working with Type

CREATE AND MOVE TYPE

Create a new text layer (when editing text)	Shift-click	Shift-click
Show/Hide selection on selected type	Command-H	Control-H
Display bounding box (when editing text)	Command	Control
Activate Move tool (cursor is inside bounding box)	Command	Control
Scale text when resizing bounding box	Command-drag bounding box handle	Control-drag bounding box handle
Move text box while creating text box	Spacebar-drag	Spacebar-drag

FORMAT PARAGRAPH ATTRIBUTES

Align left (Horizontal Type tool active)	Command-Shift-L	Control-Shift-L
Align center (Horizontal Type tool active)	Command-Shift-C	Control-Shift-C
Align right (Horizontal Type tool active)	Command-Shift-R	Control-Shift-R
Align top (Vertical Type tool active)	Command-Shift-L	Control-Shift-L
Align center (Vertical Type tool active)	Command-Shift-C	Control-Shift-C
Align bottom (Vertical Type tool active)	Command-Shift-R	Control-Shift-R
Justify paragraph	Command-Shift-J	Control-Shift-J
Force justify paragraph	Command-Shift-F	Control-Shift-F
Choose Auto leading	Command-Shift-Option-A	Control-Shift-Alt-A
Decrease leading 2 pts/px	Option-Down Arrow	Alt-Down Arrow
Increase leading 2 pts/px	Option-Up Arrow	Alt-Up Arrow
Toggle paragraph hyphenation on/off	Command-Shift-Option-H	Control-Shift-Alt-H
Toggle single/every-line composer on/off	Command-Shift-Option-T	Control-Shift-Alt-T

FORMAT CHARACTER ATTRIBUTES

Return to default font style	Command-Shift-Y	Control-Shift-Y
Choose 100% horizontal scale	Command-Shift-X	Control-Shift-X
Choose 100% vertical scale	Command-Shift-Option-X	Control-Shift-Alt-X
Decrease type size of selected text 2 pts/px	Command-Shift-<	Control-Shift-<
Increase type size of selected text 2 pts/px	Command-Shift->	Control-Shift ->
Decrease baseline shift 2 pts/px	Shift-Option-Down Arrow	Shift-Alt-Down Arrow
Increase baseline shift 2 pts/px	Shift-Option-Up Arrow	Shift-Alt-Up Arrow
Choose 0 tracking	Command-Shift-Q	Control-Shift-Q
Decrease kerning/tracking 20/1000 ems	Option-Left Arrow	Alt-Left Arrow
Increase kerning/tracking 20/1000 ems	Option-Right Arrow	Alt-Right Arrow

Task	Macintosh	Windows

Working with Type (Cont'd)

NAVIGATE AND SELECT TEXT

Task	Macintosh	Windows
Select from insertion point to mouse click	Shift-click	Shift-click
Move 1 character left	Left Arrow	Left Arrow
Move 1 character right	Right Arrow	Right Arrow
Move 1 word left	Command-Left Arrow	Control-Left Arrow
Move 1 word right	Command-Right Arrow	Control-Right Arrow
Move 1 line down	Down Arrow	Down Arrow
Move 1 line up	Up Arrow	Up Arrow
Select 1 character left	Shift-Left Arrow	Shift-Left Arrow
Select 1 character right	Shift-Right Arrow	Shift-Right Arrow
Select 1 word left	Shift-Command-Left Arrow	Shift-Control-Left Arrow
Select 1 word right	Shift-Command-Right Arrow	Shift-Control-Right Arrow
Select 1 line down	Shift-Down Arrow	Shift-Down Arrow
Select 1 line up	Shift-Up Arrow	Shift-Up Arrow
Select word	Double-click	Double-click
Select line	Triple-click	Triple-click
Select paragraph	Quadruple-click	Quadruple-click
Select story	Quintuple-click	Quintuple-click

Working with Actions

Task	Macintosh	Windows
Change action set options	Option-double-click action set	Alt-double-click action set
Display Options dialog box	Double-click set or actions	Double-click set or actions
Play entire action	Command-double-click an action	Control-double-click an action
Collapse/expand all components of an action	Option-click the triangle	Alt-click the triangle
Play a command	Command-click the Play button	Control-click the Play button
Create new action and begin recording	Option-click New Action button	Alt-click New Action button
Select contiguous items of the same kind	Shift-click the action/command	Shift-click the action/command
Select non-contiguous items of the same kind	Command-click the action/command	Control-click the action/command

Task	Macintosh	Windows

Working with Brushes

Task	Macintosh	Windows
Delete brush	Option-click brush	Alt-click brush
Rename brush	Double-click brush	Double-click brush
Decrease brush size	[	[
Increase brush size	]	]
Decrease brush hardness in 25% increments	Shift-[	Shift-[
Increase brush hardness in 25% increments	Shift-]	Shift-]
Select previous brush size	Comma (,)	Comma (,)
Select next brush size	Period (.)	Period (.)
Select first brush	Shift-Comma (,)	Shift-Comma (,)
Select last brush	Shift-Period (.)	Shift-Period (.)
Display precise crosshair for brushes	Caps Lock	Caps Lock

Working with Blending Modes

Task	Macintosh	Windows
Cycle through blending modes	Shift-Option-Plus (+)	Shift-Alt-Plus (+)
Normal	Shift-Option-N	Shift-Alt-N
Dissolve	Shift-Option-I	Shift-Alt-I
Behind	Shift-Option-Q	Shift-Alt-Q
Clear	Shift-Option-R	Shift-Alt-R
Darken	Shift-Option-K	Shift-Alt-K
Multiply	Shift-Option-M	Shift-Alt-M
Color Burn	Shift-Option-B	Shift-Alt-B
Linear Burn	Shift-Option-A	Shift-Alt-A
Lighten	Shift-Option-G	Shift-Alt-G
Screen	Shift-Option-S	Shift-Alt-S
Color Dodge	Shift-Option-D	Shift-Alt-D
Linear Dodge	Shift-Option-W	Shift-Alt-W
Overlay	Shift-Option-O	Shift-Alt-O
Soft Light	Shift-Option-F	Shift-Alt-F
Hard Light	Shift-Option-H	Shift-Alt-H
Vivid Light	Shift-Option-V	Shift-Alt-V
Linear Light	Shift-Option-J	Shift-Alt-J

Task	Macintosh	Windows

Working with Blending Modes (Cont'd)

Task	Macintosh	Windows
Pin Light	Shift-Option-Z	Shift-Alt-Z
Hard Mix	Shift-Option-L	Shift-Alt-L
Difference	Shift-Option-E	Shift-Alt-E
Exclusion	Shift-Option-X	Shift-Alt-X
Hue	Shift-Option-U	Shift-Alt-U
Saturation	Shift-Option-T	Shift-Alt-T
Color	Shift-Option-C	Shift-Alt-C
Luminosity	Shift-Option-Y	Shift-Alt-Y
Desaturate	Sponge tool-Shift-Option-D	Sponge tool-Shift-Alt-D
Saturate	Sponge tool-Shift-Option-S	Sponge tool-Shift-Alt-S
Dodge/burn shadows	Dodge tool/Burn tool-Shift-Option-S	Dodge tool/Burn tool-Shift-Alt-S
Dodge/burn midtones	Dodge tool/Burn tool-Shift-Option-M	Dodge tool/Burn tool-Shift-Alt-M
Dodge/burn highlights	Dodge tool/Burn tool-Shift-Option-H	Dodge tool/Burn tool-Shift-Alt-H

Working with Channels

Task	Macintosh	Windows
Set options for Save Selection as Channel button	Option-click button	Alt-click button
Create a new spot channel	Command-click Create New Channel button	Control-click Create New Channel button
Select/deselect multiple color-channel selection	Shift-click color channel	Shift-click color channel
Select/deselect alpha channel and show/hide as a rubylith overlay	Shift-click alpha channel	Shift-click alpha channel
Display channel options	Double-click channel thumbnail	Double-click channel thumbnail
Display composite	~ (tilde)	~ (tilde)
Load as a selection	Command-click channel thumbnail	Control-click channel thumbnail
Add to current selection	Command-Shift-click channel thumbnail	Control-Shift-click channel thumbnail

Working with Slices

Task	Macintosh	Windows
Toggle between Slice tool and Slice Selection tool	Command	Control
Draw square slice	Shift-drag	Shift-drag
Draw from center outward	Option-drag	Alt-drag
Draw square slice from center outward	Shift-Option-drag	Shift-Alt-drag
Reposition slice while creating slice	Spacebar-drag	Spacebar-drag
Open context-sensitive menu	Control-click on slice	Right-click on slice

GLOSSARY

4/1 A job printed with four colors of ink on one side of the sheet, and one color of ink on the other.

4/4 A job printed with four colors of ink on both sides of the sheet. *See* process colors, subtractive color.

achromatic By definition, having no color, therefore, completely black, white, or some shade of gray.

actions A recorded series of steps and commands that can be played back to automate repetetive processes. Actions are particularly useful for resizing a number of images, changing resolution, saving a folder full of images in a different file format, and many other common tasks that rely on a defined series of steps.

adaptive palette A sampling of colors taken from an image and used in a special compression process, usually to prepare images for the World Wide Web.

additive color The process of mixing red, green, and blue light to achieve a wide range of colors, as on a color television screen. *See* subtractive color.

adjacent color An adjoining color. Since the eye responds to strong adjoining color, its perception of a particular color is affected by any nearby colors. This means that a color with adjacent colors may look different than it does in isolation.

algorithm A specific sequence of mathematical steps to process data. A portion of a computer program that calculates a specific result.

alignment Positioning content to the left, right, center, top, or bottom.

alpha channel An additional channel in an image that defines what parts of the image are transparent or semitransparent. Programs such as Adobe Illustrator, Photoshop, Premiere, and After Effects use alpha channels to specify transparent regions in an image.

animated GIF A type of sequential file format where multiple bitmap images are displayed one after another.

animated graphics Images of any type that move.

animation The technique of simulating movement by creating slight changes to an object or objects over time.

anti-aliasing A graphics software feature that eliminates or softens the jaggedness of low-resolution curved edges.

archiving The process of storing data in a secure and safe manner. Archived data, recorded on tape or optical media, is typically stored offsite to prevent total data loss in case of a catastrophic event. *See* backing up.

art Illustrations and photographs in general. All matter other than text that appears in a mechanical.

artifact Something that is artificial or not meant to be there. An artifact can be a blemish or dust spot on a piece of film, or unsightly pixels in a digital image.

ascender Parts of a lowercase letter that exceed the height of the letter "x". The letters b, d, f, h, k, l, and t have ascenders.

ASCII American Standard Code for Information Interchange. Worldwide, standard ASCII text does not include formatting, and therefore can be exchanged and read by most computer systems.

aspect ratio The width-to-height proportions of an image.

asset An image, sound, video, or other file that may be in use in a Web page.

audience Viewers of a movie, videotape, or commercial.

auto white balance Feature on most cameras to achieve white balance with no user intervention.

background A static object or color that lies behind all other objects.

backing up The process of making copies of current work or work in progress as a safety measure against file corruption, drive or system failure, or accidental deletion. *See* archiving.

balloons Small boxes containing text that identifies objects on the screen and explains their use. You can hide or show balloons by choosing the appropriate command from the Help menu.

banding A visible stair-stepping of shades in a gradient.

bandwidth The transmission capacity, usually measured in bits per second, of a network connection.

baseline The implied reference line on which the bases of capital letters sit.

baseline shift A formatting option that moves selected characters above or below the baseline of normal text.

beta test A part of the software testing process before the completed software is released.

Bézier curves Vector curves that are defined mathematically. These curves can be scaled without the "jaggies" inherent in enlarging bitmapped fonts or graphics.

binary Any downloadable file that doesn't simply contain ASCII text. Typically it refers to an executable program available for downloading, but it can also refer to pictures, sounds, or movies, among others.

binding In general, the various methods used to secure signatures or leaves in a book. Examples include saddle-stitching (the use of staples in a folded spine), and perfect-bound (multiple sets of folded pages sewn or glued into a flat spine).

binding edge The edge of a page that is inserted into the publiation's binding.

bit depth A measure of how many colors can be contained in an image. 8-bit color is 256 colors ($2 \times 2 \times 2 \times 2 \times 2 \times 2 \times 2 \times 2$), 16-bit color is 32,768 colors ($2 \times 2 \times 2 \times 2 \times 2 \times 2 \times 2 \times 2 \times 2 \times 2 \times 2 \times 2 \times 2 \times 2 \times 2$), and so on.

bitmap image An image constructed from individual dots or pixels set to a grid-like mosaic. The file must contain information about the color and position of each pixel, so the disk space needed for bitmap images can be very large.

bitmapped Forming an image with a grid of pixels whose curved edges have discrete steps because of the approximation of the curve due to a finite number pixels.

bitmapping The stairstepped appearance of graphics, caused by enlarging raster images.

black The absence of color. An ink that absorbs all wavelengths of light.

blanket In offset printing, the intermediate step between the printing plate and the substrate. The image is transferred from the plate to a blanket, then from the blanket to the substrate.

bleed Page data that extends beyond the trim marks on a page.

bleed allowance The extra portion of an element that extends beyond the page trim edge.

bleed size An element of page geometry; the trim size plus the bleed allowance.

bleeding A key whose edges are not sharp, and allows the background to show through.

blend *See* gradient.

blind emboss A raised impression in paper made by a die, without being inked. It is visible only by its relief characteristic.

blow up An enlargement, usually of a graphic element such as a photograph.

BMP A Windows bitmap image format with low-quality and large file sizes.

body copy The text portion of the copy on a page, as distinguished from headlines.

border A continual line that extends around an element.

bounding box An area that defines the outer border of an object.

brightness 1. A measure of the amount of light reflected from a surface. 2. A paper property, defined as the percentage reflection of 457-nanometer (nm) radiation. 3. The intensity of a light source. 4. The overall percentage of lightness in an image.

browser Software program that allows you to surf the Web. The most popular browsers are Netscape Navigator and Microsoft Internet Explorer. The very first browsers, such as Lynx, only allowed users to see text. Also called "Web browser."

browser compatibility A term that compares the way a Web page functions on different browsers. Incompatibilities often exist due to the way a browser interprets the HTML. The differences may be very slight or significant.

bullet A marker preceding text, usually a solid dot, used to add emphasis; generally indicates the text is part of a list.

burn 1. To expose an image onto a plate. 2. To darken a specific portion of an image.

button An element a user can click to cause an effect, such as the submission of a form.

button state A visual version of a button. For example, when clicked, the button is in its Down state; when dormant, it is in its Up state. When the mouse is hovered over the button, the button is in its Over state.

cache A copy of files the browser has already seen and can reference without downloading again.

calibration Making adjustments to a color monitor and other hardware and software to make the monitor represent as closely as possible the colors of the final production.

calibration bars A strip of color blocks or tonal values on film, proofs, and press sheets, used to check the accuracy of color registration, quality, density, and ink coverage during a print run.

callout A descriptive label referenced to a visual element, such as several words connected to the element by an arrow.

camera-ready A completely finished mechanical ready to be photographed to produce a negative, from which a printing plate will be made.

cap line The theoretical line to which the tops of capital letters are aligned.

caption The lines of text that identify a picture or illustration, usually placed beneath it or otherwise in close proximity.

CCD Charge-Coupled Device. A light-sensitive, solid-state semiconductor consisting of image elements (photosites) arranged in a linear or area array. Light illuminates the source, which reflects the light through optics onto the silicon sensors in the array.

cel In conventional animation jargon, a single sheet of clear acetate that contains a single frame of an animation.

center marks Press marks that appear on the center of all sides of a press sheet to aid in positioning the print area on the paper.

character count The number of characters (letters, figures, signs, or spaces) in a selected block of copy.

character style sheet A style sheet that defines only character formatting attributes, including font, type size, text color, and type style.

choke   The process in which a lighter background object is extended slightly into a darker foreground object to prevent paper-colored gaps caused by misregistration. *See* trapping.

chroma   The degree of saturation of a surface color in the Munsell color space model.

chroma keying   Special effect that uses color (usually blue or green) for the background. This color is replaced by another picture during the key. *See* color key.

chromatic adaptation   The ability of the human visual system to adjust to changes in light and still differentiate colors according to relative saturation.

chromaticity diagram   A graphical representation of two of the three dimensions of color. Intended for plotting light sources rather than surface colors. Often called the CIE diagram.

Cicero/Didot point   A unit of horizontal distance slightly larger than the pica, used widely in Europe. A Cicero equals 0.178 inches, or 12 Didot points.

CIE   Commission Internationale de l'Eclairage. An international group that developed a universal set of color definition standards in 1931.

CIE diagram   *See* chromaticity diagram.

class   A style designation that can be added to multiple elements.

click-through rate   A measure that reflects the percentage of users who clicked through to a Web site divided by the total number of messages that were delivered inviting them to do so.

client   A computer system or application that requests a service of another computer system on the network.

client-side   Scripting or other actions that take place within the browser, as opposed to the server.

clip art   Collections of predrawn and digitized graphics.

clipboard   The portion of computer memory that holds data that has been cut or copied. The next item cut or copied replaces the data already in the clipboard.

clipping path   A path that determines which parts of an image will show on the page. Anything inside the path will show and print. The clipping path knocks out the unwanted part of the image.

cloning   Duplication of pixels from one part of an image to another.

close-ended question   An item on a questionnaire, survey, or test that has a single correct response.

CMM   Color-Management Module. The engine of a color-management system.

CMS   Color Management System. A process or utility that attempts to manage color of input and output devices in such a way that the monitor will match the output of any CMS-managed printer.

CMYK   Cyan, Magenta, Yellow, Black. The subtractive primaries, or process colors, used in four-color printing.

coated   Printing papers that have a surface coating (of clay or other material) to provide a smoother, more even finish with greater opacity.

collate   To gather together separate sections or leaves of a publication in the correct order for binding.

color balance   The combination of yellow, magenta, and cyan needed to produce a neutral gray.

color cast   The modification of a hue by the addition of a trace of another hue, such as yellowish green, or pinkish blue. Normally, an unwanted effect that can be corrected.

color chart   A printed chart of various combinations of CMYK colors used as an aid for the selection of colors during the design phase of a project.

color composition   The ink components that are combined to make up a specific color.

color control strip   A printed strip of various reference colors used to control printing quality. This strip is normally placed on a press sheet outside the area of a project, used as a guide and visual aid for the press operator.

color conversion   Changing the color mode of an image. Converting an image from RGB to CMYK for purposes of conventional printing.

color correction   The process of removing casts or unwanted tints in a digital image in an effort to improve the appearance of the image or to correct obvious deficiencies.

color depth   Maximum number of colors available for an image. *See* bit depth.

color gamut   The range of colors that can be formed by all possible combinations of the colorants of a given reproduction system, such as colors that can be displayed on television screens.

color key   An overlay color proof of acetate sheets, one for each of the four primary printing inks. The method was developed by 3M Corporation and remains a copyrighted term.

color mode   A system for describing color, such as RGB, HLS, CIELAB, or CMYK.

color overlay   A sheet of film or paper whose text and art correspond to one spot color or process color. Each color overlay becomes the basis for a single printing plate that will apply that color to paper.

color picker   A function within a graphics application that assists in selecting or setting a color.

color proof   A printed or simulated printed image of the color separations intended to produce a close representation of the final reproduction for approval and as a guide to the press operator.

color separation   The process of transforming color artwork into components corresponding to the colors of ink being used, whether process or spot, or a combination of the two.

color sequence   The color order of printing the cyan, magenta, yellow, and black inks on a printing press. Sometimes called rotation or color rotation.

color shift   The result of compressing out-of-gamut colors into colors that can be reproduced with a given model. Color shift can drastically change the appearance of the final output.

color space   A three-dimensional coordinate system in which any color can be represented as a point.

color temperature   The temperature, in degrees Kelvin, to which a blackbody would have to be heated to produce a certain color radiation. The graphic arts viewing standard is 5,000 K. The norm for television lighting is 3,200 K, and for outdoors is 5,600 K.

colorimeter   An optical measuring instrument designed to measure and quantify color. It is often used to match digital image values to those of cloth and other physical samples.

commercial printing   Typically, printing on high-capacity, high-resolution presses; processes include offset lithography, flexography, gravure, and screen printing. Offset printing is the most widely used commercial printing process.

comp   Comprehensive artwork used to present the general color and layout of a page.

complementary color   Opposite colors on the color wheel.

composite proof   A version of an illustration or page in which the process colors appear together to represent full color. When produced on a monochrome output device, colors are represented as shades of gray.

compression   A technique used to reduce file size by analyzing occurrences of similar data. Compressed files occupy less space, and their use improves digital transmission speeds. Compression can sometimes result in a loss of image quality and/or resolution.

configuration   The total combination of hardware components — central processing unit (CPU), video display device, keyboard, and peripheral devices — that comprise the computer system.

continuous tone   An image (such as a photograph) in which the subject has continuous shades of color or gray tones through the use of an emulsion process. Continuous tone images must be screened to create halftone images to be printed.

contrast   The relationship and degree of difference between the dark and light areas of an image.

coordinates   Numbers signifying a place in a Cartesian plane, represented by (x,y).

copy   1. Written matter intended to be reproduced in printed form. 2. The text of a news story, advertisement, television commercial, etc., as distinguished from related visual material.

creep   The minute and progressive extension of the edges of each spread in a folded signature.

crop marks   Printed lines used as guides for final trimming of the pages within a press sheet. Also called "trim marks."

cropping   The elimination of parts of a photograph or other original that are not required to be printed.

CSS   Cascading Style Sheet. Part of a Web page file listing properties that affect the appearance of content, the content to which those properties apply, and their values.

custom printer description file   A file containing information specific to a type of output device; used in conjunction with a standard PPD file to customize the printing process.

DCS   Desktop Color Separation. A version of the EPS file format. DCS 1.0 is composed of five files for each color image plus a separate low-resolution image to place in a digital file. DCS 2.0 has one file that stores process and spot color information.

default   A specification for a mode of computer operation that occurs if no other is selected.

densitometer   An electronic instrument used to measure optical density; reflective for paper, and transmissive for film.

density   The ability of a material to absorb light. In film, it refers to the opacity of an area of the image. A maximum density of 4.0 refers to solid black. Improper density in film results in washed-out or overly dark reproduction.

depth of field   The area in which all objects, regardless of their distance from the camera, appear in focus. Depth of field depends heavily on the lens type selected.

descender   The part of a lowercase letter that extends below the baseline (lower edge of the x-height) of the letter. The letters g, j, p, and y contain descenders.

descreening   A technique used to obscure the halftone dot pattern when scanning printed material.

desktop   1. The area on a monitor on which the icons appear before an application is launched. 2. A reference to the size of computer equipment (system unit, monitor, printer) that can fit on a normal desk, thus, desktop publishing.

desktop proof   A proof made on a desktop laser or inkjet printer, used to check overall design and positioning.

device-dependent color   Reproduction in which the output color is determined by the output device characteristics.

device-independent color   Reproduction in which the output color is absolute, and is not determined by the output device characteristics.

digital   The use of a series of discrete electronic pulses to represent data. In digital imaging systems, 256 steps (8 bits) are normally used to characterize the gray scale or the properties of one color.

dithering A technique in which a color is represented using dots of two different colors displayed or printed very close together. Often used to compress digital images and in special screening algorithms. *See* stochastic screening.

Dmax The maximum density in an image, or the maximum density that can be captured with a scanner or digital camera.

Dmin The minimum density in an image, or the minimum density that can be captured with a scanner or digital camera.

dot gain The growth of a halftone dot that occurs whenever ink soaks into paper. Failure to compensate for this gain in the generation of digital images can result in very poor results on press. Also known as "tone value increase."

dot pitch In computer monitors, the distance (in millimeters) between the holes in the shadow mask: the smaller the number, the sharper the image. Generally, the smaller the number, the higher the resolution of a given monitor size.

downsampling A technique for reducing the amount of digital data used to represent an image; part of the data compression process.

DPI Dots Per Inch. The measurement of resolution for page printers, phototypesetting machines, and graphics screens. Currently graphics screens use resolutions of 72 to 96 dpi; standard desktop laser printers work at 600 dpi.

drag To position the pointer on an object, press and hold the mouse button, move the mouse and release the button.

drop shadow A duplicate of a graphic element or type placed behind and slightly offset, giving the effect of a shadow.

duotone The separation of a photograph into black and a second color. Duotones are used to enhance photographic reproduction in two-, three-, or sometimes four-color work. Often the second, third, and fourth colors are not standard CMYK inks.

dye transfer A photographic color print using special coated papers to produce a full-color image. Can serve as an inexpensive proof.

dynamic range The difference between the lightest and darkest area of an image. Also used to describe the range of color capture capability in a scanner or digital camera.

effective resolution The final resolution of an image, calculated by dividing the image resolution (pixels per inch) by the magnification percentage.

elliptical dot screen A halftone screen having an elliptical dot structure.

emulsion The coating of light-sensitive material (silver halide) on a piece of film or photographic paper.

EPS Encapsulated PostScript. File format used to transfer PostScript data within compatible applications. EPS files can contain text, vector artwork, and images.

file A specific collection of information stored on the computer disk, separate from all other information. Can be randomly accessed by the computer.

file compression The process of reducing the number of bytes in a file, file compression is usually used when transferring files between computers.

fill To add a tone or color to the area inside a closed object in a graphic illustration program.

filter In image-editing applications, a small program that creates a special effect or performs some other function within an image.

flat color Color that lacks contrast or tonal variation. Also called "flat tint."

flexographic printing A rotary letterpress printing process using a rubber plate that stretches around a cylinder making it necessary to compensate by distorting the plate image. Flexography is used most often for printing on metal or other non-paper material.

flop To make a mirror image of visuals such as photographs or clip art.

focal length The size of the angle of view of a camera lens.

Focoltone A special-color library used in the United States.

folder The digital equivalent of a paper file folder, used to organize files in the Macintosh and Windows operating systems. Double-clicking the icon opens it to reveal the files stored inside.

folding dummy A template used for determining the page arrangement to meet folding and binding requirements.

font A font is the complete collection of all the characters (numbers, uppercase and lowercase letters, and in some cases, small caps and symbols) of a given typeface in a specific style; for example, Helvetica Bold.

font embedding The technique of saving font data as a part of a PDF file, which eliminates problems caused by missing font files.

font family In Web design, a grouping of (supposedly) similar fonts, which will be used to display text in the Web page. *See* Cascading Style Sheets.

font license The legal right to use a font you have paid for; most licenses limit fonts to use on a single computer.

font metrics The physical characteristics of a font, as defined in the data file.

font subsetting Embedding only the used characters of a font into the final file. The advantage of font subsetting is that it decreases the overall size of your file. The disadvantage is that it limits the ability to makes corrections at the printing service.

font substitution A process in which your computer uses a font other than the one you used in your design to display or print your publication. Usually occurs when a used font is missing on the computer used to output the design.

force justify A type alignment command that causes the space between letters and words in a line of type to expand to fit within a line.

four-color process Process color printer. *See* process colors.

FPO For Position Only. A term applied to low-quality images or simple shapes used to indicate placement and scaling of an art element on mechanicals or camera-ready artwork.

frequency-modulated (FM) screening A method of creating halftones in which the size of the dots remains constant but their density is varied; also known as stochastic screening.

f-stop The calibration on the lens indicating the aperture or diaphragm opening. Controls the amount of light that can pass through the lens.

full measure A line set to the entire line length.

gamma A measure of the contrast, or range of tonal variation of the midtones in a photographic image.

gamma correction 1. Adjusting the contrast of the midtones in an image. 2. Calibrating a monitor so midtones are correctly displayed on screen.

gamut *See* color gamut.

gamut shift *See* color shift.

gang 1. Changes made to multiple tracks simultaneously. If you want to simultaneously change the audio volume levels in tracks 1, 3 and 4, gang those tracks. 2. The process of printing more than one job on the same press sheet to minimize paper waste.

GASP Graphic Arts Service Provider. A firm that provides a range of services somewhere on the continuum from design to fulfillment.

GB Gigabyte. A unit of measure equal to one billion (1,073,741,824) bytes.

GCR Gray Component Replacement. Technique for adding detail by reducing the amount of cyan, magenta, and yellow in chromatic or colored areas, replacing them with black.

GIF Graphics Interchange Format. A popular graphics format for online clip art and drawn graphics. Graphics in this format are acceptable at low resolution. *See* JPEG.

gradient A gradual transition from one color to another. The shape of the gradient and the proportion of the two colors can be varied. Also known as blends, gradations, graduated fills, and vignettes.

grain Silver salts clumped together in differing amounts in different types of photographic emulsions.

graininess Visual impression of the irregularly distributed silver grain clumps in a photographic image, or the ink film in a printed image.

granularity The level of detail of an outline.

gray balance The values for the yellow, magenta, and cyan inks that are needed to produce a neutral gray when printed at a normal density.

grayed out Any option (menu selection, button, etc.) that is not available.

grayscale 1. An image composed in grays ranging from black to white, usually using 256 different tones. 2. A tint ramp used to measure and control the accuracy of screen percentages. 3. An accessory used to define neutral density in a photographic image.

grid A division of a page by horizontal and vertical guides into areas where text or graphics may be placed accurately.

gripper edge The leading edge of a sheet of paper that the grippers on the press grab to carry the paper through a press.

hairline rule The thinnest rule that can be printed on a given device. A hairline rule on a 1200-dpi imagesetter is 1/1200 of an inch; on a 300-dpi laser printer, the same rule would print at 1/300 of an inch.

halftone An image generated for use in printing in which a range of continuous tones is simulated by an array of dots that create the illusion of continuous tone when seen at a distance.

halftone tint An area covered with a uniform halftone dot size to produce an even tone or color. Also called "flat tint" or "screen tint."

hex values Numbers specified in the hexadecimal system, commonly used for specifying colors on Web pages.

Hexachrome Six-color printing process developed by PANTONE, in which green and orange are added to the process colors to extend the printable gamut. Also called "HiFi".

high key A photographic or printed image in which the main interest area lies in the highlight end of the scale.

highlight The lightest areas in a photograph or illustration.

high-resolution file An image file that typically contains four pixels for every dot in the printed reproduction. High-resolution files are often linked to a page-layout file, but not actually embedded in it, due to their large size.

HLS A color model based on three coordinates: hue, lightness (or luminance), and saturation.

horizontal scale A technique used for creating artificially condensed type.

HSB Model used to define color in terms of hue, saturation, and brightness.

HSL A color model that defines color based on its hue, saturation, and luminosity (value), as it is displayed on a video or computer screen.

HSV   A color model based on three coordinates: hue, saturation, and value (or luminance).

HTML   Hypertext Mark-Up Language. A tagging language that allows content to be delivered over the World Wide Web and viewed by a browser.

hue   The wavelength of light of a color in its purest state (without adding white or black).

ICC   International Color Consortium. A standards-making body for color reproduction technology.

icon   A small graphic symbol used on the screen to indicate files, folders, or applications, activated by clicking with the mouse or pointing device.

illumination   Hand-drawn illustration, often in color, that was added to medieval manuscripts.

imagesetter   A raster-based device used to output a digital file at high resolution (usually 1000–3000 dpi) onto photographic paper or film, from which printing plates are made, or directly to printing plates (called a "platesetter").

imposition   The arrangement of pages on a printed sheet, which, when the sheet is finally printed, folded, and trimmed, will place the pages in their correct order.

impression cylinder   In commercial printing, a cylinder that provides back pressure, allowing the image to be transferred from the blanket to the substrate.

indexed color image   An image that uses a limited, predetermined number of colors; often used in Web images. *See* GIF.

ink-film thickness   The amount of ink that is transferred to the substrate.

intellectual property   Any product of human intelligence that is unique, novel, unobvious, and valuable (such as a literary work, idea, or invention).

intensity   Synonym for degree of color saturation.

international paper sizes   The International Standards Organization (ISO) system of paper sizes based on a series of three sizes — A, B, and C. Each size has the same proportion of length to width as the others.

interpolated resolution   "Artificial" resolution that is created by averaging the color and intensity of adjacent pixels. Commonly used in scanning to achieve resolution higher than the scanner' optical resolution.

Java   A platform-independent programming language, invented by Sun Microsystems, that Web developers use to create applets. Java-enabled Web pages can include animations, calculators, scrolling text, sound effects, and games.

JavaScript   A scripting language, designed by Netscape, which can be embedded into HTML documents.

job package   The collected group of all elements that must be sent to a service provide or printer, including a desktop proof, the project file, any images or graphics placed in the layout, and all fonts used in the design.

job specifications   Detailed information about a particular job, required to complete the design and print the final product. Includes page geometry, number of ink colors, type of paper being used, special finishing requirements, delivery instructions, and any other relevant information.

JPEG   A compression algorithm that reduces the file size of bitmapped images, named for the Joint Photographic Experts Group, which created the standard. JPEG is "lossy" compression; image quality is reduced in direct proportion to the amount of compression.

justified alignment   Straight left and right alignment of text — not ragged. Every line of text is the same width, creating even left and right margins.

Kelvin (K)   Unit of temperature measurement based on Celsius degrees, starting from absolute zero, equivalent to –273 Celsius (centigrade); used to indicate the color temperature of a light source.

kerning   Moving a pair of letters closer together or farther apart, to achieve a better fit or appearance.

keyline   A thin border around a picture or a box that indicates where to place pictures. In digital files, keylines are often vector objects while photographs are usually bitmap images.

knockout   A printing technique that prints overlapping objects without mixing inks. The ink for the underlying element does not print (knocks out) in the area where the objects overlap. Opposite of overprinting.

L*a*b* color   The lightness, red-green attribute, and yellow-blue attribute in the CIE L*a*b* color space, a three-dimensional color mapping system.

LAN   Local Area Network. Computer network limited to one single location, usually an office.

landscape   Printing from left to right across the wider side of the page. A landscape orientation treats a letter-size page as 11 inches wide and 8.5 inches long.

layer   A function of graphics applications in which elements may be isolated from each other, so a group of elements can be hidden from view, reordered, or otherwise manipulated as a unit, without affecting other elements.

leading   Space added between lines of type. Named after the strips of lead that used to be inserted between lines of metal type. In specifying type, lines of 12-pt. type separated by a 14-pt. space is abbreviated "12/14," or "twelve over fourteen."

lens   Optical device, essential for projecting an optical (light) image of a scene in front of the surface of the camera. Lenses come in various fixed focal lengths, or in variable focal lengths and with various aperture (iris) openings.

ligature   Letters that are joined together as a single unit of type such as œ and fi.

light meter   Device used to measure the amount of light that falls on a subject.

lightness   The property that distinguishes white from gray or black, and light from dark color tones on a surface.

line art   A drawing or piece of black-and-white artwork with no screens. Line art can be represented by a graphic file having only 1-bit resolution.

line screen   *See* LPI.

lithography   A mechanical printing process based on the principle of the natural aversion of water to grease. In modern offset lithography, the image on a photosensitive plate is first transferred to the blanket of a rotating drum, and then to the paper.

lossy   A data compression method characterized by the loss of some data.

LPI   Lines Per Inch. The number of lines per inch used when converting a photograph to a halftone. Typical values range from 85 for newspaper work to 150 or higher for high-quality reproduction on smooth or coated paper. Also called "line screen."

luminosity   The amount of light or brightness in an image. Part of the HLS color model.

LUT   Look-Up Table. A chart of numbers that describe the color reproduction characteristics of a specific device.

LZW compression   Lempel-ziy-welch compression. A method of reducing the size of image files.

makeready   The process of starting a printing press and manipulating the controls until the press is running at its optimum capability.

marching ants   The blinking lines at the edge of a text box, indicating that it is selected.

marquee   The blinking lines indicating the area selected with the selection tools. Also called "marching ants."

masking   A technique used to display certain areas of an image or design; the shape and size of the top-most object or layer defines what is visible on lower layers.

mechanical   A pasted-up page of camera-ready art that is photographed to produce a plate for the press.

mechanical dot gain   *See* dot gain.

medium   A physical carrier of data such as a CD-ROM, video cassette, or floppy disk, or a carrier of electronic data such as fiber optic cable or electric wires.

memory color   The tendency to evaluate color based on what we expect to see rather than what is actually there.

metallic ink   Printing inks which produce gold, silver, bronze, or other metallic colors.

metamerism   Phenomenon in which the same color appears differently in different lighting conditions.

metric   Any method of measurement used to determine whether a goal has been reached.

midtones   The tonal range between highlights and shadows. Also called "middletones."

minimum printable dot   The smallest dot that can be accurately and consistently reproduced on film or a printing plate.

mismatched color   A problem that occurs when a defined, named color has two different values — one defined in the page layout and one defined in a placed picture file.

misregister   The unwanted result of incorrectly aligned process inks and spot colors on a finished printed piece. Misregistration can be caused by many factors, including paper stretch and improper plate alignment. Trapping can compensate for misregistration.

moiré   An interference pattern caused by the overlap of two or more regular patterns such as dots or lines. In process-color printing, screen angles are selected to minimize this pattern.

monochrome   An image or computer monitor in which all information is represented in black and white, or with a range of grays.

montage   A single image formed by assembling or compositing several images.

mottle   Uneven color or tone.

neutral   Any color that is absent of hue, such as white, gray, or black.

neutral density   A measurement of the lightness or darkness of a color. A neutral density of zero (0.00) is the lightest value possible, and is equivalent to pure white; 3.294 is roughly equivalent to 100% of each of the CMYK components.

noise   Unwanted signals or data that can reduce the quality of output. On a television screen, it resembles snow.

non-reproducible colors   Colors in an original scene or photograph that are impossible to reproduce using process inks. Also called "out-of-gamut" colors.

normal key   A description of an image in which the main interest area is in the middle range of the tone scale, or distributed throughout the entire tonal range.

object-oriented art   Vector-based artwork composed of separate elements or shapes described mathematically rather than by specifying the color and position of every point. This is in contrast to bitmap images, which are composed of individual pixels.

offset   The distance at which rules are placed above or below paragraphs of text; can be defined as a specific measurement or as a percentage of paragraph spacing.

offset lithography   A printing method whereby the image is transferred from a plate onto a rubber-covered cylinder, from which the printing takes place. *See* lithography.

opacity   1. The degree to which paper will show print through it. 2. The degree to which images or text below one object, whose opacity has been adjusted, are able to show through.

OpenType   A font format developed by Adobe and Microsoft that can be used on both the Windows and Macintosh platforms, can contain over 65,000 distinct glyphs, and offers advanced typographic features.

OPI   Open Prepress Interface. A system in which high-resolution images are scanned and stored, while low-resolution representations are placed in a page layout. When the layout is output, the OPI server swaps out the high-resolution file in place of the low-resolution version.

optical resolution   The actual resolution of a scanner's optics. *See* interpolated resolution.

options bar   Automatically displays in the menu bar area of your Photoshop window, revealing the options available for the tool in use.

out-of-gamut   Color that cannot be reproduced with a specific model.

output device   Any hardware equipment, such as a monitor, laser printer, or imagesetter, that depicts text or graphics created on a computer.

overlay   A transparent sheet used in the preparation of multicolor mechanical artwork showing the color breakdown.

overprint color   A color made by overprinting any two or more of the primary yellow, magenta, and cyan process colors.

overprinting   Allowing an element to print over the top of underlying elements, rather than knocking them out. Often used with black type. *See* knockout.

page geometry   The physical attributes of a layout page. *See* trim size, live area, bleed size.

palette   1. As derived from the term in the traditional art world, a collection of selectable colors. 2. Another name for a dialog box or menu of choices.

palette well   An area in Photoshop's Menu bar to which often-used palettes can be stored for quick and easy access.

PANTONE Matching System   PMS. A system for specifying colors by number for both coated and uncoated paper; used by print services and in color desktop publishing to ensure uniform color matching.

pasteboard   In a page-layout program, the desktop area outside the printing-page area.

PDF   Portable Document Format. Developed by Adobe Systems, Inc. (read by Acrobat Reader), this format has become a de facto standard for document transfer across platforms.

peripheral devices   Other pieces of hardware that are plugged into your computer.

perspective   The effect of distance in an image, achieved by aligning the edges of elements with imaginary lines directed toward one to three "vanishing points" on the horizon.

pica   A traditional typographic measurement of 12 points, or approximately 1/6 of an inch. Most applications specify a pica as exactly 1/6 of an inch.

PICT/PICT2   A common format for defining bitmapped images on the Macintosh. The more recent PICT2 format supports 24-bit color.

pixel   Picture Element. One of the tiny rectangular areas or dots generated by a computer or output device to constitute images. A greater number of pixels per inch results in higher resolution on screen or in print.

platform   The type of computer or operating system on which a software application runs. Common platforms are Windows, Macintosh, UNIX and NeXT. When a program can be used on more than one of these platforms, it is termed cross-platform compatible.

plug-in   Small piece of software, usually from a third-party developer, that adds new features to another (larger) software application.

PMT   Photomechanical Transfer. Positive prints of text or images used for paste-up to mechanicals.

PMT   Photomultiplier Tube. Very sensitive color-capture technology used in high-end drum scanners.

PNG   Portable Network Graphics. A graphics format similar to GIF. It is a relatively new file format, and is not yet widely supported by most browsers.

point   A unit of measurement used to specify type size and rule weight, equal to approximately 1/72 inch.

pop-up menu   A menu of choices accessed by clicking and dragging the current choice.

pop-up window   A new window that can be created and controlled through scripting. This window is in addition to the current window.

portrait   Printing from left to right across the narrow side of the page. Portrait orientation on a letter-size page uses a standard 8.5-inch width and 11-inch length.

posterize, posterization   1. Deliberate constraint of a gradient or image into visible steps as a special effect. 2. Unintentional creation of steps in an image due to a high lpi (lines per inch) value used with a low dpi (dots per inch) printer.

PostScript   1. A page-description language, developed by Adobe Systems, Inc., that describes type and/or images and their positional relationships on the page. 2. A computer-programming language.

PPD   PostScript Printer Description File. A file format developed by Adobe Systems, Inc., that contains device-specific information that enables software to produce the best results possible for each type of designated printer.

PPI Pixels Per Inch. Used to denote the resolution of an image.

preferences A set of modifiable defaults for an application.

prepress All work done between writing and printing, such as typesetting, scanning, layout, and imposition.

primary colors Colors that can be used to generate secondary colors. For the additive system (a computer monitor), these colors are red, green, and blue. For the subtractive system (the printing process), these colors are yellow, magenta, and cyan.

printer driver The device that communicates between the software program and the printer. When using an application, the printer driver tells the application what the printer can do, and also tells the printer how to print the publication.

printer fonts The image outlines for type in PostScript that are sent to the printer.

printer's marks *See* trim marks, registration marks.

printer's spread The two pages that abut on press in a multi-page document.

process colors The four inks (cyan, magenta, yellow, and black) used in four-color process printing. A printing method in which a full range of colors is reproduced by combining four semi-transparent inks. *See* color separation, CMYK.

profile A file containing data representing the color reproduction characteristics of a device determined by a calibration of some sort.

progressive download A characteristic of JPEG files, in which the file will be displayed in increasingly greater detail as it is downloaded.

proof A representation of the printed job that is made from plates (press proof), film, or electronic data (prepress proofs). Gnerally used for customer inspection and approval before mass production begins.

property An aspect or quality of an element.

proportional spacing A method of spacing whereby each character is spaced to accommodate the varying widths of letters or figures, thus increasing readability. For example, a proportionally spaced "m" is wider than an "i."

pt. Abbreviation for point.

public domain Any created work, including software, the public may copy and use without paying royalty fees.

que A set of files input to the printer, printed in the order received unless otherwise instructed. Also spelled "queue."

query Request for specific information from a database.

radio button A single round button that can be clicked to cause a form to send a name-value pair to an action.

radio group A group of radio buttons with the same name. Only one radio button may be selected at a time within a radio group.

RAM Random Access Memory. The "working" memory of a computer that holds files in process. Files in RAM are lost when the computer is turned off, whereas files stored on the hard drive or floppy disks remain available.

range kerning Another term for tracking.

raster A bitmapped representation of graphic data.

raster graphics A class of graphics created and organized in a rectangular array of bitmaps. Often created by paint software or scanners.

raster image A type of picture created and organized in a rectangular array of bitmaps. Often created by paint software, scanners, or digital cameras.

rasterize The process of converting digital information into pixels. For example, the process used by an imagesetter to translate PostScript files before they are imaged to film or paper.

ratios The difference between the highlight and shadow brightness.

reader's spread The two (or more) pages a reader will view when the document is open.

reflective art Artwork that is opaque, as opposed to transparent, that can be scanned for input to a computer.

registration Aligning plates on a multicolor printing press so the images will superimpose properly to produce the required composite output.

registration color A default color selection that can be applied to design elements so they will print on every separation from a PostScript printer. "Registration" is often used to print identification text that will appear outside the page area on a set of separations.

registration marks Figures (often crossed lines and a circle) placed outside the trim page boundaries on all color separation overlays to provide a common element for proper alignment.

render A real-time preview of clips and all effects as your production plays.

rendering intent The method used to convert color from one space to another.

repurposing Converting an existing document for another different use; usually refers to creating an electronic version of existing print publications.

resample Resizing an image to decrease the physical size of the file, not just change the appearance on the page.

resolution The density of graphic information expressed in dots per inch (dpi) or pixels per inch (ppi).

resolution dependent A characteristic of raster images, in which the file's resolution is determined when the file is created, scanned, or photographed.

resolution independent A characteristic of vector graphics, in which the file adopt its resolution at the time of output based on the capabilities of the device being used.

retouching Making selective manual or electronic corrections to images.

reverse out To reproduce an object as white, or paper, within a solid background, such as white letters in a black rectangle.

RGB 1. The colors of projected light from a computer monitor that, when combined, simulate a subset of the visual spectrum. 2. The color model of most digital artwork. *See* CMYK, additive color.

rich black A process color consisting of solid black with one or more layers of cyan, magenta, or yellow. Also called "superblack."

right-reading A positive or negative image that is readable from top to bottom and from left to right.

RIP Raster Image Processor. That part of a PostScript printer or imagesetting device that converts the page information from the PostScript Page Description Language into the bitmap pattern that is applied to the film or paper output.

rollover The act of rolling the cursor over a given element on the screen.

rosette The pattern created when color halftone screens are printed at traditional screen angles.

Rubylith A two-layer acetate film having a red or amber emulsion on a clear base used in non-computer stripping and separation operations.

ruler Similar to a physical ruler, a feature of graphics software used for precise measurement and alignment of objects. Rulers appear in the top and left edges of the project window. *See* grid.

ruler guides Horizontal and vertical guides that can be placed anywhere on the page by dragging from the rulers at the edge of the project window.

rules 1. Straight lines. 2. Lines that are placed above or below paragraphs of text.

saddle-stitching A binding method in which each signature is folded and stapled at the spine.

saturation The intensity or purity of a color; a color with no saturation is gray.

scaling The means within a program to reduce or enlarge the amount of space an image occupies by multiplying the data by a factor. Scaling can be proportional, or in one dimension only.

screen To create a halftone of a continuous-tone image.

screen angle The angle at which the rulings of a halftone screen are set when making halftones for commercial printing.

screen frequency The number of lines per inch in a halftone screen, which may vary from 85 to 300.

screen ruling *See* LPI.

screen shot A printed output or saved file that represents data from a computer monitor.

secondary color The result of mixing two primary colors. In additive (RGB) color, cyan, magenta, and yellow are the secondary colors. In subtractive (CMY) color, red, green, and blue are the secondary colors.

selection The currently active object/s in a window. Often made by clicking with the mouse or by dragging a marquee around the desired object/s.

selective color The addition of color to certain elements of a grayscale image, usually to draw attention to the colored object or area.

separation The process of preparing individual color components for commercial printing. Each ink color is reproduced as a unique piece of film or printing plate.

separation proof A type of proof in which individual ink colors in a layout are each printed to different pieces of paper; commonly used to check for accurate use of spot colors.

service bureau An organization that provides services, such as scanning and prepress checks, that prepare your publication to be printed on a commercial printing press. Service bureaus do not, however, print your publication.

service mark A legal designation that identifies and protects the ownership of a specific term or phrase.

service provider Any organization, including a commercial printer, that processes design files for output.

silhouette To remove part of the background of a photograph or illustration, leaving only the desired portion.

snap-to An optional feature in graphics applications that drives objects to line up with guides, margins, or other objects if they are within a preset pixel range. This eliminates the need for very precise manual placement of an object with the mouse.

special color Colors that are reproduced using premixed inks, often used to print colors that are outside the CMYK gamut.

spectral absorption Light wavelengths that are absorbed by the pigments in an object's surface.

spectral output Color balance.

spectral reflectance Light wavelengths that are not absorbed by the pigments in an object's surface.

spectrophotometer A device used to precisely measure the wavelengths that are reflected from an object's surface.

specular highlight The lightest highlight area that does not carry any detail, such as reflections from glass or polished metal. Normally, these areas are reproduced as unprinted white paper.

spot color   Any pre-mixed ink that is not one of the four process-color inks.

spot-color printing   The printing method in which special ink colors are used independently or in conjunction with process colors to create a specific color that is outside the gamut of process-color printing.

spotlight   A lighting instrument that produces directional, relatively undiffused light with a fairly well-defined beam.

spread   1. Two abutting pages. 2. A trapping process that slightly enlarges a lighter foreground object to prevent white paper gaps caused by misregistration.

stacking order   1. The order of elements on a PostScript page, where the topmost item can obscure underlying items. 2. The order in which elements are placed on a page; the first is at the bottom and the last is at the top. 3. The order of layers, from top to bottom.

startup disk   The disk from which the computer is set to start.

static   Fixed content.

static graphics   Graphics with no animation or interactivity. The computer-image equivalent of a photograph or a painting.

step-and-repeat   A command in most desktop-publishing applications that makes multiple copies of selected objects using defined offset values.

stochastic screening   *See* frequency-modulated (FM) screening, dithering.

stock images   Images available from a commercial source that can be used for a fee — either once or multiple times.

stroke   The width and color attributes of a line.

sub-pixel   A point based on a calculated distance that is less than the size of a single pixel.

subsampling   A technique for reducing the amount of digital data used to represent an image; part of the data compression process.

substrate   Any surface that is being printed.

subtractive color   Color that is observed when light strikes pigments or dyes, which absorb certain wavelengths of light; the light that is reflected back is perceived as a color. *See* CMYK, process color.

superblack   *See* rich black.

SVG   Scalable Vector Graphics. A language for the creation of graphics using only tags.

swatch book   A book of printed color samples; can be process-color swatches showing various combinations of the four primary inks, or spot-color swatches, showing samples of individual spot-color ink.

SWOP   Specifications for Web Offset Publications. Industry standards for web-offset printing; SWOP specifications provide the necessary information to produce consistent high-quality printing.

system folder   The location of the operating system files on a computer.

table   A grid used for displaying data or organizing information in columns and rows. It is also used to control placement of text and graphics. A row and column structure for organizing information.

target audience   The audience selected or desired to receive a specific message.

target market   The market to whom you hope to sell your product.

telephoto lens   An optical device that gives a narrow, close-up view of an event relatively far away from the camera. Also called long focal-length lens or narrow-angle lens.

template   A document file containing layout, styles, and repeating elements (such as logos) by which a series of documents can maintain the same look and feel. A model publication you can use as the basis for creating a new publication.

text   The characters and words that form the main body of a publication.

text attribute   A characteristic applied directly to a letter or letters in text, such as bold, italic, or underline.

text box   A box into which users can type.

text editor   An application used to create or make changes to text files.

text effects   Means by which the appearance of text can be modified, such as bolding, underlining, and italicizing.

texture   1. A property of the surface of the substrate, such as the smoothness of paper. 2. Graphically, variation in tonal values to form image detail. 3. A class of fills in a graphics application that create various appearances, such as bricks, grass, tiles.

throughput   Measure of data transmission speed (in Kbps).

thumbnails   1. The preliminary sketches of a design. 2. Small images used to indicate the content of a computer file.

TIFF   Tagged Image File Format. A common format used for scanned or computer-generated bitmapped images.

tile   1. Reproducing a number of pages of a document on one sheet. 2. Printing a large document overlapping on several smaller sheets of paper.

tint   1. A halftone area that contains dots of uniform size; that is, no modeling or texture. 2. A percentage of a color; a 10% tint is one part of the original color and nine parts substrate color.

toggle   A command that switches between either of two states at each application. Switching between Hide and Show is a toggle.

tone value increase   *See* dot gain.

tool tip   Small text explaining the item to which the mouse is pointing.

Toyo   A special-color library commonly used in Japan.

tracking   Adjusting the spacing of letters in a line of text to achieve proper justification or general appearance.

trademark   A legal designation that identifies and protects the ownership of a specific device (such as a name, symbol, or mark).

transfer curve   A curve depicting the adjustment to be made to a particular printing plate when an image is printed.

transparency   1. A full-color photographically produced image on transparent film. 2. The quality of an image element that allows background elements to partially or entirely show through.

transparent ink   An ink that allows light to be transmitted through it.

trapping   The process of creating an overlap between abutting inks to compensate for imprecise registration in the printing process. Extending the lighter colors of one object into the darker colors of an adjoining object.

trim marks   Printer's marks that denote the edge of the layout before it is printed and cut to final size.

trim size   Area of the finished page after the job is printed, folded, bound, and cut.

TrueType   An outline font format used in both Macintosh and Windows systems that can be used both on the screen and on a printer.

Trumatch   A special-color library used in the United States.

tweening   A process by which the in-between frames of an animation are automatically generated by the developing application.

Type 1 fonts   PostScript fonts based on Bézier curves encrypted for compactness.

typeface   A unique and distinctive design of a font alphabet; the combined group of all the letters, figures, and punctuation of a specific font.

type family   A set of typefaces created from the same basic design but in different variations, such as bold, light, italic, book, and heavy. 2. In Web design, a list of fonts that will be used to display text in a Web page. *See* CSS.

typesetting   The arrangement of individual characters of text into words, sentences, and paragraphs.

type size   Typeface as measured (in points) from the bottom of descenders to the body clearance line, which is slightly higher than the top of ascenders.

typographer's quotes   The curly quotation marks used by typographers, as opposed to the straight marks on the typewriter. Use of typographer's quotes is usually a setup option in a word-processing or page-layout application.

typography   The art and process of placing, arranging, and formatting type in a design.

UCR   Undercolor Removal. A technique for reducing the amount of magenta, cyan, and yellow inks in neutral or shadow areas and replacing them with black.

undertone   Color of ink printed in a thin film.

unsharp masking   A digital technique performed after scanning that locates the edge between sections of differing lightness and alters the values of the adjoining pixels to exaggerate the difference across the edge, thereby increasing edge contrast.

vector graphics   Graphics defined using coordinate points and mathematically drawn lines and curves, which may be freely scaled and rotated without image degradation in the final output.

vignette   An illustration in which the background gradually fades into the paper; that is, without a definite edge or border.

virtual   Simulation of the real thing. You will see this term appear before various computer terms to indicate simulation technology that enables you to cross boundaries and experience something without requiring its physical presence.

WAN   Wide Area Network. A network that connects computers over a large geographic area.

watermark   An impression incorporated in paper during manufacturing showing the name of the paper and/or the company logo. A watermark can be applied digitally to printed output as a very light screened image.

Web-safe color   A color palette used for images that will be displayed on the Internet; a specific set of colors that can be displayed by most computer-operating systems and monitors.

weight   1. The thickness of the strokes of a typeface. The weight of a typeface is usually denoted in the name of the font; for example, light, book, or ultra (thin, medium, and thick strokes, respectively). 2. The thickness of a line or rule.

white balance   Equal amounts of red, green, and blue light components to create white.

white light   Light containing all wavelengths of the visible spectrum. Also known as 5000K lighting.

work for hire   Any creative product that is prepared by an employee as a normal part of employment, or any product commissioned for several specific purposes (such as a compilation or translation).

XLin   An emerging specification defining advanced functionality for hypertext.

XML   An acronym for eXtensible Markup Language.

INDEX